STUDIES IN MEDIEVAL AND RENAISSANCE HISTORY

Volume XIII

(Old Series, Volume XXIII)

STUDIES IN
Medieval and Renaissance History

Volume XIII
(Old Series, Volume XXIII)

EDITORS:

J. A. S. EVANS

R. W. UNGER

AMS PRESS
New York

AMS PRESS INC.
56 EAST 13TH STREET
NEW YORK, NY 10003

ISSN 0081-8224
ISBN 0-404-62850-8 (Set)
ISBN 0-404-62863-X (Vol. XIII)

Library of Congress Catalog Card Number 63-22098

All AMS books are printed on acid-free paper that meets the guidelines
for performance and durability of the Committee on Production
Guidelines for Book Longevity of the Council on Library Resources.

Manufactured in the United States of America

CONTENTS

INTRODUCTION

Studies in Medieval and Renaissance History is a series designed for original major articles in all fields of medieval and renaissance history. Volumes appear once a year.

Studies in Medieval and Renaissance History was formerly published by the University of Nebraska Press, and the impetus for the creation of the series came from the belief that there was a need for a publication that would accommodate the study that was too long to be included regularly in scholarly journals, but too short to appear as a book. The editors will consider articles in all areas of history from approximately the third to the sixteenth centuries—economic, social and demographic, political, intellectual and cultural, and studies that do not fit neatly into a single traditional category of historical investigation.

While the series is devoted primarily to the publication of major studies, it contains occasional bibliographic essays, and briefer articles dealing with unpublished archival and manuscript resources. The *Studies* also makes available in translation original articles by scholars who do not write in English or French.

Studies in Medieval and Renaissance History is published by AMS Press for the Committee for Medieval Studies at the University of British Columbia, and the editors welcome submissions from all scholars doing research in medieval and renaissance fields, including those whose interests are not strictly historical.

J. A. S. Evans

HISTORY AND THE TECHNOLOGICAL PRISM

The late Lynn White, jr., one of the advisory editors of "Studies in Medieval and Renaissance History," was a founding supporter of The Association Villard de Honnecourt for the Interdisciplinary Study of Medieval Technology, Science and Art (AVISTA). We are printing here two studies first presented at the AVISTA 1990 session at Kalamazoo, Michigan, with a preface by the coordinator, Barbara M. Kreutz, Dean Emeritus of the Graduate School of Arts and Science, Bryn Mawr College.

History and the Technological Prism

History has always served, in part, as a tool, strengthening self-identification and both reflecting and shaping a people's values. But in western culture the methods employed for constructing written history—historiography's tools, so to speak—have changed significantly since the medieval period.

Modern historiography essentially began in the seventeenth century, with a marked increase in the collection, scrutiny and publication of documents; the pursuit of written evidence has never slackened since. In the twentieth century, however, tools over and above written evidence have been increasingly used. Aerial photography has revealed ancient farming and settlement patterns, archaeology has explored changing construction methods and fortification, the evidence supplied by art and artifacts has been combed and recombed—all with a view to better understanding early societies through establishing their material circumstances and tracking the ways in which they interacted with the physical (and animal) world.

No one better exemplified new approaches than the late Lynn White, jr., with his creative probing of technology's semiological aspects. Together with Jean Gimpel, Lynn White was one of the founding supporters of AVISTA (the Association Villard de Honnecourt for the Interdisciplinary Study of Medieval Technology, Science and Art). Since 1986, AVISTA has sponsored sessions at the annual Medieval Institute meetings at Kalamazoo, ranging widely across the medieval spectrum: "The Technical Revolution," "The Use and Iconography of Wheels and Circles," "Building Technology," "Villard de Honnecourt, the Artist and his Drawings," and in 1990, "Transportation as Depicted in Medieval Art and Literature."

The papers in the 1990 sessions touched on many topics under the general rubric of transportation (or "transport"), from medieval ship depictions to Elijah's ascension to heaven as portrayed in the Dover Bible. In opening the sessions, Albert C. Leighton noted remarkable advances in the field of "transport studies" in recent years; as he observed, we have come a long way from Ginzrot's fanciful nineteenth-century drawings of early wheeled vehicles. Nonetheless, there are still many issues to explore—or to explore in new ways—and the sessions demonstrated this.

The following two articles are based on papers delivered in these 1990 AVISTA sessions. Each investigates events or developments typically passed over with little comment or analysis in general histories of medieval Europe. Carroll Gillmor (coincidentally, one of Lynn White's last Ph.D.'s) makes us look hard at the training of horses for medieval combat and tournaments, and then suggests that tournaments were in fact the principal justification for undertaking such extensive and expensive training. In her conclusion, she pictures a medieval world in which the elite became increasingly obsessed not with warfare but with violent sport; it is a new and provocative hypothesis. Michael Jones's article takes us much farther back in time, to that obscure and seldom visited period in which the Angles and Saxons made their way across the North Sea to England. Jones asks, quite properly, how they managed this, and in the course of his answer he dissects the literary evidence and considers the relevance of archaeological findings. His analysis is thorough; his conclusion seems persuasive.

Altogether the Gillmor and Jones studies seem admirably to illustrate the value of examining those physical realities that underlie the sweep of history.

PRACTICAL CHIVALRY: THE TRAINING OF HORSES FOR TOURNAMENTS AND WARFARE

Carroll Gillmor

The University of Utah
Salt Lake City, Utah

Practical Chivalry: The Training of Horses for Tournaments and Warfare

Inventions harness the physical environment for human needs, and sometimes become potent symbols. A classic symbol of restraint has been the bridle bit of the horse. Indeed, the prospect of putting a bit into the pernicious mouth of Catiline seemed as appropriate an image to Cicero as to those medieval iconographers who placed bits into the mouth of the Virtue Temperance.[1] Later, the symbolic association of the horse with aristocratic status emerged from the perception of the mounted knight as the cornerstone of tactical decisiveness in medieval battles.[2]

Scholarship of the last twenty years has largely disproven the central role of mounted shock combat in medieval warfare, but has also increased our understanding of the basic ecological, veterinary, and biological factors that both enhanced and limited the military uses of horses in the Middle Ages. The work of Bernard Bachrach has been particularly valuable.[3] Nonetheless, something fundamental still has been overlooked: specifically, how the horse moves at a canter or a gallop, and the effects in combat and sport of training a horse to alter his natural stride. Not considered in recent research has been the question of how the training of medieval war horses affected their performance in military operations. For example, a recent article on the medieval cavalry charge provided ample instruction on what the riders were to do, but said virtually nothing about how the horses were to move.[4] Recent studies have emphasized that the function of the tournament was to train knights in the handling of their weapons and accustom them to fight in groups,[5] but the schooling of the horses to maneuver in tactical units has escaped attention. This article attempts to remedy that omission. It also explores the actual role of the tournament and its place in medieval society.

7

Managing a horse in combat was not simple. Not only the riders but also the horses had to be trained to deliver charges; no medieval knight would have entered the battlefield or the tournament field unless he had spent many hours schooling his horse first. Moreover, too many scholars have apparently assumed that a medieval horseman communicated only simple commands with the bit and spur, using the bit to make the horse turn right or left or to stop and the spur only as a goad. The mechanics of equine locomotion indicate that much more than this underlies the military performance of a horse. As we shall see, in the hands of experienced horsemen, these technological devices perform much more subtle functions of communicating the rider's wishes, through the hands with the bit and through leg cues with the spur. Juliet Barker, in her recent work on the English tournament, emphasized the importance of training the horse not to be afraid of the noise and crush of combat and to gallop head on for the encounter, something which went against a horse's natural inclinations.[6] But apparently she was unaware of the significance of lead change in the performance of military sports and real battle. A horse in combat, or any other kind of equestrian activity, has to be trained on cue to reorient the motion of his entire body to perform maneuvers vital to the success of military operations.

Crucial to the performance of a horse and one of the finer points of horse training is the change of leg or lead at a canter or gallop. A horse must be taught the use of the left and right leads. The gallop is not a symmetrical gait, and the gait may be led on either side. At a canter or gallop a horse leads each stride with one front leg, just as a swimmer doing a sidestroke leads each stroke with one arm. When a horse gallops, one front leg strikes out in front of the other. A horse can change leads in either of two ways. Lead change ideally takes place at a gallop during the period of suspension, when all four feet are off the ground. At this instant, the horse can reverse the order in which the hind feet land, the front feet following suit by reversing their order. Changing leads in this manner, from back to front, can be done almost simultaneously, with no change in speed. The incorrect form of lead change, from front to back, is called "disunited," because the fore legs are on one lead and the hind legs on the other. To be more specific, in a disunited lead change the front feet change order after the hind feet have struck the ground, and the hind feet then change order in the next stride, after the period of suspension.[7] A disunited gallop makes the gait extremely rough and uncomfortable for the rider.

Training a horse to change leads correctly is important for

balance and turning. A horse leading with the left front foot actually receives his power stroke from the right hind leg which tends to push diagonally to the left. The diagonal push from behind is what gives propulsion and explains why lead change from behind is so extremely important. The cue to change leads is directed towards the propulsion leg; to induce a horse to lead with the left leg, the rider moves his right leg just behind the girth on the right side. The ability of a horse to change leads quickly could be decisive in military games and battlefield maneuvers, since a horse can turn right faster if leading with the right leg, or left if leading with the left leg.[8] In a modern dressage performance, lead change is performed on a perfectly manicured surface; this does not provide useful comparative data for the conditions a horse would have experienced in the forms of medieval combat. However, the modern sport of three-day eventing (with dressage trained horses) does place demands on the horse that more nearly approximate those of medieval combat, specifically, in jumping, in cross-country endurance, and in movements requiring facility in lead change. A good event horse above all must have courage, a quality equally as important as stamina and athletic ability.

In the late nineteenth century Edweard Muybridge took sequence photographs of galloping horses to disprove the widely held view that a horse had at least one foot on the ground while galloping.[9] Before then, artists, with the notable exception of the creators of the Parthenon frieze,[10] had failed to portray the correct position of the legs during a canter or gallop.[11] Lead change, or at least the basic reorientation of the horse's bodily motion from left to right or vice versa, is clearly observable by the human eye, but before the appearance of slow motion photography, the precise action of the horse's legs during lead change was usually too fast for the human eye to see.[12] At the beginning of lead change, the leading left leg receives its propulsive force from the right hind leg. When in suspension, the precise time of lead change, the horse raises the left hind foot almost as soon as the right hind foot strikes the ground. At this instant, when the left hind foot is off the ground and the right on the ground, the horse can reorient his stride so as to gallop leading with the left front foot.

As early as the fourth century B.C., mounted warriors perceived the valuable use of the lead in mounted combat.[13] Xenophon, in his treatise on the training of war horses, emphasized the importance of schooling a horse in figure-eights so as to develop facility in changing leads.[14]

Between the time of Xenophon's treatise and the publication

of Frederico Grisone's *Ordini di Caualcare* in 1551, few detailed description of horse-training appeared in western Europe. Nevertheless, these
two treatises, written at either end of the chronological spectrum, suggest that techniques for training horses to change leads remained
remarkably similar. Horse-training was, and to a large extent still is, primarily a function of oral tradition. Even today, comparatively few articu-
lations of training techniques appear in print; hands-on teaching is still
the normal (and best) course. And in the absence of manuals from the
Roman period through the Middle Ages we can deduce the way in
which horses were trained from the maneuvers they were performing.

We do know that the Romans appreciated the significance of
flying changes in military operations. In describing the equestrian
maneuvers of the Germans, Tacitus in his *Germania* wrote: "Nor are
they [the horses] taught to change their turns according to our custom,
but are driven straight forward, or so as to make one wheel to the right
in such a compact body that none is left behind another."[15] Accustomed
to maneuver their horses to the right,[16] the Germans represented a
practice different from the Romans, who had developed through practice the flexibility to maneuver in either direction.[17] In the maneuver
described by Tacitus, the Germanic horsemen approached the enemy
side by side and then pivoted to the extreme right. Turning clockwise,
they maintained their relative position in relation to the enemy. In this
formation the Germans would have appeared to the enemy as a continuous row of shields riding in a circle.[18]

An equestrian maneuver similar to the one described in
Tacitus appeared in Regino Prüm, a ninth-century chronicler, who
described Breton horsemen in battle. In his account of the battle of
Juvardeil in 851, in which the forces of Charles the Bald were defeated
by the Bretons, Regino wrote:

> When battle was engaged, the Saxons were placed in the front line to
> cut off the round and round retreats of the swift horses, but on the
> first attack, terrified by the javelins of the Bretons, the Saxons retreat-
> ed into the battle line. The Bretons, according to their practice, run-
> ning here and there with horses well-trained for a fight of this kind,
> first attacked the Frankish battle line drawn up in close formation
> and turned their javelins to all men in the center. Then, as the
> Bretons simulated flight, their javelins pierced the chests of the pur-
> suers. The Franks, who were accustomed to fight hand to hand with
> drawn swords, stood thunderstruck. Overwhelmed by the novelty of
> the distance between themselves and the Bretons, which the Franks

had not experienced before, they were neither capable of pursuing nor were they safe crowded together in a body.[19]

The round and round retreats *(anfractuosos recursus)* described by Regino evoke the image of a continuous body of horsemen riding in a circle before enemy forces. Although Regino's passage may suggest similarities from the time of the Germanic tactics explained by Tacitus, the evidence is much too slender to make an argument for absolute continuity of horsemanship practices.[20] However, maneuvering horses here and there in Regino's account suggests making sharp turns, which indicates that horses were trained in lead change. In describing the tactics of Magyar horsemen later in 889 and mentioning the similarity with the Breton maneuvers, Bachrach noted that "The Bretons do not push their attack home but swerve their horses after each attack..."[21] This turning maneuver demands extensive drilling to coordinate the occurrence of lead change at the same time.

It is true that not all of Regino's account of the earlier 851 battle can safely be used as evidence for Breton tactics, since Regino copied parts of the passage from a classical source.[22] (The most significant feature of the copied text is the passage on the Breton feigned retreat of 851, which actually described Syrian tactics of the Seleucid army at the battle of Magnesia in 190 B.C.)[23] Moreover, as Leyser rightly suggested, Regino's material describing Magyar tactics of 889 casts a long shadow over his description of the Breton feigned retreat in 851.[24] In other words, one feature of Regino's work appears to have been a carryover of information from one battle scene to the next. All of this information on Breton feigned retreats would therefore have to be discarded were it not for Nithard's report of the military exercises in 842 and the sophisticated horsemanship maneuvers described by Ermoldus Nigellus.

Commenting on Ermoldus Nigellus' observations on the Breton mode of fighting, Bachrach noted, "Bretons fight on horseback, wear armor as do their horses, and hurl javelins at their enemies."[25] However, Bachrach did not mention what is for our purposes the most interesting phrase of the text, that with a Breton "holding the reins, the horse performed various turns." The text implies that the Breton proudly demonstrated the skill of his horse in executing turns, suggesting the aesthetic pleasure derived by experienced horsemen in observing a horse practiced in the art of flying changes and cantering in figure-eights with lead change at the center.

A few years earlier, Nithard, a grandson of Charlemagne, had described the performance of military training exercises which would have required the horses to have been trained in the fast and accurate changing of leads:

> The entire group of Saxons, Gascons, Austrasians, and Bretons were divided into two units of equal size. They charged forward from both sides and came toward each other at full speed. Then [before contact was made] one side turned its back and under the protection of their shields pretended to be trying to escape. Then those who had been engaged in a feigned retreat counter-attacked and the pursuers simulated flight. Then both kings [Louis the German and Charles the Bald] and all the young men, raising a great yell, charged forward on their horses brandishing their spear shafts. Now one group feigned retreat and then the other. It was a spectacle worthy of being seen as much because of its nobility as because of its discipline.[26]

In analyzing this passage, Bachrach emphasized "the officers who orchestrated such training exercises were acutely aware of how potentially dangerous it was for men to practice these complicated maneuvers at high speed."[27] As he observed, the troops were performing these military games so as to function as cohesive tactical units and "From these formations they were required to carry out repeated complicated redeployments that entailed sharp directional changes at high speed."[28] However, we should also note that in order for groups of horses to turn sharply at a gallop, they would have to have been trained to respond on cue to change leads immediately and correctly. As mentioned above, a horse best changes leads from back to front, simultaneously and with no change in speed. In this case, had any of the horses performed disunited lead changes, from front to back, there would have been a disastrous loss of balance.[29] Some horses would either have bumped into the adjacent horse or even worse, taken a fall. Thus extensive training was needed, not only to drill the riders to retain orderly formations, but also to school the horses in swift lead change. Maintaining the correct lead was absolutely vital for mounted units moving at a canter or gallop, to retain the integrity of their formations.

Closely related to the functioning of tactical units, military exercises were also needed "to perfect the execution of the feigned retreat, ... the single most important tactic in the repertoire of the medieval mounted fighting man."[30] The mechanics of this maneuver required expert coordination in the timing of the withdrawal, the planning of the distance to be covered, and the turning movement itself.[31]

The success of this manuever requires schooling to perfection of both horse and rider. Lead change must have been the primary feature of training horses to function in tactical units for a feigned retreat. Pre-arranged coordination of the turns away from the enemy and then the wheel for the charge was all-important. Performing the turns in a syn-chronized manner could not have been accomplished unless the horses all received simultaneously the cue to lead right, so that the shield would face the enemy. The lead indicates the basic alignment and directional orientation of the horse's body. Horses had to be trained to change leads on command, otherwise the body of horsemen could not turn as one, thereby functioning as a tactical unit.[32]

Lead change was also important in single combat. Such encounters on the battlefield were rare, but one description appeared in the work of Liudprand of Cremona:

> The Bavarian wheeling his horse, first urged him forward in a vigor-ous manner, then he pulled up on the reins and drew him back. In the meantime, Hubald drove his mount straight at his opponent. When the two horsemen were in striking distance of each other, the former turned his horse around in his accustomed manner and then veered him to the left and to the right in a convoluted series of encir-cling movements that were intended to frustrate the straight attack of Hubald. However, as the Bavarian turned his horse in retreat with the intention of wheeling suddenly and striking a frontal blow, Hubald spurred his horse straight on and drove his spear through his oppo-nent before the latter could wheel around.[33]

Several passages in this text indicate that a reasonably sophisticated level of horse-training existed in the tenth century. The Bavarian pulling on the reins and drawing back the horse is clearly a reference to the practice of collection, whereby the rider makes the horse atten-tive to receive a command by arching the neck with the action of the bit which in turn causes the horse to shorten his base of movement with hind legs drawn a little further underneath his body.[34] This passage also describes the Bavarian veering his horse left and right in a convo-luted series of encircling movements; the horse could not have execut-ed these movements in the facile manner described by Liudprand with-out extensive schooling in rapid change of leads. Liudprand explained that the turns were done to avoid showing a predictable line of advance to the opponent, so the cues must not have been given according to regular numbers of strides. The horse thus would not have been able to predict precisely when he would receive the next command to turn; this irregularity in turning surely indicates the sensitivity of the horse to the rider's cues.

In examining this text, Bachrach rightly raised the question as to whether the Bavarian was riding *à la jineta* (with short stirrups) to provide the mobility described by Liudprand.[35] In modern dressage the cue or "aid" given to the horse is provided by the spur applied just behind the girth; for a left lead gallop, the rider, with his left leg on the girth, places his right leg just behind the girth so that the right spur can make contact with the flank of the horse.[36] Because lead change takes place at the moment of suspension, the rider must give the horse sufficient warning so that the horse will be able to anticipate the rider's wishes and perform the change correctly. The rider must be attuned to every stage in the horse's stride in order to feel the exact moment of suspension.[37] In Liudprand's description, the horse will have been changing leads just before he entered each turn. The rider necessarily would have been riding with stirrups short enough to signal the lead changes with his spurs.

Scholars have been so deeply immersed in evaluating the evidence about the adoption of the stirrup in combat that they have neglected the initial step of investigating fully the stirrup's function in horsemanship. While the stirrup could assist the rider to mount, the real significance of the stirrup begins once horse and rider are in motion.[38] The stirrup assists in supporting the weight of the rider's legs (not the entire body) so as to center the rider's body in alignment with the movement of the horse. The weight of the rider in the stirrups provides lateral stability to keep him on the horse, especially during the sharp turns required of maneuvers such as a feigned retreat.[39] Without stirrups, the rider would be more preoccupied with gripping the horse with his legs; moving the spur into position to give the signal for lead change would be much more difficult, as surely must have been the case in ancient feigned retreats. The flexibility of the strap which attaches the stirrup and positions the rider's legs makes it possible for the boot and spur to swing easily, just behind the girth, to communicate the directional aids to change leads. The stirrup leather also provides flexibility in allowing the rider to move the other foot away from the horse during lead change; the rider turns his toe outwards and away from what is becoming the lead shoulder.[40] For this other foot, the stirrup serves as a balance point or pivot. In a series of flying changes, the movements of the rider resemble a scissors action.

The applicability of the stirrup to combat techniques lies in its cue-giving role in lead change. This point of horsemanship is not apparent to the casual observer and would not easily lend itself to portrayal in the iconographical evidence, thus justifying Bachrach's statement that "extensive research during the past half century has failed to identify a single piece of ninth century evidence that *illustrates* [italics mine] how stirrups were used in combat."[41] However, he also says that "A careful examination of the written and pictorial sources indicates that the stirrup had no identifiable impact on the combat techniques of the eighth and ninth century."[42] One must question this conclusion. For in fact we know that feigned retreats were practiced in the ninth century and that without horses schooled in lead change, communicated by spur through the action of the rider's foot in the stirrup, these maneuvers would have been very difficult to accomplish, as they must have been in the ancient world.

Not until the sixteenth century did treatises appear which elaborated on the refinements of horse training. Chief among these writers was a Neapolitan, Federico Grisone, whose *Ordini di Caualcare* (mentioned earlier) exerted a tremendous influence on the popularization of horsemanship practices in northern Europe.[43] These treatises surely recorded knowledge communicated by the oral traditions of aristocratic culture.

According to Grisone, a rider induced lead change on the right leg of the horse by holding his right foot against the horse's shoulder and his left foot a little behind the girth. Lead change on the horse's left leg was a reversal of this process.[44] In jousting contests, Grisone said, the two opponents should first come along the length of the barrier ten steps opposite each other, and then ride gently at a trot in opposite directions until they reached the marked or appointed starting line. Then, each rider took a turn on the right lead and charged his opponent. When both came to the end of the barrier, both riders took a turn on the left lead.[45] Taking a turn on the right lead with lance held to the left of the horse's head while charging prevented the horse from being thrown off stride upon impact of the lances. Of course, not all jousts ran so smoothly as portrayed in Grisone's training manual. Horses frequently crashed, crossed over their paths, bolted, swerved or completely refused to run the length of the course.[46] Nonetheless, Grisone indicated how it was supposed to be done.

In Grisone's treatise, just as in modern dressage handbooks, spurs act not simply as goads to make the horse go faster, but have the more refined task of communicating the rider's signals, directing the horse to perform certain maneuvers. The spur signal, with a stroking action just behind the girth to communicate lead change, is the same in modern dressage as in Grisone. Treatises on the techniques for training war horses to perform complicated maneuvers, proliferating after the publication of Grisone's work, developed eventually into a genre of manuals for training horses to execute the intricate movements of dressage.

Before a horse can be trained to change leads correctly and swiftly for tournament-style engagements, the trainer must work on flexion first; he must practice diagonal movements before the horse will be strong enough to move at the rear. A horse must learn to bend at the stifle and reach with his hindlegs; bend with the forehand; develop flexibility below the point of the hip. A modern manual suggests about two months of flexion work as necessary preparation for training in lead change.[47] The training for lead change is then a lengthy coordinating activity involving variables such as teaching the horse to change leads at different speeds; lead change is executed more easily the faster the horse is galloping. Today, training a horse for lead change usually involves two steps. A modern authority says that concentrated schooling with emphasis on precision should usually last only five to fifteen minutes at a time, the attention span of a horse.[48] In addition, there should be daily aerobic exercise, lasting two to three hours: this serves to build stamina, wind, and heart capacity, vital to performance in modern three-day eventing. Mêlée tournaments surely required a somewhat similar training schedule.[49]

The constant necessity of maintaining his mounts in combat readiness must have affected the chivalric lifestyle, for this activity undoubtedly occupied a substantial portion of a knight's day. And if we apply the data developed by Bachrach on the nutritional requirements for maintaining a horse in combat condition, we can appreciate the enormous cost in economic resources as well.[50] During a three-month summer of tourneying, a destrier would consume about 180 lbs. of grain; each knight normally had a string of destriers, which would place tremendous demands on available grain supplies,[51] no doubt to the detriment of the local peasants. In the last half of the twelfth century, when rich nobles dominated the sport,[52] huge retinues of 80 to 200 knights competed in tournaments.[53]

To assess the overall significance of horse training, we need to reexamine the relevance of tournaments and jousts to real warfare. Many historians have said that the tournaments of the twelfth and thirteenth centuries were military exercises designed to train knights for actual combat.[54] This functional relationship assumes the frequent occurrence of set battles. Yet examination of battles fought in the twelfth and thirteenth centuries, the period when the interaction of tournaments and battles was presumed to exist, will indicate that tournaments did not serve merely as military exercises to prepare for battle, but had an independent importance as aristocratic games.

Feigned retreats may have been the most important tactic used by mounted troops during the Middle Ages, but even their occurrences were few and far between, with considerable geographical distance: Riade in Italy 933; Pontlevoy under Fulk Nerra of Anjou in 1016; St. Aubin le Cauf near Arques in 1052–3; near Messina in 1060; Hastings 1066; by Robert le Frison of Flanders at Cassel in 1071.[55] Given the enormous cost of training horses to perform this maneuver, it is hardly arguable that pitched battles involving feigned retreats justified the need for continuous training.

The Crusades exemplify repeated attempts to apply tournament tactics to actual warfare. Yet during the Crusades the principal striking forces proved to be squadrons of mailed horsemen who relied for victory only a frontal charge, a single directional orientation that could be changed only with difficulty once the charge began. The devastating impact of the successful charge against concentrated light forces was recognized in the *Alexiad* of Anna Comnena.[56] However, the mounted archers of the Muslims practiced swarming tactics; dispersed in small groups, these mounted archers sought to envelop the flanks or rear of their enemies. Only rarely were the Franks therefore able to close with the elusive enemy and deliver a decisive mounted charge, as at Dorylaeum (1097), when the horsed archers concentrated their forces on one of the Frankish flanks and then received a charge from a relief force.[57]

In the most significant French and English battles of the Anglo-Norman age, the mounted knights did not fight in battles but functioned as dragoons or mounted infantry, riding to the site of the battle and then dismounting to fight on foot: specifically, at Conquereuil (992), Hastings (1066), Dorylaeum (1098), Tinchebrai (1106), Bremule (1119), Bourg Theroulde (1124), Northallerton (1138), Lincoln (1141).[58]

And in the pitched battles of this period there were some notable failures of mounted forces when hurled against disciplined forces fighting on foot, as for example Conquereuil (992), Saint Michel en l'Harm (1014), the first charge at Pontlevoy (1016), the first few charges at Hastings (1066), Legnano (1176), Courtrai (1302), Bannockburn (1314).[59] At the battle of Bouvines (1214), traditionally regarded as a victory by French mounted troops, the Saxon infantry was actually superior to King Philip's horsemen in the center of the line.[60]

In battles where horsemen were tactically decisive, some evidence does exist that the maneuvers were those learned in tournaments. At Lewes in 1264 and Evesham in 1265, a mounted charge delivered the decisive blow.[61] The battle of Falkirk (1298) demonstrated the efficiency of combined arms, with a victory of longbowmen and armored horsemen over the Scottish pikemen.[62] However, the thirty-year chronological gap, nearly a generation, in the occurrence of major set battles in thirteenth-century England surely challenges the idea that tournaments were held to train knights for real war; in the same century, tournaments occurred at least every year. It is difficult to escape the conclusion that a tournament, although a paramilitary operation, was a separate equestrian activity having only occasional application to real warfare.

The predominance of siege warfare in medieval Europe provided few opportunities for mounted knights to be tactically decisive.[63] During the frequent stalemates, however, tournaments often served to relieve the monotony of the besiegers.[64] And, in addition, the medieval rural landscape (networks of castles spaced by the distance a horse could cover in a day) was well-suited for the paramilitary activities of horsemen maintaining lines of communication and patrolling the countryside against raids and skirmishes which were actually logistical wars to reduce the material resources of rivals.[65]

Overall, however, in light of the relative ineffectiveness of mounted knights on the battlefield, and the infrequency of major battles, it can no longer be argued that a close pragmatic relationship ever really existed between tournaments and actual warfare. Recent scholarship discussing tournaments, especially the works of Malcolm Vale and Juliet Barker, rightly emphasizes that tournaments did teach knights how to wield the weapons of their profession and fight in tactical units.[66] Both the narrative sources containing the tactical descriptions of actual battles and the battle descriptions of the *Chansons de Geste* agree that knights were trained to fight in tactical units with disciplined maneuvers.[67] Yet, the compelling need for horsetraining could not have come solely from pitched battles; these engagements occurred too seldom to justify the intense schooling of a horse in lead change.

The infrequency of set battles in the period 1050–1300 and the relative unimportance of mounted knights when set battles did occur, must mean that horses were primarily trained to fight in tournament-style contests.

Often ranging over the extensive countryside, the *mêlée* tour-

nament did resemble real warfare. As Sidney Painter observed,
"Tournaments were pitched battles fought for amusement and gain;
only the provision for refuges differentiated them from ordinary battles."[68] Tournaments were engagements for which horses were trained
to confront other horses, even though they did not prepare medieval
knights to face a massed infantry formation presenting a wall of
bristling pikes as at Courtrai in 1302. Tournaments in fact were *the* "cavalry" battles of the Middle Ages.[69] If we wish to consider the tournament
a training exercise for warfare, we must modify what we mean by "warfare." Scholars have erroneously assumed that its function as a training
exercise constituted the tournament's sole link with "wars" that otherwise they were totally separate activities. In actuality, *mêlée* tournaments
often developed into real battles. The tournament was a sporting event
which, when it lost its formalized structure, could and did erupt into
outright violence. What knights were mostly training for was the anticipated eventuality that a tournament might escalate into a major confrontation.[70]

A schedule of these spectacles appeared every summer in
northern France; in some areas tournaments were held every two
weeks.[71] Like modern cowboys on the rodeo circuit, knights errant such
as William Marshal competed for prize money in the form of captured
horses and armor. And just as modern race cars are not driven to the
sites of auto races, but are hauled on trailers, medieval destriers probably were hardly ever used as a means of transportation.[72] Once adequate
wagons were developed and the practice of horse hauling became relatively widespread, war horses were likely carried around the countryside in horse-drawn vans in the entourage of knights on the tournament circuit.[73]

The paucity of set battles in the Middle Ages indicates that
tournaments and jousts were the only confrontations where mounted
shock combat was practiced regularly. The present state of the evidence
suggests that this distinctive style of mounted warfare emerged in its
final form in the second half of the eleventh century with the appearance of the couched lance position.[74] The impact would combine the
weight of horse and rider, with lateral support provided by the stirrup,
and a high-backed saddle to stabilize the rider on the horse.

The adulation of the "invincible" mounted knight appears to
have been derived from knightly performances in tournaments, which
were not practice for war but a form of professional sport.[75] The eleva-
tion of the mounted knight had little to do with military activity in
pitched battles.[76] Sidney Painter, in *French Chivalry* and *William Marshal*,

listed the most desirable quality of a knight as prowess in battle, but the sources Painter cited were actually not tactical descriptions of set battles, but descriptions of tournaments.[77] Not the battlefield but the tournament field provided the stage for the adulation of the medieval mounted knight. Since prowess in battle was in fact demonstrated mainly in tournaments, the medieval mounted knight was not a "cavalryman." He more resembled what we would consider a professional athlete, admired by his peers for his athletic ability in a rough sport.

To receive adulation, the medieval knight needed an audience. Set battles in warfare, primarily because they did not occur often enough, normally would not provide a stage for demonstrating fighting skills, a place where the same individuals could be observed repeatedly and thereby build a reputation for valor. By contrast, tournaments and jousts occurred frequently, eventually becoming the primary form of spectator sport in medieval Europe.

Training the horses to perform in these contests involved extensive investment of personal time by the knights and a huge consumption of scarce resources. Contemporaries liked to think of this as justified because tournaments prepared knights for war but in fact we know that tournament skills were seldom put to effective use on actual battlefields. In reality, we must conclude that practitioners of the chivalric lifestyle were heavily involved in professional sports, and this is what justified the elaborate training they and their horses undertook.

Notes

1. Lynn White, Jr., "The Iconography of *Temperantia* and the Virtuousness of Technology," *Medieval Religion and Technology, Collected Essays* (Berkeley, Los Angeles, 1978), 181–204.
2. For an assessment of this view, *v* Bernard S. Bachrach, "Animals and Warfare in Early Medieval Europe," in *L'uomo di fronte al mondo animale nell'alto medioevo,* Settimane di Studio 31 (Spoleto, 1985), I: 732.
3. *V* especially Bachrach, *"Caballus* and *Caballarius* in Medieval Warfare," in *The Study of Chivalry: Resources and Approaches,* ed. Howell Chickering and Thomas B. Seiler (Kalamazoo, 1988), pp. 173–211, and "Animals and Warfare in Early Medieval Europe," pp. 707–64. Also, R. H. C. Davis, *The Medieval Warhorse* (London, 1989).
4. Matthew Bennett, *"La Règle du Temple* as a Military Manual, or How to Deliver a Cavalry Charge," *Studies in Medieval History Presented to R. Allen Brown,* ed. Christopher Harper-Bill, Christopher J. Holdsworth, and Janet L. Nelson (Woodbridge, Suffolk, 1989), 7–19. Bennett overlooked the information in the 1937 British cavalry manuals which he cites as instructing the rider in the techniques of

lead change. *V Manual of Horsemastership, Equitation, and Animal Transport* (HMSO, London, 1937), 76, 101, 105, and *Cavalry Training* (Horsed) (HMSO, London, 1937), 50, 67–68.

5. Malcolm Vale, *War and Chivalry, Warfare and Aristocratic Culture in England, France and Burgundy at the End of the Middle Ages* (London, 1981), p. 68. Juliet Barker, *The Tournament in England, 1100–1400* (Woodbridge, Suffolk, 1986), pp. 20–22. Also, Sydney Anglo, "How to Win at Tournaments: The Technique of Chivalric Combat," *Antiquaries Journal* 68 (1988), pp. 252-64.

6. Barker, *Tournament in England,* 173. Also, David Nicolle, "The Impact of the European Couched Lance on Muslim Military Tradition," *Journal of the Arms and Armour Society,* 10 (1980), p. 14.

7. The clearest explanations of equine movement and the horse's interaction with the rider appear in dressage manuals. Henry Wynmalen, *The Horse in Action* (London, 1954), pp. 42–46, and his *Dressage, A Study of the Finer Points of Riding* (New York, 1975), pp. 240–47. Also, Jennie Loriston-Clarke, *The Complete Guide to Dressage* (Philadelphia, 1987), pp. 62–63, 96–99; Charles de Kunffy, *Dressage Questions Answered* (New York, 1985), pp. 130–41. For the motion picture evidence, *v* Edweard Muybridge, *Animals in Motion* [1897], ed. Lewis S. Brown (New York, 1957), 10. On the importance of lead change in modern flat racing, *v* William Nack, *Secretariat: The Making of a Champion* (New York, 1975), pp. 51–52.

8. This observation appeared as early as Xenophon, writing on the training of war horses in the fourth century B.C. *V* J. K. Anderson, *Ancient Greek Horsemanship* (Berkeley, Los Angeles, 1966), p. 168, for his translation of Xenophon, 7. 12.

9. Eadweard Muybridge, *Animals in Motion,* 64–65 for the gallop; Pl. 56–73 for change of lead.

10. The fact that the artists of the Parthenon frieze portrayed the precise movement of the horses' legs at a canter indicates that horses they observed had been trained to move with a high degree of collection, a technical term in advanced horsemanship referring to the ability of the horse to shorten his base of movement by placing his hind quarters further underneath his body. This shortened outline allows his steps to be higher and more mobile, having impulsion, a dressage term denoting the potential energy of a coiled spring. The overall impression is one of slow and deliberate motion. *V* Anderson, *Ancient Greek Horsemanship,* pp. 123; 176 –77 for his translation of Xenophon 11. 2–3. giving a description of a collected horse which closely matches the horses portrayed on the Elgin marbles. *V* also Loriston-Clarke, *Complete Guide to Dressage,* p. 154, and Wynmalen, p. *Dressage,* 114.

11. On this, *v* Salomon Reinach, "La représentation du galop dans l'art ancien et moderne," *Revue Archéologigue* 36.1 (1900) pp. 229, 237; Robert Lefort des Ylouzes, "Les images du galop dans l'Antiquité," *Revue Archéologigue* 14 (1939), 45–47 and his "Les images du galop 'ramassé' dans l'Antiquité," *Revue Archéologigue* 19 (1942–43), 18–23.

12. Anderson, *Ancient Greek Horsemanship,* pp. 104–5, observed that Xenophon and Henry Wynmalen, the noted dressage expert, gave the same directions for obtaining the left lead from a trot, with the difference that Xenophon (7. 10–11) concentrated first on the action of the horse's front legs, mandating the signal to gallop at the exact instant when the horse raises his right front foot. By contrast, Wynmalen, *(Equitation* [London, 1938], p. 105), with the advantage of slow motion photography to analyze the canter, directed his attention to the horse's hind legs. With the knowledge that the propulsion of the canter (with the near forefoot leading) comes from

the off hind foot, Wynmalen emphasized that the cues should be given "at the precise moment when the right diagonal is in the air."

13. Anderson, *Ancient Greek Horsemanship*, pp. 104–105; and p. 168 for a translation of Xenophon 7. 10–12.

14. Anderson, *Ancient Greek Horsemanship*, pp. 168–69, translating Xenophon 7. 13. *V* also, Paul Vigneron, *Le cheval dans l'antiquité gréco-romaine*, Annales de l'Est, Mémoire, 35 (Nancy, 1968), I, p. 95. *V* the passage of Tacitus, n. 17 below. Also, *v* Federico Grisone, *Ordini di Caualcare* (Venice, 1551), 85ff: the author is indebted to the Folger Shakespeare Library of Washington, D.C. for providing a copy of this work. Some evidence of this practice exists in the Middle Ages, as implied in the passage of the ninth century Aquitanian poet, Ermoldus Nigellus, in n. 25 below. Writing c. 1198, William fitz Stephen (cited in) *Norman London*, with an essay by Sir Frank Stenton, introduction by F. Donald Logan [New York, 1990], p. 57) noted, "Every Sunday in Lent after dinner a fresh swarm of young gentles goes forth on war horses, steeds skilled in the contest, of which each is apt and schooled to wheel in circles round. From the gates burst forth in throngs the lay sons of citizens, armed with lance and shield, the younger with shafts forked at the end, but with steel point removed. They make war's semblance and mimic contest exercise their skill in arms." For this reference to William fitz Stephen the author is grateful to Judith Feller of East Stroudsburg University.

15. Tacitus, *Germania*, 6, 3: "Sed nec variare gyros in morem nostrum docentur: in rectum aut uno flexu dextros agunt, ita coniuncto orbe, ut nemo posterior sit." The range of possibilities for interpreting this passage rest largely on the meaning of "coniuncto orbe." Rodney Potter Robinson, *The Germania of Tacitus, A Critical Edition* (Middletown, CT, 1935), pp. 281–82, offered several ways of construing the text. In the first, a line of horsemen moved as the radius of a circle with the man on the extreme right acting as the pivot and the remaining horsemen moving in such a straight line that no rider lagged behind. The principal objection to this rendering is that Tacitus was describing the equipment and practices of actual combat, and this maneuver, while suited to the riding school, was not practicable on the battlefield. More recently, this interpretation was accepted by L. L. Hammerich, "Ein Reiterstück (Tacitus, Germania, c. 6)," *Fragen und Forschungen im Bereich und Umkreis der germanischen Philologie. Festgabe für Th. Frings* (Berlin, 1956), 286–87. Following H. Schneider ("Zu Tacitus Germania 6.3," *Blätter für das Gymnasial-schulwesen* 36 [1900], 238–56) Robinson implied his acceptance of an alternative view that orbs referred not to a circle but to a mass formation of horsemen. In Robinson's and Schneider's rendering of the passage, Tacitus was describing two ways of attacking practiced by the Germans, specifically, a frontal attack and an oblique attack to the right against the enemy's right. This maneuver likewise seems risky on the battlefield; moving diagonally in the direct path of the center and left forces would invite a flank attack from the enemy's left. Herbert W. Benario ("Tacitus. Germania 6.3," *The Classical World*, 60 [1967], 270 argued that Tacitus drew his inspiration from a passage of the *Aeneid* (10.885): "ter circum adstantem laevos equitavit in orbes." Mezentius rode in a circle around Aeneas so as to keep the shield on his left arm facing Aeneas while retaining the capacity to throw weapons with his right arm. Benario's explanation that the Germans could not encircle an enemy line so they swept past it and veered to the right, protected by their shields and able to hurl their weapons, nevertheless did not account for the phrase that no one was left behind. The interpretation accepted here is of horsemen riding around clockwise in a circle, which also conveys the appearance of no rider lagging behind. Construing *Germania* 6.3 in this way makes the maneuver similar to the

Cantabrian gallop, a Roman maneuver where one group of riders galloped in a circle and hurled their spears at the shields of the second group as they rode past in a straight line. See Arrian's *Tactica*, c. 40, a work written not long after the *Germania*, and Roy W. Davies, *Service in the Roman Army*, ed. David Breeze and Valerie A. Maxfield (New York, 1989), p. 142. The Cantabrian gallop required the horses to maintain the right lead, while the javelin maneuvers in Arrian 36-39 nessitated facility in both the left and right leads. A similar maneuver to *Germania* 6.3 appears to have been practiced by the Bretons at the battle of Juvardeil; *V* below n. 19.

16. Frauke Stein *(Adelsgräber des achten Jahrhundert in Deutschland* [Berlin, 1967] I pp. 216–396) provided a catalogue of the grave goods of some 704 fighting men who were buried throughout eastern Francia from the late seventh through the early ninth century. Bachrach ("Charles Martel, Mounted Shock Combat, the Stirrup and Feudalism," *Studies in Medieval and Renaissance History*, 7 [1970], p. 65) noted that of the eighty-five sure equestrian graves, sixty-two had at least one spur, and that single spur was on the left foot, but Bachrach did not note the significance of this apparent irregularity. Wearing the spur on the left foot strongly suggests the practice of emphasizing the right lead. As we have seen, when signalling a horse to lead with the right foot the rider must touch the left side of the horse's side with his spur. This practice was recognized in the older scholarship; for example, L. Lindenschmidt, *(Handbüch der deutschen Alterthumskunde, Übersicht der Denkmale und Gräber frühgeschichtlicher und vorgeschichtlicher Zeit* [Braunschweig, 1889], I, p. 287) also noticed that graves revealed that warriors wore only one spur on the left foot, and explained, "Wahrscheinlich bestimmte dazu die Absicht, beim Anlegen desselben das Pferd in Galopp nach Rechts zu versetzen, welcher die bewaffnete Hand zuerst an den Gegner bringt." Also, O. Olshausen, "Beitrag zur Geschichte des Reitersporns," *Zeitschrift für Ethnologie* 22 (1890), p. 207.

17. Vigneron, *Le cheval*, I, p. 95 and n. 7. Hammerich ("Ein Reiterstück," 285–86) indicated that *variare gyros* referred to a change in the direction of the circles so that a horse would be galloping in successive figure eights, always maintaining the inside lead, with lead change occurring in the center of the two circles.

18. J. C. G. Anderson, ed., *Cornelii Taciti, De Origine et Situ Germanorum* (London, 1938), p. 65. The use of the right lead would indicate that warriors held their shields on the left arm. According to Anderson, "The right wheel lead was preferred in order to avoid exposing to the enemy the side unprotected by the shield." Since warriors in battle array held their shields on the left arm, the horse had to lead with the right leg to diminish the distinct possibility that he would be thrown off stride upon the clash of weapons. Ann Hyland, *Equus: The Horse in the Roman World* (New Haven, 1990) did not discuss this passage, but did interpret on p. 117, the *toulotlegon* maneuver of Arrian, c. 43, rightly observing that the shield on the left arm caused the lose of the directional use of the left rein. In her view, the rider pressed his shield against the left side of the horse's neck to keep him turning in a circle combined with correct leg pressure for turns. However, without the continuous pressure of the shield against the horse's neck, the horse would continue the right lead orientation, but would drift from a circular path. Obviously, using the shield as a tool to direct the horse would compromise the effectiveness of the shield as a defense weapon, making this maneuver more suitable for the parade ground than the battlefield. The shield as a substitute for correct leg pressure overlooks the capability of the spur to achieve the same effect. A practice of using the arms for signalling lead change would not have been a viable option in ancient or medieval warfare.

19. Regino of Prüm, *Chronicon*, ed. Fridericus Kurze (Hanover, 1890), 79: "Pugna com-

mittitur, Saxones, qui conducti fuerant, ad excipiendos velocium equorum anfractuosos recursus in prima fronte ponuntur, sed primo impetu spiculis Brittonum territi
in acie se recondunt. Brittones more solito huc illucque cum equis ad huiuscemodi
conflictum exercitatis discursantes modo confertam Francorum aciem impetunt ac
totis viribus in medio spicula torquent, nunc fugam simulantes insequentium
nihilominus pectoribus spicula figunt. Franci, qui comminus strictis gladiis pugnare
consueverant, attoniti stabant, novitate ante inexperti discriminis perculsi, nec ad
insequendum idonei nec in unum conglobati tuti."

20. Bachrach ("The Origins of Armorican Chivalry," *Technology and Culture*, 10 [1969],
    166–71) has however argued for continuity of horsemanship practices from the
    Alans of late Antiquity to the Bretons of the ninth century.

21. Bachrach, *History of the Alans*, p. 88, and n. 29, quoting Regino of Prüm (*Chronicon*,
    p. 133): "Pugnant aut procurrentibus equis aut terga dantibus, saepe etiam fugam
    simulant. Nec pugnare diu possunt: ceterum intolerandi forent, si quantus est impe-
    tus, vis tanta et perseverantia esset. Plerumque in ipso ardore certaminis prelia
    deserunt ac paulo post pugnam ex fuga repetunt, ut cum maxime vicisse te putes,
    tunc tibi discrimen subeundem sit."

22. In the above passage Bachrach, *History of the Alans*, p. 88 and n. 29, explained that
    Regino was comparing the Hungarians with the Bretons as derived from a description
    of Scythian tactics as found in Justin, a second century A.D. historian who wrote an
    epitome of the *Historiae Philippicae* by Pompeius Trogus, a contemporary of Livy. For a
    discussion of Regino's reliance on Justin, *v* Heinz Löwe, "Regino of Prüm und das his-
    torische Weltbild der Karolingerzeit," *Rheinische Vierteljahrsblätter*, 17 (1952), 163.

23. A comparison of the passages from Regino on the 851 battle and Justin on the battle
    of Magnesia describing these equestrian maneuvers appeared in an article by Max
    Manitius, "Regino und Justin," *Neues Archiv* 25 (1899), p. 193.

24. Karl Leyser, "Henry I and the Beginning of the Saxon Empire," *English Historical
    Review* 83 (1968), p. 18, n. 2. On the swarming tactics of the Magyars, *v* Leyser, "The
    Battle at the Lech, 955. A Study in Tenth Century Warfare," *History* 50 (1965), pp.
    15–16.

25. Ermold Le Noir [Ermoldus Nigellus] *Poème sur Louis le Pieux et épîtres au roi Pépin*, ed. E.
    Faral (Paris, 1932), III, 1630–31, p. 124: "Scandit equum velox, stimulis praefigit acu-
    tis/Frena tenens; giros dat quadrupes varios." Bachrach, History of the Alans, p. 88.

26. Nithard, *Histoire des fils de Louis le Pieux*, ed. and trans. Ph. Lauer (Paris, 1926), Bk. 3.
    ch. 26; I have used here Bachrach's translation of the text in *"Caballus et Caballarius,"*
    p. 187.

27. Bachrach, *"Caballus et Caballarius,"* p. 187.

28. Ibid.

29. Wynmalen, *Horse in Action*, p. 46.

30. Bachrach, *"Caballus et Caballarius,"* p. 188.

31. *V* Charles H. Lemmon, "The Campaign of 1066," in *The Norman Conquest: Its Setting
    and Impact*, ed. N. T. Chevallier (New York, 1966), p. 109, and his argument that the
    Norman knights lacked sufficient discipline to execute the maneuver. For a criticism
    of Lemmon's assumption, *v* Bachrach, "The Feigned Retreat at Hastings," *Mediaeval
    Studies* 33 (1971), pp. 345–47. Also, on the requirements for a successful feigned
    retreat, *v* Ian Peirce, "The Knight, his Arms and Armour in the Eleventh and
    Twelfth Centuries," *The Ideals and Practice of Medieval Knighthood*, ed. Christopher
    Harper-Bill and Ruth Harvey (Woodbridge, Suffolk, 1986), p. 153.

32. Infantry formations experienced with charges of horsemen operating in tactical

units may have been able to detect the intention of a feigned retreat by observing the leads of the oncoming horses, or even by noting the cohesion of mounted tactical units during the first turn away from the enemy forces. The right wheel lead was necessary to protect the left side of the Knight so that his shield would be facing the enemy. All horses of a tactical unit turning right on the right lead would indicate a high degree of discipline and purpose. At the battle of Hastings, possibly two attempts at feigned retreats were unsuccessful against disciplined Huscarls. But events immediately preceding the battle of Hastings explain why, later, the shire levies did follow the feigned retreat. Harold had taken with him to the north the first-string shire levies, who then fought at the battle of Stamford Bridge; but the Norman landing required Harold to leave these shire levies in the north, so that he could hurry south. Consequently, he had to collect another army in the south, a second mobilization of shire levies. These men doubtless would have had less military experience, and thus would have been more likely to follow a feigned retreat. (On the mobilization of these shire levies, *v* Richard Glover, "English Warfare in 1066," *English Historical Review*, 67 [1952], 11.) Who also downplayed the occurrence of a feigned retreat at Hastings, emphasizing that "panic could become infectious." Against this, see recent discoveries below n. 66 that Knights fought in disciplined tactical units.

33. Liudprand of Cremona, *Antapodosis*, ed. Joseph Becker, 3rd. ed. (Hanover and Leipzig, 1915), Bk 1, ch. 21, 19–20; I have used here Bachrach's translation in *"Caballus et Caballarius,"* p. 193.

34. The practice of collecting the horse by pulling on the reins to get the horse's attention before giving commands is explained by Xenophon (11.3. in Anderson, *Ancient Greek Horsemanship*, p. 123); Grisone, *Ordini di Caualcare*, 47–48. *V* also, Vigneron, *Le cheval*, p. 94; Loriston-Clarke, *Dressage*, pp. 74–75; de Kunffy, *Dressage Questions Answered*, pp. 77–83, and esp. p. 80.

35. Bachrach, *"Caballus et Caballerius,"* p. 209.

36. Wynmalen *(Dressage*, p. 98) pointed out the exceeding sensitivity of the trained horse to the rider's slightest movements. A schooled horse readily associates one movement with another, so almost every cue given by the rider is preceded by some introductory movement. The contact of the spur with the horse is always preceded by a gradual tightening of the calf of the leg against the horse's flank. Responding to this subtle pressure the horse will not wait for the prick of the spur, but will act upon feeling the pressure of the calf muscle, or even any action usually preceding the approach of the calf. These "aids by association" are extremely important; they demonstrate the ability of the schooled horse to anticipate what the rider wants him to do next. The use of cues or aids by a skilled rider on a schooled horse becomes so refined as to appear almost invisible to the casual observer. *(V* Loriston-Clarke, *Dressage*, p. 63; de Kunffy, *Dressage Questions Answered*, pp. 83–84). Some question exists as to whether these invisible cues were an objective of medieval horsetraining as they are in modern dressage. The medieval knight more likely used his spurs to induce lead change rather than concentrate on communication through his calf muscles, as in Grisone, *Ordini di Caualcare*, p. 25. Unlike the dressage rider who can devote his full attention to the performance of the horse, the medieval knight was also preoccupied with wielding his weapons, and also wore mailed leggings or plate armor which prevented the use of calf muscles.

37. Loriston-Clarke, *Dressage*, p. 96.

38. Bachrach ("Charles Martel, Mounted Shock Combat, the Stirrup, and Feudalism,"

p. 60) observed that the list of weapons and horses which appeared in Charlemagne's new recension of the law code of the Ripuarian Franks did not include stirrups. But stirrups surely would have been considered simply part of the saddle. Further (p. 62), Bachrach argued that the Carolingians could not have appreciated the military value of the stirrup since they were not mentioned in Rabanus Maurus' revision of Vegetius's *Epitoma rei militaris* (dedicated to King Lothair I). He noted that Rabanus departed from his model to update to existing conditions, describing for example the use of wooden horses to teach recruits how to mount; Bachrach suggested that if stirrups had any military importance they surely would have been mentioned here. In fact, however, Vegetius emphasized the importance of the ability to leap upon a horse's back from the left, right and rear. In the heat of combat, the length of time to mount a horse with stirrups could give an enemy the advantage to strike a decisive blow; leaping on the horse's back would ensure a much faster escape. Lacking the skill to leap upon the back of a fractious horse during battle could prove fatal. Nicolle ("The Impact of the European Couched Lance," p. 15) referred to a Muslim warrior during the siege of Acre who "had dismounted to pick up his lance, and was trying to remount his horse, which was very restive, when the Franks swooped down on him and killed him." In view of the need for agility to mount a horse in battle without stirrups, Rabanus Maurus' revision of Vegetius should not be used as proof positive to argue that the stirrup had no military significance in the ninth century.

39. This function of the stirrup was readily recognized in tournaments, where squires and men-at-arms would join in the fray, cutting the stirrup leathers of knights to encourage falling. Benson, "Tournament," p. 150 n. 28, citing Matthew Paris (*Chronica Majora*, ed. Henry Richards Luard, *Rerum Britannicarum Medii Aevi Scriptores* [Rolls Series], 57 [London: Longaman, 1874] IV: 135) referring to a tournament of 1241. Also, Nicolle ("The Impact of the European Couched Lance," p. 13), drawing on a passage from the mid-eleventh century Turkish romance *Warqa wa Gulshah*, "He struck him a cutting blow of the lance to make him lose his stirrups."

40. The artist of the tenth-century illustration of the Maccabees, the earliest depiction of the use of stirrups in combat (*v* Bachrach, "Animals and Warfare," p. 742 and pl. 3), may have been attempting to capture the instant the rider turns his toe out during lead change for the final charge of the Israelites against the "Forces of Evil." This appears to be a viable explanation of why the rider's foot is turned outwards so prominently. In this depiction, the horse would have been changing to the right lead, which would have been correct in relation to the lance in the right hand and the shield on the left arm.

41. Bachrach, "Animals in Warfare," p. 741, n. 109.

42. Bachrach, "Animals and Warfare," p. 739.

43. F. H. Huth, *Works on Horses and Equitation: A Bibliographical Record of Hippology* (London, 1887), pp. 7–11, indicates that a translation appeared in Paris in 1559. In 1565, the first edition of Thomas Blundeville's *The Four Chiefest Offices Belonging to Horsemanship* appeared in England; his work was an abridged translation of Grisone. Johann Fayser of Augsburg's translation into German of Grisone appeared in 1570. The wide dissemination of Grisone's treatise in the mid-sixteenth century coincided with the period when the tournament reached its peak as an expression of aristocratic values. On the progressive rather than degenerate development of the tournament, *v* Larry Benson, "The Tournaments in the Romances of Chrétien de Troyes and *L'Histoire de Guillaume Le Maréchal,*" in *Chivalric Literature: Essays on Relations*

between Literature and Life in the Later Middle Ages, ed. Larry D. Benson and John Leyerle (Kalamazoo, 1980), pp. 1–2.

44. Grisone, *Ordini di Caualcare,* p. 25.
45. Grisone, *Ordini di Caualcare,* pp. 201–02.
46. Juliet Barker, *Tournament in England,* p. 175, citing Froissart (xiv, 105–51) on the St. Inglevert jousts of 1390. A well-worn trail of scholarship rightly has indicated concern about the behavior ascribed to horses performing the maneuvers of mounted shock combat. *V* Bachrach, "Animals and Warfare," 738. John Keegan, *The Face of Battle* (New York, 1976), pp. 94–96. Also, Nicolle, "The Impact of the European Couched Lance on Muslim Military Tradition, pp. 33–34.
47. On longitudinal flexion and lateral bending, *v* de Kunffy, *Dressage Questions Answered,* pp. 57–111.
48. George H. Waring, *Horse Behavior, The Behavioral Traits and Adaptations of Domestic and Wild Horses, Including Ponies* (Park Ridge, NJ, 1983), p. 242.
49. A horse can travel about twenty miles per day and still retain combat effectiveness. *V* Bachrach, "Animals and Warfare," 718–19, for the literature dating back to Vegetius. Sidney Painter *(William Marshal,* 59) indicated that mêlée tournaments often lasted several days. To ensure success on the tournament circuit, a horse must have received daily exercise, to reach this level of endurance. Three-day eventing is the modern equestrian activity most comparable to mêlée tournaments and their demands on equine endurance. Both modern eventing and the medieval mêlée tournament require a horse to have genuine athletic ability, combining endurance, facility in lead change, and jumping skills to negotiate the obstacles commonly found in the European countryside. The modern training schedule entails about two hours of road work daily. *V* Jane Holderness Roddam, *Play to Win: Eventing* (London, 1988), p. 15: chart for fitness programs.
50. The daily average ration for a horse consists of about ten kilograms of feed; while half could be grass or hay, an equal amount was needed in grain such as barley or oats, comprising the half of the ration indispensable for combat activity. *V* Bachrach, "Animals and Warfare," pp. 718–19 and n. 49, and his *"Caballus et Caballarius,"* p. 179.
51. The number of horses in a string of destriers could depend on a knight-errant's success on the tournament circuit. Painter *(William Marshal,* p. 24) noted that on his first tournament William captured the war horses of three knights.
52. Benson, "The Tournament in the Romances of Chrétien de Troyes and *L'Histoire de Guillaume Le Maréchal,"* p. 5.
53. At Lagny-sur-Marne in 1179 Young King Henry, duke of Burgundy, led a retinue of 86 knights; in 1175 Count Baldwin of Hainault brought 200 knights (and 1,200 foot soldiers) to a tournament. *V* Benson, "Tournament," p. 5, citing *L'Histoire de Guillaume Le Maréchal,* ed. Paul Meyer, 3 vols. (Paris, 1891–1901) III, p. xxxvii; and Sidney Painter, *William Marshal,* p. 45.
54. Most recently, *v* Helmut Nickel, "The Tournament, an Historical Sketch," in *The Study of Chivalry,* 214; Richard Barber and Juliet Barker, *Tournaments, Jousts, Chivalry, and Pageants in the Middle Ages* (Woodbridge, Suffolk, 1989), 14; Juliet Barker, *The Tournament in England,* 17–19. Michel Parisse, "Le tornoi en France, des origines à la fin du XIIIe siècle," in Josef Fleckenstein, ed, *Das ritterliche Turnier im Mittelalter: Beiträge zu einer vergleichenden Formen-und Verhaltengeschichte des Rittertums* (Göttingen, 1985), p. 177.
55. R. Allen Brown, "The Battle of Hastings," *Proceedings of the Battle Conference on Anglo-*

° Not true. See David Crouch, Tournament (which has pretty well superceded all the stuff cited here).

Norman Studies 3 (1980), ed. R. Allen Brown (Woodbridge, Suffolk, 1981), p. 16. Bachrach, "Animals and Warfare," p. 731, n. 84; "The Feigned Retreat at Hastings," pp. 344–347; *"Caballus et Caballarius,"* pp. 188–92.

56. The *Alexiad of Anna Comnena,* trans. E. R. A. Sewter (Harmondsworth, 1969), pp. 171, 349, 416.

57. Raymond C. Smail, *Crusading Warfare,* 1097–1193 (Cambridge, 1956), p. 169. J. F. Verbruggen, *The Art of Warfare in Western Europe during the Middle Ages,* trans. S. Willard and S. C. M. Southern (New York, 1976), p. 95.

58. C. Warren Hollister, Anglo-Saxon Military Institutions (Oxford, 1962), pp. 131–32. Bachrach, History of the Alans, pp. 89–90; *"Caballus et Caballarius,"* p. 184.

59. Bachrach, *"Caballus et Caballarius,"* p. 184.

60. Bachrach, *"Caballus et Caballarius,"* p. 184, stated that, "The mounted charge by the French left flank against the Brabantine foot, who withdrew after little resistance, was the decisive phase of the battle," but Bachrach suggested that this retreat was probably caused by the duke of Brabant's duplicity instead of the tactical superiority of the French horse.

61. Barker, *The Tournament in England,* 1100–1400, p. 20.

62. C. M. Gillmor, "Cavalry, European," in Dictionary of the Middle Ages, ed. Joseph R. Strayer (New York, 1983), p. 205.

63. On the predominance of siege warfare, *v* Bachrach, *"Caballus et Caballarius,"* p. 204, n. 53.

64. Barker, *Tournament in England,* p. 32.

65. Bachrach, "The Angevin Strategy of Castle Building in the Reign of Fulk Nerra," *American Historical Review* 88 (1983), 533–59. John Gillingham, "War and Chivalry in the History of William the Marshal," *Thirteenth Century England,* ed. P. R. Coss and S. D. Lloyd (Woodbridge, Suffold, 1988), pp. 1–13.

66. Malcolm Vale, *War and Chivalry,* p. 68; Barker, *Tournament in England,* pp. 20–22. For general scholarly agreement that medieval battles were fought in tactical units, *v* Verbruggen, *The Art of Warfare,* pp. 72–76, and especially his "La tactique militaire des armées des chevaliers," *Revue du Nord* 30 (1948); 161–80, and "Le problème des effectifs et de la tactique à la bataille de Bouvines (1214)," *Revue du Nord* 31 (1949); 181–93. For an exhaustive bibliography and French translations of the sources on this battle, *v* Georges Duby, *Le dimanche de Bouvines, 27 juillet 1214* (Paris, 1973). For the opposite view, *v* Claude Gaier, "La cavalerie lourde en Europe occidentale du XIIe au XVIe siècle," *Revue internationale d'histoire militaire* 31 (1971), 385–96.

67. Paul Erfurth, *Die Schlachtenschilderungen in den älteren Chansons de Geste* (Halle, 1911), pp. 11–17.

68. Painter, *William Marshal,* p. 58.

69. Parisse, "Le tournoi en France," p. 177, construed a passage of William of Newburgh, *(Historia rerum Anglicarum,* ed. R. Howlett in *Rerum Brittannicarum medii aevi scriptores* 82, 2 [London, 1885], IV, pp. 422–23) to mean that Richard I sent knights to France to become more praticed in tournaments as preparation for war. But training to compete successfully in continental tournaments instead of actual warfare seems to be a more accurate motivation. Barker *(Tournament in England,* p. 17) interpreted a passage from Roger of Hoveden (II, pp. 166–7) to mean that Richard I legalized tournaments in England to train knights for war. The sense in which these chroniclers defined "warfare" should be reevaluated in view of the infrequency of pitched battles.

70. Maurice Keen, *Chivalry* (New Haven and London, 1984), pp. 85–86. Barker *(Tournament in England*, pp. 48–52) showed that mêlée tournaments sometimes became occasions for settling private feuds.

71. Painter *(William Marshal*, 43) citing *Histoire de Guillaume le Maréchal*, 11. 3884–4284.

72. On the importance of the medieval destrier, Anne-Marie Bautier, "Contribution à l'histoire du cheval au moyen âge," *Bulletin philologique et historique (jusqu'à 1610)*, 1976 (Paris, 1978), pp. 224–25; Robert-Henri and Anne-Marie Bautier, "Contribution à l'histoire du cheval au moyen âge, l'élevage du cheval," *Bulletin philologique et historique (jusqu'à 1610)*, 1978 (Paris, 1980), 59–75. Also, R. A. Brown, "The Status of the Norman Knight," in *War and Government in the Middle Ages: Essays in Honour of J. O. Prestwich*, ed. J. B. Gillingham and J.C. Holt (Woodbridge, Suffolk, 1984), pp. 28–29.

73. John Langdon, "Horse Hauling: A Revolution in Vehicle Transport in Twelfth and Thirteenth Century England," *Past and Present* 103 (1984); 37–66. Vehicles with the capacity to haul a destrier weighing around 1300 pounds (Bachrach, "Caballus et Caballarius," p. 179) did not appear until the late thirteenth century. *V* Bachrach, "Animals and Warfare," p. 717 and "Caballus et Caballarius," p. 203, n. 36, on carts and wagons.

74. Bachrach, "Animals and Warfare," p. 744, and especially p. 738, for the valuable distinction between the lance at rest and the couched lance position; Barker, *Tournament in England*, p. 4; Barker and Barber, *Tournaments, Jousts, Chivalry*, pp. 14, for the view that the origins of the tournament coincide with the introduction of the couched lance position. *V* also, Victoria Cirlot, "Techniques guerrières en Catalogne féodale: le maniement de la lance," *Cahiers de civilisation médiévale* 28 (1985), 35–43. Jean Flori, "Encore l'usage de la lance… La technique du combat chevaleresque vers l'an 1100," *Cahiers de civilisation médiévale* 31 (1988), pp. 213–40.

75. The professional sports dimension of the tournament was appreciated by Nickel, "Tournament," p. 238. *V* also, John Marshall Carter, *Sports and Pastimes of the Middle Ages* (Lanham, MD, 1988), and William J. Baker, *Sports in the Western World* (Totowa, NJ, 1982).

76. Benson ("The tournament in the romances of Chrétien de Troyes and *L'Histoire de Guillaume Le Maréchal*, p. 11) pointed out but did not develop the idea of the tournament as a form of professional sport. Instead, he focused on the tournament as an inexpensive form of amusement. In view of the cost of training and feeding destriers, this conclusion does not seem warranted.

77. Painter *(William Marshal*, p. 57) says the first priority was the search for military glory. Also, *Histoire de Guillaume le Maréchal*, 11. 3010–3012. But Benson ("Tournaments," 20) pointed out that Jean the Minstrel, who was commissioned to write the poem on William Marshal, relegated his military activities in the Holy Land to a mere 62 lines, and devoted thousands of lines to his performance in tournaments, which he clearly regarded as more important for attaining recognition for prowess in battle than going on a Crusade.

THE LITERARY EVIDENCE FOR MAST AND SAIL DURING THE ANGLO-SAXON INVASIONS

Michael Jones

Bates College
Lewiston, Maine

The Literary Evidence for Mast and Sail During the Anglo-Saxon Invasions

One of the very few certainties associated with the Anglo-Saxon invasions of Britain in the period A.D. 400–600 is that the invaders, however many there were, must all have come by ship. Given this circumstance, there must be a significant, perhaps even a controlling relationship between the quality and quantity of shipping available to the Anglo-Saxons and the nature and scale of the Anglo-Saxon migration and the subsequent early demographic, political, and economic order in England. The extremes of choice traditionally lie between an exceptionally large-scale folk movement involving entire agricultural communities and many tens of thousands of people, or the movement of isolated, relatively small militarized groups.[1]

The archaeological evidence relating to shipbuilding and the Anglo-Saxon migrations in the period c. 400–600 A.D. is drawn from England as well as the Anglo-Saxon continental homelands of the North Sea coastal regions, the Jutland peninsula and the lower Elbe. The most significant material is the actual remains or impressions of the ships themselves, supplemented with information gleaned from depictions of ships on coins, metal work, pottery, and stone. Because the evidence is thinly and unevenly scattered over several centuries, conclusions based on the archaeological record are necessarily somewhat speculative. Depictions of ships add little sure information concerning the Anglo-Saxon invasions because they are either too imprecisely dated or too late and too far afield to be directly relevant. For example, although depictions of ships with sails on the rock carvings of Gotland are sometimes cited as evidence for Scandinavian sailing ships as early as the sixth century A.D., the stones themselves cannot be securely dated even to within a particular century. Dating relies on decorative themes and styles tied to art historical typological arguments, a very inexact method. In fact, there is no consensus regarding the dating of these figures and they are as likely to be from the seventh century or later as the sixth century.[2] Ultimately the picture stones will probably be dated on the basis of excavations of ship types rather than the reverse. Sune Lindqvist, the Scandinavian scholar who pioneered the classification of the ships in the Gotland record, divided the progression of ship types into three phases (A,B,C). Crudely speaking, the Anglo-Saxon invasions fall into phase A (400–600) of his scheme with some overlap with the beginning of phase B (500–700). He classified ships without sails as phase A, and ships with sails as phase B.[3] Even in this very speculative chronology, therefore, there is no necessary or certain overlap between the Anglo-Saxon invasions and the earliest use of sails in Scandinavia. If the sailing ships of the Gotland stones are seventh century or later, of course, there is no overlap in any case.

Recently a Merovingian strap-end from northern France has been cited as possible evidence for the early use of sail by the Anglo-Saxons and Scandinavians. The strap-end is decorated with a crude depiction of a ship with mast and rigging. Several considerations make it irrelevant for the Anglo-Saxon ships of the invasions. It is evidently of seventh-century date and thus too late. Moreover, it may not be from an Anglo-Saxon or Scandinavian context. If the outline of the ship's hull is a realistic depiction, it is more likely to be a representation of a Romano-Celtic or perhaps Frisian type than a Scandinavian ship. In fact, the ship may not be a seagoing vessel at all but a small river craft.[4] Perhaps the most noteworthy depiction of a ship comes from an early seventh-century urn from Caistor-by-Norwich. This is distinctly an Anglo-Saxon context, and in time and location provides a good analogue for the boat finds from East Anglia, including the seventh-century ship from Sutton Hoo. Detlef Ellmers, Director of Deutsches Schiffahrtsmuseum, Bremerhaven, is almost certainly correct in identifying the freehand drawing of a ship chased by a wolf with the ship Naglfar, the Fenriswolf and the Götterdämmerung, an appropriate theme for a cremation urn. The ship is crudely drawn. The crew seem to be represented by thirteen vertical furrows placed just above the outline of the hull. Significantly, there is no attempt to show either mast or sail.[5]

Evidence of the ships themselves could obviously be highly useful. However, although hundreds of fragments of ships have been found, in only a handful of cases can reconstructions of ships' hulls be

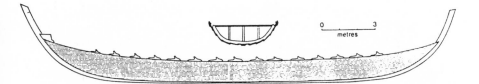

Figure 1. The Nydam boat, showing the low rake of the end-posts, and the narrow, shallow midships section. After Angela Evans, "The Clinker-built Boats of the North Sea," in The North Sea, *ed. Arne Bang-Andersen, Basil Greenhill, and Egil Harald Grude (Oslo, 1985).*

attempted. The crucial examples are summarized in Table I; the examples most relevant to the Anglo-Saxon invasions are the finds from Nydam, Sutton Hoo and Gredstedbro.

Surprisingly, as the table indicates, there is no positive archaeological evidence for the use of mast and sail by the Anglo-Saxons in the period of the migrations, 400–600 A.D. The case of the larger Sutton Hoo ship is inconclusive because when the ship was used as a funerary memorial, a burial chamber replaced the area amidships where a hypothetical keelson and mast partner (the normal Scandinavian structural support for a mast) might theoretically have been. However, all the surviving ships, fragments and impressions of vessels seem to be examples of clinker-built, undecked, double-ended rowing galleys. It is always difficult and awkward to prove a negative, but the archaeological evidence suggests that the North European or Scandinavian tradition of boatbuilding did not incorporate the use of mast and sail until the seventh century or later, after the Anglo-Saxon movement to Britain had ended.[6] The first positive archaeological evidence for mast and sail in Scandinavia is associated with the Oseberg and Askekarr ships of c. 800 A.D. This coincides roughly with the beginning of the Viking expansion in the late eighth century. If the Anglo-Saxons moving to Britain did indeed lack sails, this would have constituted a severe technological restriction, imposing in turn a significant limitation on the logistics of any transmarine movement.[7] Such a restriction and its implications have led a number of scholars to posit the existence during the migration of an unknown, undiscovered type of sail-driven vessel, or to modify the ships of the archaeological record with speculative additions such

Table I.

Ship	Location	Estimated Date	Possible origin	Approximate length	Excavated	Details
Halsnøy	S. Norway	c. 200 A.D. votive?	?	?	1896	fragments only found in bog
Nydam Oak	Schleswig	c. 350–400 A.D. votive	S. Scandinavia N. Germany	75'	1864	complete hull 30 oars
Nydam Fir	Schleswig	c. 400 A.D. votive	S. Norway N. Germany	51'	1864	Survives from 19th century plan 24 oars
Larger Sutton Hoo	Suffolk	c. 600 A.D. funerary	East Anglia	89'	1939 re-excavated 1965/67	nearly intact impression in sand & rivets c. 40 oars
Sutton Hoo Mound 2	Suffolk	7th Century funerary	East Anglia	22'	1939	poorly preserved as impression in sand
Snape	Suffolk	c. 650 A.D. funerary	East Anglia	50'	1862	poorly recorded [a second ship has been recently discovered]
Gredstedbro	S.W. Jutland	600–650 A.D.? wreck?	Jutland	65'	1945	fragments
Kvalsund	W. Norway	disputed: 7th or 8th century? votive	Norway	60'	1920	complete hull 20 oars accompanied by small boat
Ashby Dell	Suffolk	? pre-viking funerary	?	54'	1830	local newspaper record only, 14 oars, no iron

as the Sutton Hoo ship equipped with a purely hypothetical mast and sail.[8]

As this illustrates, arguments based on archaeology often resemble jigsaw puzzles with many critical pieces forever lost. Even the surviving pieces can be reinterpreted with new discoveries. In contrast, the literary evidence is relatively fixed. The small corpus includes brief observations in the writings of Tacitus, Claudian, Sidonius, Gildas, and Procopius. Periodically since 1953, some historians and archaeologists have cited passages from Claudian, Sidonius, and Gildas to support the case for a hypothetical mast and sail technology in use during the Anglo-Saxon migrations into Britain.[9] Sean McGrail, Chief Archaeologist at the National Maritime Museum (Greenwich), restated the case in 1981. Critical judgment of these primary sources involves several considerations. In all of these records the nautical information is inconsequential to the main objective of the authors. This adds a dimension to normal problems of obscurity and unclear meaning. Another problem lies with the nautical "competence" of the authors and their observations. These particular documents, with the exception of Gildas, can be closely placed in time and space, but the usual problems of translation blur the authors' intended meanings.[10] This article reviews the literary primary evidence and uses it to confront both the archaeological record and also the dissenting sail-related hypotheses of some modern scholars.

Tacitus

In 98 A.D., the Roman historian Tacitus described vessels in use in Scandinavia.

> Beyond these tribes the states of the Suiones, not on, but in, the ocean, possess not merely arms and men but powerful fleets: the style of their ships differs from normal in this respect, that there is a prow at each end, with a beak always ready to be driven forwards; they *neither work it with sails* [italics mine], nor fix oars in banks to the side: propulsion is by means of free paddles as on certain rivers, and reversible as occasion demands, for movement in either direction. (Suionum hinc civitates, ipso in Oceano, praeter viros armaque classibus valent. forma navium eo differt, quod utrimque prora paratam semper adpulsui frontem agit. nec velis ministrant nec remos in ordinem lateribus adiungunt: solutum, ut in quibusdam fluminum, et mutabile, ut res poscit, hinc vel illinc remigium.)[11]

There are a number of reasons for including this passage, even though the reference obviously long predates the era of the migrations. Tacitus has some claim to credibility, and the fact that the Germans he singles out for their maritime power lack mast and sail is of interest. This description confirms the archaeological evidence of the Halsnøy and Hjortspring boats (c. 200 B.C.–c. 200 A.D.) and provides an unambiguous starting point for our discussion.[12] The time of Tacitus' writing can be closely fixed. Finally, there is a distant tie between the Swedes, the Baltic, the tribal homelands of the Anglo-Saxons and the later Anglo-Saxon migration into Britain. A number of scholars have drawn connections between this description by Tacitus and the fourth-century Nydam vessel. Sutton Hoo, the famous seventh-century burial, shows strong Swedish influence. The Sutton Hoo vessel also seemingly lacked mast and sail.[13]

Claudian

From Tacitus we jump across a textual gap to the immediate period of the migrations, with the work of the court poet Claudian.[14]

> Next spoke Britain clothed in the skin of some Caledonian beast, her cheeks tattooed, and an azure cloak, rivalling the swell of ocean, sweeping to her feet: "Stilicho gave aid to me also when at the mercy of neighbouring tribes, what time the Scots roused all Hibernia against me and the sea foamed to the beat of hostile oars. Thanks to his care I had no need to fear the Scottish arms or tremble at the Pict, or keep watch along all my coasts for the Saxon who would come *whatever wind might blow* [italics mine]. (Inde Caledonio velata Britannia monstro, ferro picta genas, cuius vestigia verrit caerulus Oceanique aestum mentitur amictus: "me quoque vicinis pereuntem gentibus" inquit "munivit Stilicho, totam cum Scottus Hivernen movit et infesto spumavit remige Tethys. illius effectum curis, ne tela timerem Scottica, ne Pictum tremerem, ne litore toto prospicerem dubiis venturum Saxona ventis").[15]

This passage, written in A.D. 400, is sometimes cited as support for the idea that Saxons used wind-driven vessels during the fifth-century invasions. The basic argument associates reference to wind with an implied mast and sail. Of course weather and sea conditions, including specifically the strength and direction of the wind, affect the movement of all vessels, not just sailing craft. Tacitus recorded of the seas around Britain, "The sea was sluggish and *heavy to the oars* [italics mine], and was not set in motion as much as other seas even by the winds." An Anglo-Saxon Gnomic verse points out "weary shall be he who rows against the wind." According to the understanding of the fifth century and after, the three elements of water, the lower air, and the wind were an interacting system.[16] A reference to wind therefore need not imply any special significance in terms of the possible presence of mast and sail. This idea of where there is wind there is sail is repeated in connection with other texts, including Gildas' *De excidio* (see below). In the particular case of Claudian, the argument looks weak.

Claudian's description is drawn from a work of propaganda written in a highly ornate and stylized fashion, for an audience at the imperial Roman court in Milan, far removed from the scene of Saxon activity. It is part of a panegyric, not an offhand, incidental eyewitness description of Saxon raiding. In this literary context, the allusion to the wind is probably a metaphor for the unexpected, the sudden and unpredictable rather than an oblique reference to mast and sail. A literary topos underlies the image. Roman authors stereotypically associated particular groups of barbarians with particular traits. Just as Burgundians were extraordinarily tall and Britons (or Picts) tattooed, Saxons were a byword for savage surprise based on their great mobility and the sea. Ammianus described Saxons of the fourth century in a number of passages.[17] He was the last great Roman historian, a soldier who had campaigned against the Germans in Gaul.

The Franks and Saxons ... burst in by sea or by land, savagely robbing and burning. (Franci et Saxones ... quo quisque erumpere potuit, terra vel mari, praedis acerbis incendiisque, et captivorum funeribus ominum violabant).

27.8.5 (A.D. 368)

The Saxons are feared beyond all other enemies because of the suddenness of their incursions. (quam ob causam prae ceteris hostibus Saxones timentur ut repentini)

28.2.12

The Saxons had broken out with fearful violence, and always in parts where they were least expected. (conversos ad metuendam rabiem Saxonas, semper quolibet inexplorato ruentes)

30.7.8

A later description by the Spanish presbyter Orosius written c. 417 conveys the same basic image.[18]

> The Saxons ... are terrible by reason of their valour and mobility.
> *History Against the Pagans* 7.32

"Shifting winds" in Claudian is thus a natural poetic image to use in describing the sudden, savage, and unexpected attacks by Saxons along the shores of Roman Britain.

In fact, one of the examples drawn from Ammianus makes clear that it is the idea of the unexpected, not a veiled reference to mast and sail, that is brought to mind in classical literature by the association of Saxons with the wind.

> No one could guard against their unexpected coming, since they [the Maratocupreni, a brigand race from inland Syria] did not assail previously chosen places ... *breaking out wherever the wind took them* [italics mine] (quocumque ventus duxerat)—the same reason that makes the Saxons feared before all other enemies for their sudden raids.
> 28.2.12 (trans. J. C. Rolfe)

In this last example, the wind could hardly have less to do with ships and the sea; even so, the image that comes to Ammianus as a parallel is the Saxons, equally sudden and unpredictable, like the shifting winds.[19] In relation to Claudian and the Saxons, a century ago Hugh Williams, an editor and translator of Gildas, caught the root of Claudian's meaning in a charming rhymed translation that does not even mention the wind.

> When Seas did foame with strokes of oars
> That beat the billowes back,
> His force effecting with his cares,
> Prevented still my wracke:
> He bade me fear no forraine powers,
> That Picts or Scots could make,
> Nor of the Saxons that on seas
> Uncertain courses take.[20]

Finally, if Claudian's statement that the Saxons could arrive on any wind ("whatever wind might blow") is taken strictly and literally, this must suggest a motive power independent of the wind, in other words oars rather than sails. In this sense Claudian might be taken as evidence against associating mast and sail with Saxon shipping. The only technology he specifically mentioned, lumped vaguely with raiding Picts, Scots, and Saxons, is oars: "the sea foamed to the beat of hostile oars."

However, it is best not to press these last points too closely, for Claudian is an inappropriate witness for the fine details of Saxon marine technology. He was probably a native Egyptian, and very possibly never traveled west or north of Italy. The details of his career and travels in the west are not well documented, but it seems unlikely that Claudian ever saw a Saxon, let alone one of their ships. He apparently first visited Rome c. 394, embarking on his career in Latin poetry in 395. Probably early in that year Claudian moved to the imperial court at Milan. His detailed movements over the next five years are uncertain. He was at one time a tribune and notary. Certainly he must have frequented the court at Milan, for he directed panegyrics to court officials or the emperor in 396, 395–97, 398 and 399. Late in 399 or perhaps early in 400 he returned to Rome. During the period 396–400 Claudian may have traveled in the west outside Italy. Our ignorance concerning his movements permits such a speculation. He may have seen something of Gaul although the evidence for this is thin.[21] No one has ever suggested that he visited Britain.

Claudian's knowledge of the Rhine frontier and the Elbe, the most likely scene for Saxon activity outside of Britain, seems grossly inaccurate.[22] His general ignorance of Spain, Gaul, and Britain in contrast with Italy and the East is revealed by his use of images.[23] These western regions play a minor role in his poetry and his allusions do not suggest any close personal knowledge. Claudian's references to the Saxons reveal no specific details. He associates them with the sea and with the Scots and Picts attacking Britain. Claudian several times uses Britain and the Saxons as part of a far-flung image, paired with Africa and the Moors. He contrasts north with south, cold with hot. The Saxons seem a conventional motif. Certainly sails are never mentioned in connection with them.[24] It thus seems unlikely that Claudian had any personal or perhaps even good secondhand knowledge of the Saxons and even less likely that he knew the technical details of their ships.

To summarize, Claudian seems unlikely to be an informed or reliable source, nor are his poems a likely medium for the accurate transmission of maritime details. In any case, he never in fact describes

Saxon sails and his brief statements may actually be interpreted to support the idea that the Saxons used oars alone. He certainly does not bolster the case for the use of mast and sail by the Saxon invaders of Britain c. 400 A.D.

Sidonius

Our next literary glimpses of Saxon ships come from the pen of Sidonius Apollinaris, a Gallic aristocrat writing c. 456–77. Sidonius makes a tricky witness for matters maritime. On the one hand he sometimes shows good powers of observation and a love of detail. On the other hand, Sidonius is a typical product of late Roman education—derivative, full of classical tropes and allusions and writing in the highly conventionalized style of Roman epistolography, for an audience with similar background. It is difficult to separate Sidonius the potential firsthand witness from Sidonius the antiquarian rhetorician, captive to stylistic effect and formal stock *motifs*. As C. E. Stevens, an historian and biographer of Sidonius and his times, remarked, "in the letters the living man is smothered in the conceits of borrowed verbiage."[25]

Sidonius' letters were carefully edited and polished before publication. His later epistles, including the one describing Saxon ships, were possibly padded for publication with added "filler." These letters are thus not what a historian would most wish for, an offhand, spontaneous record of first person impressions. The passage describing Saxon ships illustrates the difficulty of distinguishing details of personal observation from convention and cliché. As we shall see, for the modern historian a triple, obscuring filter lies between Sidonius and his description of Saxon ships—the borrowed conventions of classical rhetoric; personal ignorance; and cultural prejudice.

> You ... were roving the winding shores of Ocean to meet the curving sloops of the Saxons, who give the impression that every oarsman you see in their crew is a pirate captain—so universal is it for all of them simultaneously to issue orders and obey orders, to teach brigandage and to learn brigandage. (inter officia nunc nautae, modo militis litoribus Oceani curvis inerrare contra Saxonum pandos myoparones, quorum quot remiges videris, totidem te cernere putes archipiratas: ita simul omnes imperant parent, docent discunt latrocinari).[26]

Sidonius uses *myoparon* in reference to the Saxon ships. This is an exotic term derived from the Greek and conveys the image of a light piratical galley. The term carries no evocation of sails. This part of Sidonius's description sounds promising. The "curving sloops of the Saxons," and the description of oarsmen seem appropriate when matched with archaeological discoveries such as Nydam or Sutton Hoo, or picture stones such as Häggeby, Uppland. Sidonius' source is purportedly a messenger momentarily arrived from the fleet at the very moment of the composition of the letter. The letter continues:

> That enemy [the Saxons] surpasses all other enemies in brutality. He attacks unforeseen, and when foreseen he slips away; he despises those who bar his way; and he destroys those whom he catches unawares; if he pursues, he intercepts; if he flees, he escapes. Moreover, shipwreck, far from terrifying them, is their training. With the perils of the sea ... they are familiarly acquainted; for since a storm whenever it occurs lulls into security the object of their attack and prevents the coming attack from being observed by victims, they gladly endure dangers amid billows and jagged rocks, in the hope of achieving a surprise. (hostis est omni hoste truculentior. inprovisus aggreditur praevisus elabitur; spernit obiectos sternit incautos; si sequatur, intercipit, si fugiat, evadit. ad hoc exercent illos naufragia, non terrent. est eis quaedam cum discriminibus pelagi non notitia solum, sed familiaritas. nam quoniam ipsa si qua tempestas est huc securos efficit occupandos, huc prospici vetat occupaturos, in medio fluctuum scopulorumque confragosorum spe superventus laeti periclitantur.) *Ep.* 8.6.14

Here we have strong indications of topos and convention. The fortuitously arriving messenger is a common convention in epistolography. The emphasis on surprise, as we have already seen, is the expected stereotypic quality associated with Saxons. The presence of these conventions tends to undermine the technical value of Sidonius' description. Certainly it would be naive to accept this description as "this lifelike picture, by a contemporary hand, of the brothers and cousins ... of the very men ... under Hengest and Horsa."[27]

Taken literally, the image of Saxons practicing shipwreck amid storms and shoals seems highly improbable. However, modern historians specializing in the study of the Scandinavian ship have suggested a number of differing rationalizing interpretations of this statement by

Sidonius. For example, Charles Green accepted the description at face value and wryly remarked that, given boats such as Nydam and Sutton Hoo, shipwreck must really have been a common peril.[28] Ole Crumlin-Pedersen rationalized "shipwreck" as a confused description by a Roman author unaccustomed to the practice of beaching ships through the surf, as opposed to harbour and dock.[29] Alan Binns suggested, if Sidonius were to be believed, the crews of the Saxon ships must have expected a safe haven in the region, and their ships must have been easily replaced.[30]

There may be some truth to these rather forced rationalizations, or alternatively we could treat Sidonius's description as an exaggeration calculated to enhance the effect of his description on his Roman audience. The Saxons' hardiness and endurance, as described by Sidonius, might be profitably compared to the Caledonians as described by the third-century Roman historian Dio Cassius.

> [They] are able to endure cold, hunger and all kinds of hardship; for they plunge into the marshes and stay there for many days with only their necks above water....[31]

At the least, the difficulties and conventions within this passage of Sidonius ought to warn against a simple, literal acceptance of his description.

In the next section of Sidonius' letter comes a crucial reference to Saxon sails, the single most important element in the literary case for the use of mast and sail by the Anglo-Saxon invaders of the fifth century.

> Moreover, when ready to unfurl their *sails* [italics mine] for the voyage home from the continent and to lift their gripping anchors from enemy waters, they are accustomed on the eve of departure to kill one in ten of their prisoners by drowning or crucifixion.... (praeterea, priusquam de continenti in patriam vela laxantes hostico mordaces anchoras vado vellant....)
>
> *Ep.* 8.6.15 (trans. W. B. Anderson)

The reference to sails is highly poetic and hence deeply suspicious. The Latin has a pleasant alliteration equivalent to "swelling sails" or "anchors aweigh"— "vela laxantes ... anchoras vado vellant." The murder of captives is reminiscent of a line in Ammianus, although the practice of crucifixion looks suspiciously like an invention of Bishop Sidonius, with allegorical overtones, and is not elsewhere attested. O. M. Dalton, who edited Sidonius' letters, translated the key phrase as "when the Saxons are setting sail from the continent, and are about to drag their firm-holding anchors from an enemy's shore." In his translation "setting sail" may be taken as idiomatic, and the phrase loses special technical significance in terms of actual mast and sail.[32]

It would be tempting to focus on the first part of Sidonius' description of pirate oarsmen and curving ships and dismiss the rest, including the reference to sails, as an embellishment invented by Sidonius for the delectation of his aristocratic Christian audience. This smacks of false selectivity, of course, and it may be better simply to dismiss Sidonius, in matters maritime, as an uncertain and ambiguous witness. As O. M. Dalton pointed out, "we learn nothing of naval matters" from Sidonius. It is by no means certain that he ever saw a Saxon ashore, let alone on board ship. For the most part the Saxons were active in northern Gaul while Sidonius was busy in the south. He did refer to travel to Bayeux, an area of Saxon settlement, but there is no mention of Saxons in the relevant letter.[33] The other occasions where Sidonius does mention Saxons tend to reinforce skepticism concerning the historical value of his descriptions. For example, a blue-eyed and strangely shaven Saxon at Bordeaux appears in a typical barbarian catalog redolent with stereotypic convention.

> We see in his courts the blue-eyed Saxon, lord of the seas, but a timid landsman here. The razor's keen blade, content no more to hold its usual course round the head's extremity, with clean strokes shearing to the skin, drives the margin of the hair back from his brow, till the head looks smaller and the visage longer.... (istic Saxona caerulum videmus assuetum ante salo solum timere; cuius verticis extimas per oras non contenta suos tenere morsus artat lammina marginem comarum et sic crinibus ad cutem recisis decrescit caput additurque vultus.)

This is peculiar but conceivable, but there follows a sea-green Herulian and a seven-foot Burgundian.

> Here strolls the Herulian with his glaucous cheeks, inhabitant of ocean's furthest shore, and of one complexion with its weedy deeps. here the Burgundian bends his seven feet of stature on suppliant

knee.... (hic glaucis Herulus genis vagatur, imos Oceani colens reces-
sus algoso propre concolor profundo. hic Burgundio septipes fre-
quenter flexo poplite supplicat quietem.)

Ep. 8.9 "To Lampridius" (trans. O. M. Dalton)

This is poetic license, not incidental firsthand detail. Sidonius did not
care for barbarians, even when they were "good" *(Ep.* 7.14.10). His
ingrained dislike seemingly prevented him from recording naturalistic,
realistic descriptions of those barbarians with whom he had personal
contact, let alone those like the Saxons whom he evidently knew only
secondhand from hearsay. Dalton called this circumstance "a great
opportunity lost."[34]

Sidonius gives one other reference to Saxon ships.

The Aremorican region too expected the Saxon pirate, who deems it
but sport to furrow British waters with hides, cleaving the blue sea in
a stitched boat. (cui pelle salum sulcare Britannum ludus et assuto
glaucum mare findere lembo.)   *Panegyric on Avitus* 369–71

Independently of its suspicious formulaic elements, this is a curious
description.[35] All other Roman authors except Sidonius treated seagoing hide boats as a peculiarly British product.[36] None linked hide boats
with Saxons or indeed any Germanic or Scandinavian peoples. For
example, in the first century B.C. Julius Caesar indicated that the hide
boats he encountered in Britain were new to the Romans. Caesar later
adopted the idea and built his own hide boats in Spain *(De bello civile*
1.4). A century later the poet Lucan referred to this same incident. He
mentioned that the Britons sailed the ocean in hide boats and also
mentioned that small hide boats were used on the river Po *(Pharsalia*
4). There may be a Celtic connection here, but if Lucan was correct,
this would add a non-British example of a hide boat to the Roman literary catalog, although not a seagoing boat. In the late first century A.D.,
Pliny made several references to hide boats. Significantly although he
had fought against Germans and spent most of twelve years with the
Roman armies on the Rhine, his references are to a specifically British,
not Germanic context *(Natural History* 4.30.16; 7.57). In the third century the geographer Solinus associated the use of hide boats specifically
with the sea between Hibernia (Ireland) and Britain *(Polyhistor* 23). In
the fourth century another geographer, Avienus, referred to skin-covered, seagoing British vessels *(Ora Maritima)*. Sidonius may actually have

taken his own reference to hide boats from the earlier work of Avienus or Pliny. The language used is suggestively similar.[37] If so, Sidonius evidently mistakenly transferred the hide boats in question from an originally Celtic British context to the Saxons. Many of the references to hide boats in Roman literature are derivative and uncritical borrowings from earlier works.[38] However, the association between hide boats and specifically British contexts is persistent and striking. Thus Sidonius seems to enjoy the dubious distinction of being the only Roman author to have confused the hide boats of the Celts of the British Isles (coracles and curraghs) with the vessels of their Saxon enemies.[39]

The idea that Sidonius has somehow confused Saxon with Celtic ships is strengthened by the context of his peculiar description. Earlier in the same piece he anachronistically proclaimed:

Caesar took his victorious legions over even to the Caledonian Britons, and although he routed the *Scot,* the *Pict,* and the *Saxon* [italics mine], he still looked for foes where nature forbade him to look any more for men. (victricia Caesar signa Caledonios transvexit ad usque Britannos; fuderit et quamquam Scotum et cum Saxone Pictum, hostes quaesivit, quem iam natura vetabat quaerere plus homines). *Panegyric on Avitus* 88–92.

This passage is revealing of Sidonius' methods and also of the historical value of the specific details he records. Here he has mistakenly connected the contemporary invaders of fifth-century Britain, the Scots, Picts, and Saxons, with the ancient figure of Julius Caesar. Caesar, of course, never fought the Scots or Picts in Britain let alone the Saxons. It may well be that the association of Saxons with hide boats or Saxons with sails is as bogus as the association of Saxons with Caesar. Very probably Sidonius has simply confused the Saxons and the Scots in his account.[40] Although we might concede that as invaders with a common victim (Britain), the Scots, Picts and Saxons might be said metaphorically to be in the same boat, Sidonius has literally and wrongly placed the Saxons in the skin boats of the rival invaders. This is an understandable but not a reassuring error. In the work of Sidonius, Saxon skin boats and Saxon sails seem equally dubious. In his own day Sidonius deliberately refused to write history *(Ep.* 4.22; 8.15). It is unreasonable to expect to find in him a scientific observer of nautical detail. Certainly he cannot serve as authoratative textual support for an otherwise unattested technology.

Gildas

Gildas is the most difficult of our small corpus of sources. His time and place of writing can be only approximated as sometime during the first half of the sixth century, somewhere in northern or western Britain.[41] Moreover, the meaning of his Latin is often difficult and obscure and creates serious problems for any translator. This is true of his description of Saxon ships in *De excidio* 23.3. The best and most recent translation gives:

Then a pack of cubs burst forth from the lair of the barbarian lioness, coming in three *keels*, as they call warships in their language. *The winds were favourable* [italics mine]; favourable too the omens and auguries, which prophesied, according to a sure portent among them, that they would live for three hundred years in the land towards which their prows were directed, and that for half the time, a hundred and fifty years, they would repeatedly lay it waste. (Tum erumpens grex catulorum de cubili leaenae barbarae, tribus, ut lingua eius exprimitur, cyulis, nostra longis navibus, *secundis velis* [my italics] omine auguriisque, quibus vaticinabatur, certo apud eum praesagio, quod ter centum annis patriam, cui proras librabat, insideret, centum vero quinquaginta, hoc est dimidio temporis, saepius vastaret, evectus....)[42]

In terms of an argument for mast and sail, we seem to have at best an example analogous to Claudian's shifting winds, with the weak association of a reference to wind and an assumed mast and sail.[43] The Latin in this passage is ambiguous, however, and the key phrase "secundus velis" may be translated either to mean favourable wind (through metonymy), as above, or as favourable sail (or perhaps more ambiguously as smooth sailing). The structure of the complicated sentence allows the critical phrase to be associated either with the Saxon ships or with the omens and auguries. The context greatly influences the translation. This ambiguity and the obscurity of Gildas's intended meaning is echoed in the various editions and translations of *De excidio*. For example in the sometimes flawed but still valuable Cymmrodorian edition of 1899–1901, Hugh Williams translated the passage to mean:

Then there breaks forth a brood of whelps from the lair of the savage lioness, in three cyulae (keels), as it is expressed in their language, but in ours, in ships of war *under full sail* [italics mine], with omens and divinations. In these it was foretold, there being a prophecy firmly relied upon among them, that they should occupy the country to which the bows of their ships were turned, for three hundred years....[44]

Williams's translation thus seems to indicate the use of sails by the Saxons, or, just possibly, by the Romans. This interpretation was echoed by A. W. Wade-Evans in 1959, whose work on Gildas is controversial: "under favourable sails with omen and divinations wherein it was being predicted."[45] In the earlier Bohn edition of 1848, J. A. Giles compromised between interpreting Gildas's *secundus velis* as either favourable wind or favourable sail by using both possible meanings and linking these to the omens. The Saxons arrive in "three cyuls, as they call them, that is, in three ships of war, with their *sails* wafted by the wind and with *omens and prophecies favourable* [italics mine]."[46] The confusion concerning Gildas' intended meaning is reflected not only in the various modern editions, but also in the medieval manuscript tradition. One of the principal manuscripts omits any mention of *velis*.[47]

 Unfortunately, Gildas does not write in a simple or straightforward style amenable to literal translation. The passage in question with its lioness and cubs abounds in metaphor and concludes with the reek of prophecy heavy in the air. In fact, the prophetic element seems to be the controlling feature and this strongly suggests that *secundus velis* should be associated as another favourable portent to form a triad with favourable omens and auguries. In 1928 in a translation prepared for the University of London's sourcebooks of history, R. W Chambers caught the meaning of *secundis velis* as "wind," another expression of favourable omens and portents. Thus the Saxons arrive "in three warships, with a favorable wind and with good augury. For it had been foretold them by a prophecy...."[48] This interpretation, as in the case of Winterbottom's, creates no evidence for Saxon mast and sail. Analogues are a useful clue in deciphering Gildas' intended meaning. Compare Constantius's fifth-century description of the arrival of Saint Germanus in Britain, whose success is predicted by the vanquishing of demons and the good omens of favorable weather. "He embarked under Christ's leadership and the elements permitted a calm voyage; winds, waves, and atmosphere all helped the ship along" (mare Christo auctore conscenditur; ad itineris tranquillitatem elementa consentiunt; navigium venti, fluctas, aera prosequuntur).[49] As with the earlier example of Claudian, Constantius provides a good example of the ancient and medieval perception that the three elements of water, wind and the lower air were parts of an interacting system. In this context, a reference to favorable wind suggests nothing more specific than good weather, a possible omen. Mast and sail are not necessarily or even obviously implied. In fact, *secundus* seems inappropriate when paired with *velis* (sail) unless as a literary conceit, and the more common phrase would be *secundis ventis*, meaning favorable wind or weather, or through transference, a sign of good success. An example from Cicero is instructive, "may you give to my talent favourable sails" (des ingenio vela secunda meo).[50] This is obviously a literary conceit. Bede provides a good example of *secundis ventis* (favorable winds) connected, as in the case of Constantius, with good omens as an expression of God's will:

No sooner was his prayer ended than he had calmed the swelling main; so that the fierce tempest ceased on all sides and favourable winds carried us over a smooth sea to land. (Et cum orationem conpleret, simul tumida aequora placauit, adeo ut cessante per omnia saeuitia tempestatis, secundi nos uenti ad terram usque per plana maris terga comitarentur.)[51]

Analogues from Latin literature thus suggest that Gildas used *secundus velis* as a literary idiom, much as we might say "smooth sailing" today. Thus we return to the most satisfactory translation "the winds were favorable, favorable too the omens...."

Gildas' other reference to Saxon ships is not helpful, unless perhaps as a warning against too literal an interpretation of his meaning.

The mother lioness learnt that her first contingent had prospered, and she sent a second and larger troop of satellite dogs. It arrived by ship.... (Cui supradicta genetrix, comperiens primo agmini fuisse prosperatum, item mittit satellitum canumque prolixiorem *catastam*, quae *ratibus* [my italics] advecta adunatur cum manipularibus spuriis.) *DE* 23.4 (trans. Winterbottom)

Hugh Williams linked *catastam* with *ratibus* to produce the following translation with its image of Saxon dogs on a raft, a deliberately contemptuous expression on the part of Gildas, one which Bede later altered to *classis* (fleet), to better suit the dignity of his countrymen.

To these the mother of the brood, finding that success had attended the first contingent, sends out also a larger raft-full of accomplices and curs....

Rafts can hardly be an accurate description of the Saxon invaders' craft, whether they had sails or not. Williams's image, however, is questionable in any case, for elsewhere Gildas also referred to Roman ships as *"ratibus."*[52]

Elsewhere in *De excidio* Gildas describes ships of other peoples in unambiguous terms indicating that the Britons, Scots, and Picts all used sails.[53] The lack of any equivalent unambiguous statement concerning the Saxons is therefore perhaps significant. Neither Bede nor the author of *Historia Brittonum,* a ninth-century British work incorporating earlier material, mention sails when describing the invading Saxons.[54]

Even Gildas's unambiguous descriptions of non-Saxon sail-powered ships present difficulties. He is fond of the formulaic and poetic phrase "swelling sails" *(velorum sinibus)* and uses the phrase to describe the ships of both the Britons and the raiding Scots and Picts.[55] Gildas described the ships of the Picts and Scots in the following way:

They came relying on their oars as wings, on the arms of their oarsmen, and on the winds swelling their sails. (alis remorum remigumque brachiis ac velis vento sinuatis vecti.) *DE* 16

This seems a clear description of craft powered by both sail and oar, quite in keeping with what we know of Celtic coracles and curraghs. However, Neil Wright pointed out that Gildas possibly borrowed the phrase describing the sails from the *Historica Ecclesiastica* of Rufinus, one of Gildas's favorite sources. Rufinus used "quasi *uelis* nauis *uento sinuatis*" (Wright's italics). Given the commonness of the image, borrowing is not certain, but the rest of Gildas's description is similar to a line from the *Aeneid,* another of Gildas's sources, "remigio alarum" ("the oarage of wings").[56]

If these are in fact examples of literary borrowings, even if they are appropriate ones, then we must treat very cautiously the highly literary passages in Gildas containing descriptions of ships, and not expect to find therein a specific and accurate reflection of naval technology. In general, the text of Gildas, in the matter of sails, will not bear much interpretive weight. He makes no clear, unambiguous or credible reference to Saxon sails. This is clearly too frayed a rope with which to rig a sail on the ships of the invading Anglo-Saxons.

Claudian, Sidonius, and Gildas constitute the conventional literary support for the use of mast and sail by the Anglo-Saxons of the invasions. Yet these three texts individually and collectively provide an unimpressive argument. At best they seem ambiguous, and inappropriate sources for such a conclusion. In fact, as we have seen in the case of Claudian and possibly also Gildas, the literary evidence seems actually to undermine the case for Saxon sail. In any case, however, a final source provides the *coup de grâce* to the textual arguments for the use of mast and sail by the Anglo-Saxons of the fifth and sixth centuries.

Procopius

Writing c. 550, roughly contemporary with Gildas and towards the end of the period of invasions, the Greek historian Procopius described the ships of the Angles in Britain.

> And there were no supernumeraries in this fleet, for all the men rowed with their own hands. Nor do these islanders have sails, as it happens, but they always navigate by rowing alone.[57]

This is a clear statement, unencumbered by idiom or metaphor. It seems to complete a sail-less circle begun by the text of Tacitus. How reliable is it?

In terms of his sources, methods, aims and language, Procopius poses formidable problems of interpretation.[58] This is particularly the case with his geographical or ethnographical digressions such as the one concerning Britain containing the description of the Angle fleet. These digressions often present a bizarre mixture of the preposterous and the plausible, so intertwined that no single statement within a passage can be used to validate or disprove another.[59] The British material, for example, besides the matter-of-fact description of oar-driven ships, also includes unbelievably inflated numbers, a romance, and a ghost story. Despite this, most scholars see within the account a genuine historical core.[60] As Averil Cameron concluded:

> There is just enough plausible detail, among the hearsay and the personal comment, to qualify as serious evidence, with sufficient distortion to make its interpretation highly problematic.[61]

In this particular case Procopius names his source, a Frankish embassy, and historical conditions linking Britain, the kingdom of Clovis and Byzantium in this period make the circumstances of transmission to Procopius of the information concerning Britain more convincing than much of the information itself.[62] The Frankish embassy at least establishes a potential credibility for Procopius' information concerning the ships of the Angles.

To deny mast and sail to the Angles seems to serve no obvious purpose in terms of Frankish or Byzantine propaganda. Nor does this seem to reflect a particular, personal or stylistic aim on the part of Procopius. Moreover, for all of his limitations, Procopius had firsthand experience with warships and transports of the sixth century. This alone sets him apart as a source for maritime details from the company of Claudian, Sidonius and Gildas. His descriptions of the ships of the Byzantines and Vandals, even if sometimes couched in archaic language, seem technically correct.[63] He certainly knew that the Romans, Celtic peoples, and even other Germans knew the use of mast and sail.[64] The distinctive ignorance of sails that he attributes to the Angles of Britain thus commands respect. The one other distinction Procopius links to the Angles is an ignorance of horses.[65] Even if overstated, the reliance on infantry rather than cavalry on the part of the Anglo-Saxons did distinguish them from the other Germans. This fact would seem to enhance the credibility of Procopius's statement concerning Angle ships.

To escape the full implications of Procopius' statement concerning the lack of sails among the Angles, some historians have suggested that his statement applied only to warships, not to (purely hypothetical) sail-powered transports.[66] Not only is this completely speculative but it then invalidates the other "proof" for sails, since Claudian, Sidonius, and Gildas also evidently described warships. In fact, however, Procopius does not describe specifically warships, but a fleet engaged in transporting an army from Britain to the continent.

Thus presumably if there were a type of Anglo-Saxon transport distinct from a warship (and there is no evidence of this), then the hypothetical transport would be included in Procopius's categorization. What he actually says is "nor do these islanders have sails...." a blanket statement independent of any specific type of ship, hypothetical or otherwise.

Procopius certainly appreciated the distinction between warship and transport in the Byzantine fleet; he is unlikely to have been

careless or insensible concerning the implications of his characteriza-
tion of the Angle fleet from Britain.[67] In general, Procopius provides
the clearest and quite possibly the best qualified statement in the textual record concerning the use of mast and sail by the Anglo-Saxons of
the migrations. He gives an unambiguously negative answer.[68]

Anglo-Saxon Sources

Because the Anglo-Saxons were illiterate during the migrations and for
some time thereafter, they left no contemporary written descriptions of
their own invading ships. Accordingly it is not possible to make a comparison with the Roman and British literary evidence. However, nothing in the later Anglo-Saxon literature contradicts the idea that they
lacked mast and sail in the period 400–600 A.D. Brief retrospective
accounts of the original invasions in Bede and the *Anglo-Saxon Chronicle*
make no mention of sails. Bede completed the *Ecclesiastical History of the
English People* c. 731. The *Anglo-Saxon Chronicle* is a complicated record,
probably begun in the ninth-century during the reign of King Alfred.
Both sources drew on earlier material.[69] Probably the earliest certain
Anglo-Saxon reference to a seagoing sailing ship is in the poem
Andreas, written perhaps c. 800 A.D. The poem *Beowulf* mentions mast
and sail (11. 36; 217; 1905–06), but although it ostensibly describes the
world of the sixth century, the poem is anachronistic and the details of
the ships should most probably be associated with vessels contemporary
with the date of composition. This last is a highly debated question.
The poem was probably recorded c. 1000 A.D., but may have been com-
posed originally in the ninth-century Anglo-Scandinavian world, eight-
century Mercia, or even seventh-century Northumbria or East Anglia.
These possible contexts are all centuries removed from the fifth-century invasions of Britain, and no one has been rash enough to press
Beowulf into service as an authority for the ships of an earlier period.
The earliest Anglo-Saxon reference to sail evidently comes from Bede's
Ecclesiastical History. In this story the priest Guthfrith goes to visit
Ethelwald (c. 687 to 699) on Farne Island and is caught in a storm: "So
fiery a wintry tempest arose that we could make no progress either by
sailing or rowing and expected nothing but death." A prayer from
Ethelwald saved the day. "No sooner was the prayer ended than he had
calmed the swelling main so that the fierce tempest ceased on all sides
and favourable winds *(secundi uenti)* carried us over a smooth sea to
land."[70] This description of a boat in use in the last decade of the sev-

Table II

	Latin	Old English	Old Norse	Old Irish	Indo-European
Row	remigare	rōwan	rōa	rāme	*erē
Oar	remus	† ār	ār	rām	*re-smos
Sail	velum	segl	sigla	sēol	? * seq
Mast	malus	maest	vida	matan	mazdos (Western Indo-European)
Anchor	ancora	ancor	akkéri	ingor	

† Old Teutonic, a North Sea word but perhaps radically akin to Greek eretmós
* = hypothetical early Indo-European form

enth century is too late to be relevant to the migrations. Even this reference has its share of problems in linking unambiguously Anglo-Saxon seagoing ships with mast and sail. Bede's account is derivative and may not be technically accurate. The last line quoted echoes Vergil *(Aen.* 1.142) and the New Testament origin for the miracle of calming the waters is obvious.[71] Moreover, the voyage is only seven miles long and the boat involved is a little vessel ("nauiculam") so portable that its crew of three can carry it. This is obviously not a seagoing clinker-built ship. Bede's description thus evidently has nothing of significance concerning the original ships of the migration era. Finally, Lindisfarne is part of the Celtic world and the context of the event is a reflection of the interface of Irish and Saxon culture. Bede's description fits best an Irish curragh or coracle and this is the most plausible identification.[72]

An earlier miracle story related by Bede concerning the voyage of Utta from Kent to Northumbria sometime after c. 642, mentions "storms and contrary winds" and an anchor, but no details of mast, sail, or oar. A timely dose of oil on the waters saved the ship *(HE* 3.15). The Biblical inspiration of the miracle of oil on the waters is obvious. The elements of prophecy, miracle, and lack of explicit detail rob the story of any significance as evidence for mast and sail.[73]

Linguistic evidence, although notoriously difficult to interpret, offers a supplemental if speculative approach to the use of literary evidence. For what it is worth, the terminology for rowing, mast, and sail in the Germanic languages may be interpreted to suggest that the art of sailing came late to Scandinavia, transmitted indirectly by intermediate contact between Scandinavia and the Roman-influenced Celtic or Frisian spheres after Roman control of northwestern Europe had ended. Dating based on linguistic evidence is of course speculative and inexact, but a date sometime after the fifth-century migrations seems indicated. There may be great significance in the fact that the words for mast in Old English and Old Norse had different origins (see table II). This suggests that the use of mast and sail was introduced into Scandinavia after the historical divergence of these languages.[74]

In contrast, the Germanic words for oar and row are similar in OE. and ON., and may be derived from Latin, an example of the diffusion of technology during the Roman period. There is some evidence to suggest that the Saxons adopted true oars and rowing as opposed to paddling sometime during the fourth century.[75]

Alternatively, the words relating to oar and row may be derived from a common Indo-European root *(erē)*. "Anchor" certainly seems to be borrowed into Germanic languages from Latin, suggesting a borrowed technology. "Sail" is more difficult to account for. The Germanic term does not come from Latin *(velum)* but is perhaps derived from the leather sails of the Celts *(zagulum)*, perhaps via the Frisians *(sigla)*. It is puzzling to find that the word for mast can differ in OE. and ON., but not the word for sail. In fact, the difficulty of determining the direction and origin of the historical circumstances of linguistic borrowing and technology is well illustrated by the sail. The Irish and Welsh borrowed a great vocabulary of nautical terms from the Norse of the Viking period, evidently greatly impressed by Viking ship technology. In this manner sail *(segl)* was ironically possibly transmitted from an immediate Norse context into Irish and Welsh *(Sēol, hwyl)*, even though the Norse word originally was perhaps borrowed from the Celtic![76] In general, the linguistic evidence seems to support the archaeological record, and the literary evidence to suggest that the use of mast and sail first reached Scandinavia and the continental homelands of the English after the Anglo-Saxon invasions of Britain had ended. It is possible to speculate that Britain played a role in the ultimate dissemination of the technology to Scandinavia, an ironic effect in light of the eventual Viking assault on Anglo-Saxon England.

At present, the archaeological evidence for the use of sail by the Anglo-Saxons of the migrations is nonexistent. It is always possible, of course, that new discoveries could dramatically alter this picture. Somewhere among the unexcavated burial mounds of Britain and Scandinavia, like the pea in a carnival shell game, may lie undiscovered evidence for the use of mast and sail in the period 400–600. Against this possibility and the small number of ships so far discovered, must be set the coherence and consistency of the existing evidence; the knowledge that boats are the most conservative of all archaeological objects in the period 300–1000; the strongly conservative and traditional character of specifically Scandinavian shipbuilding right up to the later middle ages; and the idea that larger seagoing ships have always been more uniform than the more various small craft of Scandinavia.[77]

Nor does the literary evidence lend support to the possible existence of an undiscovered type of Anglo-Saxon sailing ship within the Scandinavian tradition. A significant new discovery of literary evidence seems unlikely and close examination of those passages relating to Saxon ships reveals no convincing evidence for the use of sails by the invading Anglo-Saxons. Sidonius stands virtually alone and suspect. Although the overall representativeness of the literary evidence may be questioned, proponents of Saxon sails must seek for persuasive arguments elsewhere.

If the evident convergence of the archaeological record, the literary evidence, and the linguistic arguments explored and interpreted here is accepted, then the Anglo-Saxon migration was seemingly limited to clinker-built, oar-powered craft. The Anglo-Saxons reaching Britain must have rowed themselves there and this circumstance would have imposed a severe logistical limitation on the scale and nature of their settlement. Within reasonable limits it is possible to estimate the size of the crews and the carrying capacity of the ships of the archaeological record. The largest ships such as Sutton Hoo and Nydam oak will have carried as many as sixty to eighty men.[78] Such great ships suitable for royal burial or godly sacrifice may have been exceptional. The more modest ships along the lines of Nydam fir, Snape or Kvalsund would have carried smaller crews of fifty or fewer. In the context of warfare in the early middle ages when armies numbered but a few hundred soldiers, a single ship's company would have been a significant force and a handful of such crews would have constituted a powerful army.[79] In terms of military forces, therefore, these rowing ships would have been effective for piracy, raiding, or invasion. In contrast, such ships would not have been suitable for conveying entire agricultural communities or moving many tens of thousands of people including the old, the young, women and all the paraphernalia of agricultural stock and equipment. The difficulty here is that the "cargo" must be its own motive power. Recall the words of Procopius:

And *there are no supernumeraries in this fleet* [italics mine], for all men rowed with their own hands. Nor do these islanders have sails, as it happens, but they always navigate by rowing alone.

Allowing for a crew large enough to provide the necessary propulsion, and a minimum of water and provision for these oarsmen, even the larger vessels such as Sutton Hoo would have had little room to spare, carrying at most perhaps twenty to thirty dependents and very little non-human cargo.[80] There is general agreement that such ships would rarely or safely have risked direct crossing of the North Sea. The alternative would have involved long and expensive coasting voyages of several months to reach the narrow sea approaches to Britain from the continental homelands.[81] Moreover, the ships themselves would have represented considerable, perhaps enormous, investment of wealth. They cannot have been common. Independent of maintenance and crew, construction of a ship such as Nydam must have been expensive in time, skilled labor and material. Some idea of relative cost may be gained by a comparison with later, richer and more settled circumstances. At the beginning of the eleventh century in Anglo-Saxon England, a warship roughly comparable to the ships of Nydam or Sutton Hoo represented the taxable wealth of hundreds of families.[82] Given these considerations, a truly popular migration on a national scale in 400–600 seems logistically impossible. Instead, we should expect to find a pattern of scattered, smaller and heavily militarized emigrant groups such as those described by Gildas, Bede, the *Anglo-Saxon Chronicle*, and the *Historia Brittonum*. The clinker-built rowing ships are a logistical funnel through which all theories of the nature of the Anglo-Saxon migration into Britain must pass.

NOTES

1. Sir Frank Stenton, the most influential historian of Anglo-Saxon England in this century, referred to the Anglo-Saxon migrations as "unique in any case among contemporary movements... a series of national migrations." *Anglo-Saxon England*, 3d ed. (Oxford, 1971), p. 277. Stenton shared the perception that the Anglo-Saxon movements involved large and organized forces, not small groups of invaders acting independently of one another, with the earlier classic work of H. M. Chadwick, *Origins of the English Nation* (Cambridge, 1907), pp. 12–14, 181 ff. R. V. Lennard's criticism of the "big" invasion theory is venerable but still effective. "The Character of the Anglo-Saxon Conquests: A Disputed Point," *History* n.s. 18 (1933–34), 104–15. For a recent overview of this question emphasizing theoretical and archaeological concerns *v* C. J. Arnold, *Roman Britain to Saxon England* (Beckenham, 1984), pp. 8 ff.

For a more general historical summary see James Campbell, "The Lost Centuries: 400–600," in *The Anglo-Saxons* (Ithaca, 1982), 20–44. Campbell's book is the best recent survey of the Anglo-Saxon period. There is a recent discussion of the genesis of the Anglo-Saxon kingdoms in Steven Bassett, ed., The *Origins of Anglo-Saxon Kingdoms* (Leicester, 1989). For support of the idea that the Anglo-Saxon migration was characterized by small numbers and multiple landings largely dominated by military elements *v* note 7 below.

2. Angela Evans calls the Gotland stones "notoriously difficult to date." "Clinker-Built Boats of the North Sea, 300–1000 AD," in *The North Sea*, ed. Arne Bang-Andersen, Basil Greenhill and Egil Harald Grude (Oslo, 1985), p. 70. Alan Binns thinks the Gotland stones can be no more closely dated than the Old English poems. *Viking Voyagers* (London, 1980), p. 24. For a seventh-century date (or later) P. H. Sawyer, *The Age of the Vikings*, 2d ed. (London, 1971), p. 78.

3. Sune Lindqvist, *Gotlands Bildsteine*, 2 vols. (Stockholm, 1941–42); idem, "Fartygsbilder från Gotlands forntid," *Foreningen Sveriges Sjöfartmuseum* 1 (Stockholm, 1941), pp. 9–24. For a recent review of Lindqvist's work *v* Erik Nylen, *Bildstenar* (Visby, 1978).

4. Sean McGrail hints that the ship may be Celtic or Frisian when he suggests a possible continuity with ships in use in France before the seventh century. *The Ship: Rafts, Boats and Ships from Prehistoric Times to the Medieval Era* (London, 1981), p. 40. René Joffroy suggested that the ship might be a small river craft. "Note sur deux ferrets mérovingiens des collections du musée des antiquités nationales," in *Problémes de chronologie relativ et absolute concernant les cimetiéres mérovingiens d'entre Loire et Rhin*, ed. Michael Fleury and Patrick Périn (Paris, 1978), pp. 195–97.

5. "Die Schiffe der Angelsachsen," *Sachsen und Angelsachsen, Veröffenlichungen des Helms-Museums* 32 (1978), p. 506.

6. I have used surveys of the relevant archaeological material written by prominent specialists in the archaeology of the boat representing the opinions of German, Scandinavian and English scholars. Ellmers, "Die Schiffe der Angelsachsen," pp. 495–509; Arne Emil Christensen, "Scandinavian Ships from Earliest Times to the Vikings," in *A History of Seafaring Based on Underwater Archaeology*, ed. George Bass (London, 1972), pp. 159–68, at p. 165; Paul Johnstone, *The Sea-craft of Prehistory* (London, 1980), pp. 102–20, at 117; Evans, "The Clinker-built Boats of the North Sea, 300–1000 AD," pp. 63–78. At one time the Galtabäck ship, a sail-powered merchant vessel, was dated c. 400–600 A.D., on the basis of pollen evidence. The ship was later redated using C 14 and is now accepted to be post-Viking. Arne Emil Christensen, "Viking Age Ships and Shipbuilding," *Norwegian Archaeological Review* 15 (1982), 19–28 at p. 24.

7. This logistical restriction would have limited the invading Anglo-Saxon armies to a few hundred men each and the overall migrating population to thousands, not many tens of thousands. Michael E. Jones, "The Logistics of the Anglo-Saxon Invasions," in *Naval History*, ed. Daniel Masterson (Wilmington, 1987), 62–69. Leslie Alcock has written extensively on the size of armies in Dark Age Britain and argues persuasively that the actual "immigrant bands" described in the literary sources must have numbered individually between perhaps one hundred and two hundred and fifty men. *Arthur's Britain* (Harmondsworth, 1971, reprinted 1983), p. 335. For the specific case of Kent *v* K. P. Witney, *The Kingdom of Kent* (London and Chichester, 1982), p. 41. The small carrying capacity of the ships of early medieval northern

Europe is emphasized by the economic historian Richard Hodges, *Dark Age Economics* (New York, 1982), pp. 94–95. Armies in Anglo-Saxon England may well have continued to be small, continuing the traditions and scales of the original invading warbands. *V* Richard Abels, *Lordship and Military Obligation in Anglo-Saxon England* (Berkeley, 1988), pp. 35, 219 n. 130. The comparable archaeological evidence from the continent relating to the *adventus Saxonum* is in keeping with the idea of small scale invasion. *V* John Hines, "The Military Context of the *Adventus Saxonum*: Some Continental Evidence," in *Weapons and Warfare in Anglo-Saxon England*, ed. Sonia C. Hawkes (Oxford, 1989), pp. 25–46.

8. Speaking of great rowing boats like Nydam and the implications of a migration limited to such ships, Leslie Alcock stated: "Clearly there is an *absurdity* here [italics mine]. It can be removed if we recall that Nydam is close to the Baltic shore and if we think of the Nydam boat as designed for that tideless sea. It is probably irrelevant to the question of the vessels used by the ancestral English whether as raiders or immigrants, and we must return later to the problems which they pose *(Arthur's Britain*, pp. 280–81)." Alcock returned to this point with a discussion of Sutton Hoo and admitted "In sum, then, all the available archaeological evidence is for rowing boats, not sailing vessels, among the early English and their continental ancestors... [but] it is inconceivable that the idea of the sail, known in the Bay of Biscay before the Christian era, had not been diffused to the North Sea by the time of the migrations. Fortunately we are saved from the conclusion that the archaeological evidence has not given us the full range of Anglo-Saxon ships by the latest, authoritative reconstruction of the Sutton Hoo ship which shows it under sail before a following wind *(Arthur's Britain*, p. 301)." Alcock here refers to the work of the Scandinavian scholar H. Akerlund, who first speculated that the hull of the Sutton Hoo ship might have been strong enough to support a mast and sail. *Nydamskeppet* (Göteborg, 1963), p. 141. His speculation was incorporated into the published report on Sutton Hoo. R. Bruce-Mitford, ed., *The Sutton Hoo Ship Burial*, I (London, 1975), pp. 252, 421 ff. While it is sometimes possible to conclude with some confidence that a particular hull could not have supported the strain of a mast and a single great sail, a stronger hull need not imply the use of a sail. This is pure conjecture. In fact, the assumptions made by Akerlund and others concerning the hull and keel of the Sutton Hoo ship, or more correctly, the sand impression of a ship, are by no means secure. *V* the criticism advanced by Alan Binns of these ideas in "Sutton Hoo Published: A Review," *Anglo-Saxon England* 6 (1977): 359–62. The somewhat later Kvalsund ship, with a hull and keel evidently stronger than those of Sutton Hoo, provided no evidence of mast and sail. This is significant, because the evidence relating to Kvalsund had not been distorted by the construction of a burial chamber in the ship as was the case with Sutton Hoo. It is unlikely that all trace of mast and sail would have vanished if Kvalsund had originally been equipped with such. *V* the comments of Angela Evans, "Clinker-built Boats of the North Sea," 69. Charles Green concluded that it would have been too dangerous for the Anglo-Saxons to have made direct crossings of the North Sea in rowing ships such as Nydam or Sutton Hoo. Using a series of convincing technical arguments, he outlined the probable coasting routes and short sea crossings likely to have been used and outlined the difficulties, time, and expense involved. "North Sea Crossings" in *Sutton Hoo*, 2d ed. (Totowa, 1988), pp. 103–14. To escape the implications of his argument, some scholars have suggested that the Anglo-Saxons must have made direct crossings of

the North Sea in sailing ships of a type missing from the archaeological record. Since the neighboring Celts and Romans used sails, it is inferred, the Saxons must have seen the advantage of this technology and adopted it. D. M. Goodburn, "Do We Have Evidence of a Continuing Saxon Boat Building Tradition?" *International Journal of Nautical Archaeology and Underwater Exploration* 15 (1986), p. 45. In a review of the first edition of Charles Green's book, J. N. L. Myres cited the Roman defences along the Yorkshire coast and the northern areas of Anglian settlement in Britain as evidence that the Anglo-Saxons made direct crossings of the North Sea using sailing ships. "Review of Charles Green's *Sutton Hoo,*" *English Historical Review* 80 (1965), pp. 572–73. In terms of Myres's arguments, the Roman stations in Yorkshire may very well have been erected in response not to Saxon attack but to Pictish raiding from the north of Britain. There is a significant difference between the initial landfall of an established migration route and the area of ultimate permanent settlement. The Angles, for example, after crossing from the continent, may have coasted up the eastern seaboard to reach their final northern settlements. Richard Hodges provides a good example of an uncritical acceptance of the idea of the use of sails by the Saxons to overcome the logistical difficulties outlined by Charles Green. *Dark Age Economics,* p. 101. For a discussion of the possibility of a sail-driven type of Anglo-Saxon ship missing from the archaeological record *v* Detlev Ellmers, *Frühmittelalterliche Handelsschiffahrt in Mittel und Nordeuropa* (Neumünster, 1972), pp. 16 ff.

9. McGrail, *The Ship,* p. 40. The earliest version of this argument known to me was published in 1953. G. J. Marsden, "Mast and Sail in the North," *Mariner's Mirror* 39 (1953), 140–41. For a fuller survey of the literary evidence *v* Ellmers, *Frühmittelalterliche Handelsschiffahrt,* pp. 16–58.

10. McGrail, *The Ship,* p. 7.

11. Tacitus, *Germania* 44, trans. M. Hutton, revised E. H. Warmington (London and Cambridge, Mass., 1970). If paddles rather than true oars are being described here, it would give added support to the idea that the Saxons may also have lacked genuine oars and rowlocks until the fourth century. *V* n. 75 below.

12. Christensen, "Scandinavian Ships," 161-62.

13. Tacitus and Nydam: Richard W. Unger, *The Ship in the Medieval Economy 600–1600* (London, 1980), p. 70 n. 27; Akerlund, *Nydamskeppet,* 155–57. Sweden and Sutton Hoo: Sune Lindqvist, "Sutton Hoo and Sweden," *Antiquity* 22 (1948), 131–40; N. E. Lee, "The Sutton Hoo Ship Built in Sweden?" *Antiquity* 31 (1957), 40–41); Rupert Bruce-Mitford, *The Sutton Hoo Ship-Burial: Reflections after Thirty Years* (York, 1979), p. 18. David Wilson warns against overemphasizing the tie. "Sweden-England," in *Vendel Period Studies* 2, ed. J. P. Lamm and H.-Å. Nordström (Stockholm, 1983), 163–66.

14. For a good introduction to Claudian and his work *v* Alan Cameron, *Claudian: Poetry and Propaganda at the Court of Honorius* (Oxford, 1970).

15. Claudian *On the Consulship of Stilicho* II. 247–55, trans. M. Platnauer (London and Cambridge, Mass., 1972), II, pp. 20–21. Patrick Sims-Williams translates this as "nor look out along my whole shore for the Saxon coming with the uncertain winds." "The Settlement of England in Bede and the *Chronicle,*" *Anglo-Saxon England* 12 (1983), p. 9 n. 33. R. W. Chambers gives "watching along all the shore for the Saxon who would come with any wind." *England Before the Norman Conquest* (London, 1928), pp. viii–ix. S. Ireland translates "nor watch on all my shores for Saxons to arrive with

every shifting wind." *Roman Britain: A Source Book* (New York, 1986), p. 163. J. C. Mann and R. G. Penman give "nor watch all along my shore for the arrival of the Saxon with the shifting winds." *Literary Sources for Roman Britain* (London, 1977), p. 48. These various translations share the same perception that the shifting winds evoke uncertainty.

16. *V* n. 9 above. To speak of "Claudian, who in the fourth century tells of Saxon sails hovering off the coasts of Britain" is an inaccurate representation of what he actually says. Marsden, "Mast and Sail in the North, "p. 141. Tacitus *Agricola* (trans. H. Mattingly) 10. The Gnomic verse is quoted by Martyn J. Whittock, *The Origins of England 410–600* (Totowa, N.J., 1986), p. 134. For the interrelation of water, lower air and wind see Isidore of Seville *De natura Rerum.* A good example relevant to Britain is Constantius *Vita Germani* 25. The three elements interacted in the following way: water generated the vaporous lower atmosphere which in turn generated the winds.

17. The translations are by R. W. Chambers, *England Before the Norman Conquest,* pp. 61–62.

18. Ibid.

19. Ammianus was evidently fond of the striking juxtaposition of Saxons raiding from the sea in the north and attacks by desert tribesmen against the cities of the Mediterranean. Compare 28.2.12 with 28.5.7 and 28.6.1.

20. Hugh Williams, ed., *Gildas,* Cymmrodorion Record Series, no. 3, pt. I and II (London, 1899–1901), p. 43.

21. Cameron suggests Claudian visited Gaul. *Poetry and Propaganda,* pp. 26 ff., 345–47, 390 ff. Platnauer, the Loeb editor of Claudian, suggested Claudian stayed the entire period in Milan while serving on Stilicho's staff. *Claudian,* pp. xiii–xvi.

22. Cameron, *Poetry and Propaganda,* p. 346.

23. P. G. Christiansen, *The Use of Images by Claudius Claudianus* (The Hague and Paris, 1969), p. 74.

24. References to the Saxons and Britain may be found in the following passages of Claudian's work: *Panegyric on the Third Consulship of Honorius* 51–56; *Panegyric on the Fourth Consulship of Honorius* 24–33; *Epithalamium of Honorius and Maria* 219; *Against Eutropius* I:391–93; *Epithalamium of Palladius and Celerina* 85–90; *On Stilicho's Consulship* II. 247–55.

25. C. E. Stevens, *Sidonius Apollinaris and His Age* (Oxford, 1933), p. 174; O. M. Dalton was more blunt: "The curse of the rhetorical tradition clung to him like a chronic disease." *The Letters of Sidonius,* 2 vols. (Oxford, 1915), p. cxxii.

26. *Ep.* 8.6.13. Sidonius, *Poems and Letters,* 2 vols. trans. W. B. Anderson (London and Cambridge, Mass., 1965), vol. 2, pp. 419–33. Both Dalton's and Anderson's commentaries and translations of Sidonius are useful.

27. Thomas Hodgkin, *Italy and Her Invaders,* 8 vols. (1880–1889, reissued 1967, New York), II:365–56. Such uncritical and literal acceptance of Sidonius, even by so great a scholar as Hodgkin, has bedeviled the discussion of Saxon ships.

28. Green, *Sutton Hoo,* p. 54.

29. Ole Crumlin-Pedersen, "Viking Shipbuilding and Seamanship," *Proceedings of the Eight Viking Congress,* ed. Hans Bekker-Nielsen, Peter Foote, and Olaf Olsen (Odense, 1981), pp. 271–86 at p. 280.

30. Binns, *Viking Voyagers,* p. 5.

31. Dio Cassius *Epitome* 76.12.1–5, trans. S. Ireland, *Roman Britain: A Sourcebook* (New York, 1986), p. 23.

32. Compare Ammianus Marcellinus (trans. R.W. Chambers) 27.8.5: "The Franks and Saxons...were ravaging it wherever they could burst in by sea or by land, savagely robbing and burning, and murdering all prisoners." Dalton, *Letters*, 149.
33. Stevens, *Sidonius*, pp. 75–77. Sidonius must have had close personal contact with the Burgundians and Visigoths encountered on his estate or at Euric's court. His information concerning Saxons and other barbarians seems to be hearsay. Dalton, *Letters*, pp. xci–iv. For Sidonius on naval matters see Dalton, *Letters*, pp. cx n.3 and cxi.
34. For barbarian hairstyles *v* Dalton, *Letters*, p. cix. Nora Chadwick has a good discussion of the "catalog" as used by Sidonius and notes that he used well worn models in a mechanical way. "Intellectual Contacts between Britain and Gaul in the Fifth Century," in *Studies in Early British History*, ed. N. K. Chadwick (Cambridge, 1954), pp. 189–253 at pp. 233–36. For Sidonius and the barbarians *v* O. M. Dalton, *Letters*, pp. xci–xcv.
35. A comparison of the *Panegyric on Avitus* 369–71 with the *Panegyric on Maiorianus* 283 ff. illustrates Sidonius's tendency to use stereotype and formula. *V* specifically the use of *sulcare*. A comparison of *Panegyric on Avitus* 369–71 and *Ep.* 8.6.14 reveals the repetition of the image of the Saxon sporting amidst dangerous waters.
36. Peter Marsden concluded, "The impression gained from these short descriptions is that skinboats (hide boats), as far as the Romans were concerned, were peculiar to the British." "Ships of the Roman Period and After in Britain," in *A History of Seafaring Based on Underwater Archaeology*, ed. George F. Bass (London, 1972), p. 115. A discussion and translation of the Roman sources is provided by J. Hornell, *British Coracles* (Greenwich, 1973), pp. 6 ff. A reference in Virgil, *Aen.* 6:413–14, is to a sewn boat but not very probably a hide boat. *V* Lionel Casson, "Sewn Boats," *Classical Review* 13 (1963), 257–59. McGrail stated that Strabo described a skin boat from Spain but I have not found this reference. *The Ship*, p. 20.
37. Compare the phrases "British Ocean" and "sewn" boat in Sidonius and Pliny (*Natural History* 7.57; 4.30.16). Jonathan M. Wooding suggests that Avienus must have been the source of Sidonius's description. Both authors in short descriptions use the words *pellis* and *salum*. Wooding, however, thinks that even though Sidonius borrowed the description from an earlier work and a different context, it might still have been appropriate for Saxon ships of the period. "Saxons who Furrow the British Sea with Hides," *The Great Circle* 10 (1988), pp. 33–36.
38. In his *Natural History* Pliny refers to the earlier work of Timaeus. Solinus derived much of his material from Pliny. The 4th century A.D. *Ora Maritima* of Avienus preserves the very early reference to hide boats recorded originally in the 6th century B.C. in the *Massaliote Periplus*. C. F. C. Hawkes believes that the original description referred to Spain but was at some later stage transferred to a British context. If so, this illustrates the strength of association in Roman eyes between hide boats and Britain. *Pytheas: Europe and the Greek Explorers* (Oxford, 1977).
39. Although hide boats may have been used in Scandinavia during the Bronze Age, there is no clear evidence that their use continued into the Iron Age and Roman eras. The literary evidence for the latter is fully discussed above. For the debate over hide boats in the Bronze Age compare Sverre Marstrander, *Østfolds Jordbruksristninger* (Oslo, 1963), 117 ff. with Ole Crumlin-Pedersen, "Skin or Wood?" in *Ships and Shipyards Sailors and Fishermen*, ed. Olof Hasslöf, Henning Hennigsen and Arne Emil Christensen Jr. (Copenhagen, 1972), 208–33. Certainly during the early medieval era (400–800) contemporary references to hide boats in British, Irish, Anglo-Saxon

and Norse sources indicate that hide boats were confined to the Scots, Britons and Picts. The only literary exception is the exotic seventh-century Spanish work of Isidore, the unreliable *Etym.* 19.1.21.

40. Without explanation a number of authors have emended Sidonius and altered his Saxons into Scots (Irish) or Britons. *V* Hornell, *British Coracles*, p. 8; G.J. Marcus, *Conquest of the North Atlantic* (Oxford, 1981), p. 8; idem, "Factors in Early Celtic Navigation," *Etudes Celtiques* 6 (1953-54): 312–27. Ellmers simply dismisses Sidonius' statement as "certainly false." *Frühmittelalterliche Handelsschiffahrt*, p. 49.

41. Patrick Sims-Williams, "Gildas and the Anglo-Saxons," *Cambridge Medieval Celtic Studies* 6 (1983): 1–30.

42. Gildas, *The Ruin of Britain*, ed. trans. Michael Winterbottom (London and Chichester, 1978), p. 26.

43. Goodburn, "Do We Have Evidence of a Continuing Saxon Boat Building Tradition?" 45: "Gildas in the 6th century does hint that the 5th century Saxons had sail, but he is not explicit." Cf. McGrail, *Ship*, p. 40.

44. Williams, *Gildas*, p. 55. Archibald Lewis identified *navis longa* as *actuana*, a rowing galley. This undercuts Williams's translation. *The Northern Seas* (Princeton, 1958), p. 46.

45. *The Emergence of England and Wales*, 2nd ed. (Cambridge, 1959), p. 32.

46. *Six Old English Chronicles* (London, 1848), p. 310. Giles may have been thinking of the variant reading in Cambridge University Library MS. Ff. I. 27, a thirteenth-century text.

47. *V* Theodore Mommsen, ed., *Monumenta Germaniae historica, Auctorum antiquissimum, XIII* (Berlin, 1898), p. 38. I have not personally examined the "A" text of *De excidio* (Avranches public library MS. no. 162) but have relied on Mommsen's notes.

48. *England before the Norman Conquest*, p. 86.

49. Constantius *Vita Germani* 25, trans. F. R. Hoare in *The Western Fathers* (London, 1954), pp. 306, 306 n. 3. *v* n. 16 above.

50. *V* the *Oxford Latin Dictionary*, ed. P.W. Glare (Oxford, 1982), p. 1721. The entry gives a number of examples other than Cicero defining *secundus* as "attending" or "favourable," especially associated with wind or water.

51. *Ecclesiastical History of the English People* 5.1, trans. Bertram Colgrave and R. A. B. Mynors (Oxford, 1969), 454–57. This example is fully discussed below. Even in a passage relatively unobscured by the prophetic context and difficult language that complicates interpretation of Gildas, it is still difficult to tell whether Bede's favourable winds aided rowing, sailing, drifting or some combination of these. The boat affected was probably a small coracle. Leo Shirley-Price caught the ambiguity even in Bede: "a following wind bore us over calm water." *A History of the English Church and People*, rev. ed. (Harmondsworth, 1968), p. 271.

52. Williams, *Gildas*, p. 54.

53. Gildas *DE* 25; 16.

54. Bede *HE* 1.15; *HB* 31.

55. *DE* 25; 16.

56. Neil Wright, "Did Gildas Read Orosius?" *Cambridge Medieval Celtic Studies* 9 (1985), pp. 31–42 at p. 41. Rufinus *Historia Ecclesiastica* 4.15.37; *Aeneid* I. 301.

57. Procopius, *History of the Wars* 8.20.26–31, trans. H. B. Dewing (Cambridge, Mass., 1953), 253–71 at 261.

58. Averil Cameron, *Procopius* (London, 1985).

59. The two main digressions concerning Britain are *History of the Wars* 8.20; 3.2.31 ff.
60. For discussion of this digression and its possible interpretations see the following: A. R. Burn, "Procopius and the Island of Ghosts," *English Historical Review* 70 (1955), 258–61; E. A. Thompson, "Procopius on Brittia and Britannia," *Classical Quarterly* 30 (1980), 498–507; J. O. Ward, "Procopius *Bellum Gothicum* II. 6. 28: The Problem of Contacts between Justinian I and Britain," *Byzantion* 38 (1968): 460–71; James Campbell, "The Lost Centuries," in *The Anglo-Saxons*, ed. James Campbell (Ithaca, 1982), p. 38.
61. Cameron, *Procopius*, pp. 207-22, at p. 213.
62. The embassy is usually dated c. 533. Thompson, "Procopius on Brittia," p. 501. Alternatively, information may have reached Constantinople before 549 during the reign of Theodebert. Roger Collins, "Theodebert I, '*Rex Magnus Francorum,*'" in *Ideal and Reality in Frankish and Anglo-Saxon Society*, ed. Patrick Wormald, Donald Bullough and Roger Collins (Oxford, 1983), 10–12. *V* Ian Wood, "The End of Roman Britain: Continental Evidence and Parallels," in *Gildas: New Approaches*, ed. Michael Lapidge and David Dumville (Woodbridge, Suffolk, 1984), pp. 23–24.
63. *History of the Wars* 3.9.13–16.
64. For example, the Vandals. *History of the Wars* 3. 6. 17–22.
65. *History of the Wars* 8.20.29–31.
66. McGrail, *Ship*, p. 40; Ellmers, *Frühmittelalterliche Handelsschiffahrt*, pp. 30 ff., esp. pp. 35, 49. Archibald Lewis and Timothy Runyan suggest that reliance on oar power alone was perhaps more characteristic of the Angles from the Baltic than the Saxons of the North Sea. They cite Sidonius for evidence of Saxon sails. *European Naval and Maritime History, 300–1500* (Bloomington, 1985) pp. 12–13. This is an interesting suggestion but it rests on a false premise because Celtic and Classical authors, including Procopius, made no such clear distinction between "Saxons" and "Angles." For example, although Procopius located "Frisians" [Jutes?] in Britain, he never mentioned Saxons at all, while Sidonius never mentioned Angles. The British sources indiscriminately labelled as "Saxons" all the Germanic invaders including the Angles. *V* the comments of J. N. L. Myres, *The English Settlements* (Oxford, 1986), pp. 104 ff.
67. Procopius' description of the Byzantine naval expedition against the Vandals provides an illuminating parallel. Procopius separates the transports from the warships. Both types have sails, but the warships ("dromones") were crewed by men who doubled as rowers and warriors: "In these sailed two thousand men of Byzantium, who were all rowers as well as fighting men; for there was not a single superfluous man among them." *History of the wars* 3.11.16, trans. H. B. Dewing, pp. 106–107.
68. If I have followed his argument correctly, Detlev Ellmers discusses a passage from Procopius that might seem to support the idea that some of the Anglo-Saxon ships perhaps used sails: "There they (inhabitants of villages along the coast opposite Brittia) see skiffs ... not their own skiffs, however, but a different kind ... after rowing a single hour they put in at Brittia. And yet, when they make the voyage in their own skiffs, not using sails but rowing, they with difficulty make this passage in a night and a day." Procopius *History of the Wars* (trans. H. B. Dewing) 8.20.50–55. This passage is part of the ghost story contained in the digression on Britain describing the ferrying of dead souls from the continent to Britain. Procopius himself disclaimed it as the product of dream or myth, and it seems an unpromising source for details of shipping. Ellmers, however, concludes: "Von den Schiffen heisst es, dass

die fremden Totenschiffe keine Segel hatten. Dan wird deren Geschwindikeit mit der der eigenen Boote verglichen, und zwar für den Fall, dass jene Schiffer auf ihren eigenen Booten keine Segel setzten, sondern nur ruderten. Wahrscheinlich hatten diese Boote Segel." *Fruhmittelalterliche Handelsschiffahrt,* p. 17 n. 29. *V* also 35, 49. In fact, Procopius does not indicate that these people *sailed* to Britain in their own craft even under normal circumstances (why would anyone row to Britain over a night and a day if they could sail there?). He merely emphasizes that both elements of his comparison of travel times (one hour vs. a night and a day) are based on rowing. In any case, this section seems irrelevant in the context of the ships of the Angles and Saxons, for the people located a night and day's row from Britain (3 knots/hour would be good rowing speed) probably would be south of the continental homelands of the Angles and Saxons. The people Procopius names as subject to the Franks and living on this coast opposite to Britain might be Gauls or Bretons, or perhaps Frisians, but they were probably not the Angles living in Britain or their continental cousins.

69. A good introduction to these sources may be found in Antonia Gransden, *Historical Writing in England c. 550–c. 1307* (Ithaca, 1974), pp. 13–41.

70. Bede, *Ecclesiastical History of the English People* 5.1, trans. Bertram Colgrave and R. A. B. Mynors (Oxford, 1969), n. 455–57. *V* n.51 above.

71. J. M. Wallace-Hadrill, *Bede's Ecclesiastical History of the English People: A Commentary* (Oxford, 1988), 174–75, 241.

72. Charles Green suggested this boat was a skin-covered curragh. *Sutton Hoo,* 56f. In Bede's *Ecclesiastical History,* Book 5 alone lacks the heading "the ecclesiastical history of the English people." The book may be said to have a possibly overall Celtic theme, the winning of the Picts and Irish into the Catholic order. Wallace-Hadrill, *Bede's Ecclesiastical History,* p. 174.

73. Alan Binns rightly called the story "apparently unpromising" but his conclusion that the ship was evidently a royal sailing ship is highly speculative. *Viking Voyagers,* pp. 14–15.

74. H. Shetelig and H. Falk, *Scandinavian Archaeology,* trans. E. V. Gordon (Oxford, 1937), 345; McGrail, *The Ship,* 40.

75. Ellmers, "Schiffe der Angelsachsen,"n. 499 ff. *V* n. 11 above.

76. Peter Foote and David M. Wilson. *The Viking Achievement* (London, 1974), p. 234.

77. For the conservative nature of ships and shipbuilding traditions *v* Evans, "Clinker-built Boats of the North Sea," pp. 63–64. For the idea of larger boats as relatively uniform *v* Arne Emil Christensen Jr., *Boats of the North* (Oslo, 1968), p. 12. Although there is no consensus, many scholars suggest that it is possible to trace a cultural-historical line of evolution among the Scandinavian ships of the archaeological record. For example, *v* Arne Emil Christensen, "Viking Age Ships and Shipbuilding," *Norwegian Archaeological Review* 15 (1982): 20–22.

78. Conventional estimates number the crew as roughly twice the number of oars. This figure represents factors such as internal space, displacement and the practical necessity of having at least one full change of oarsmen for rowing at sea. This last is a crucial point. *V* Sean McGrail, *Ancient Boats in N.W. Europe* (London and New York, 1987), 198–200. Compare Alan Binns, "The Ships of the Vikings: Were They 'Viking Ships'?" *Proceedings of the Eighth Viking Congress* (Odense, 1981), pp. 287 ff. Charles Green estimated that Nydam could have carried 60 men, 80 if very crowded. *Sutton Hoo,* 103. John Coates estimated that Sutton Hoo could have carried 60 men and 7

tons of equipment. Quoted by McGrail in *The Ship*, p. 30. Some of the later Viking finds support the idea of a double crew. Gokstad, for example, had 16 pairs of oars but 64 rather than 32 shields.

79. Alcock, *Arthur's Britain*, p. 335.
80. *V* Hodges, *Dark Age Economics*, 95 ff. His chart outlining the changing relationship over time between the number of rowers and cargo capacity of ships is very suggestive. Cargo capacity is a function of internal dimensions, reserve buoyancy and the space occupied by crew and equipment. *V* McGrail, *Ancient Boats*, pp. 198 ff. Minimum necessary power has been estimated by Alan Binns as 1 hp/ton, with each oarsman producing. 5 hp. Given 40 oars for Sutton Hoo and 30 oars for Nydam, this produces ratios respectively of 20 hp/20 tons and 15 hp/9 tons. "The Ships of the Vikings," pp. 288 ff. Binns's assumption of .5 hp/oarsman is too high to be sustained for long at sea, even with frequent changes of oarsmen. McGrail suggests a figure of .3 hp/oarsman or even less, again assuming regular changes of oarsmen. *Ancient Boats*, p. 216. The important implication is that the ships of the migrations would have needed full or nearly full complements of rowers and also full changes of oarsmen. Each oarsman would have required at least 4 lbs. of food and 4 pints of water per day. A week's provisions would have provided a risky reserve. This would have left very little room for cargo or passengers. Charles Green's suggestion that 30 oarsmen in a Nydam type vessel could ferry 30 or more dependents looks entirely too optimistic. *Sutton Hoo*, pp. 103–104. This is why some scholars resort to the use of hypothetical sails or missing types of ships in order to make conceivable the movement of large numbers of Anglo-Saxon migrants. Sometimes the implications of a migration relying solely on oars are not well understood. Colin and Sarah McEvedy state that "The Nydam ship does not look up to much but a dozen of them doing a round trip a year could move 100,000 people in a century." *The Dark Ages* (New York, 1972), p. 37. They have forgotten that most of the crew would necessarily have returned home in the event of a round trip. What sort of merchant or ruler would have maintained a ship and a crew of 60 for such ventures is problematic, but if each Nydam ship of this example carried even 20 passengers to Britain (a number that seems too high) the total for a dozen ships making one round trip each year for a century is 24,000 emigrants, not 100,000. Their estimate is off by a factor of 400%.
81. Green, "North Sea Crossings," in *Sutton Hoo*, pp. 103 ff.
82. *Anglo-Saxon Chronicle* s.a. 1008. For the expense v Binns, *Viking Voyagers*, p. 10; idem, "Ships of the Vikings," p. 292. For Nydam specifically v Christensen, *Boats of the North*, p. 20; Greenhill, *Archaeology of the Boat*, 180.

MANSUS, MACHINERY, AND CO-PROPRIETORSHIP: THE TUSCAN CONTRIBUTION TO MEDIEVAL ASSOCIATIONS OF INDUSTRY

John Muendel, PhD

Wankesha, Wisconsin

Mansus, Machinery, and Co-proprietorship: The Tuscan Contribution to Medieval Associations of Industry

The Florentine Catasto, a tax survey initially drawn up for the territory of Florence between 1427 and 1430,[1] makes it possible to examine quite closely the internal economic structure of Florentine mills that were jointly owned or divided into shares. These negotiable units, held in mills owned by families, rural communes, or an assortment of individuals and institutions, were duly reported to state officials so that they could, to the best of their ability, determine an equitable assessment. Some of these mills, particularly those owned by certain branches within larger families, were limited to a small number of individuals. Since profits and losses could be easily distributed among their members, management did not create any difficulties.[2] Others, however, were composed of numerous unrelated shareholders whose parts had evolved through several divisions over many years. These progressive modifications could cause complications that nonetheless remained unchanged simply because any alterations would have upset a time-honored scheme fully comprehended by the parties involved. Take, for example, a jointly owned mill on the Arno near Mantignano. By 14 October 1428, the old suspension mill of the association had been abandoned for an entirely new structure.[3] But rather than adjust a distribution of shares that did not have a clearly determined limit, the owners retained their division into eighth, twelfth, sixteenth, and thirty-second parts. The one newcomer to the consortium did bring some semblance of order to the distribution when he purchased one-third of an eighth, or a twenty-fourth, share. However, problems in consigning flour, based on a common denominator of 96, would have still remained (v Table 1).[4]

Other jointly owned mills were organized in a more orderly fashion. The wealthy consortial mill at Ognissanti, located just outside the walls of the city on the right bank of the Arno, was made up of a definitive forty-eight parts. Some of these amounted to 7⅝, 2⅙, and 1½ of a forty-eighth part, but the common denominator of 48 was maintained by 11of the 13 consorts who reported it (v Table 2). The mountain commune of Palazzuolo owned a mill on the Senio that was divided into at least 52 *paghe*, a measure commonly used in urban complexes to determine interest gained on public debts[5] (v Table 3). Another highly organized consortial mill was placed on the Arno next to the *castello* at Empoli, some 32 kilometers downstream from Florence. This mill, like the one at Ognissanti, was apportioned into forty-eight parts, but each one was called an *ottavo* or an eighth. In other words, a specific fractional determination had become a unit of account for six citizens of the city of Florence, a resident of Montelupo, eight ecclesiastical institutions and five inhabitants of Empoli itself, and an individual from nearby Portorme (v Table 4). Since the jointly owned mills of Toulouse in southern France were organized on the same basis by utilizing the *uchau*, a corruption of *octavum*,[6] the significance of this Empolese mill has ramifications that are European rather than Tuscan. Can co-proprietorship actually be a European institution in which the ownership of mills and other industrial establishments was a contributing factor? If so, when does it begin? How does it develop? And, finally, what are its implications as far as the history of technology is concerned?

I

Joint ownership of mills may be the oldest form of co-proprietorship known to medieval Europe. It is true that aristocratic families acquired lands in common, while peasant consortia held vast uncultivated areas, such as woods, meadows, and marshes, as a means of protecting themselves against unforeseen economic crises.[7] In central-southern Italy, the heirs of Carolingian freemen, most of whom were soldiers or *exercitales*, collectively held extensive marginal areas known as *waldi*, whose origins were tied to the pre-Roman *pagus*.[8] This control by means of association must be seen, nevertheless, as a form of possession rather than ownership: each group had definite inalienable rights to the land, but not a transferable deed.[9] The case is entirely different with mills. As early as 726, the wealthy Pistoiese physician Gaidualdo, the court doctor for such Lombard kings as Liutprand, Desiderius, and Adelchus, purchased from Filiperto, a cleric who was the son of a blacksmith named Filimari, a share of a mill located on the Brana just outside the city of Pistoia.[10] The number of shares in the mill are not known, but they must have been minimal. At this time—sixteen years before the birth of Charlemagne—the general population was too small to generate adequate profits for a large number of shareholders. It would appear that this edifice, to my knowledge the only recorded jointly owned mill prior to the ninth century, is an atypical example of the Lombard ownership of mills that has been generally characterized by individual seigneurial proprietorship.[11] However, the research of Pierre Toubert concerning southern Latium and the Sabina, Italian regions directly south of Tuscany, strongly suggests that during the eighth and ninth centuries the watermill was not yet an established element of the rural seigneury. Most mills after 855 were suburban, and those in the countryside were outside the boundaries of lordships, sometimes held in co-proprietorship by small communities of allod holders.[12] Without any stretch of the imagination, we can see that the Pistoiese mill of 726 was hardly an anomaly. We must, moreover, be somewhat cautious in accepting Marc Bloch's point of view that watermills were purely seigneurial in origin.[13]

Co-proprietorship broadened in scope with the collapse of the Carolingian Empire and the steady increase in population that followed in its wake. Changes are seen in all levels of society. The *mansus* or single family farm, which was used by lords from the late seventh century as a means of assessing rents and dues within their domains,[14] began, certainly by the ninth century, to be divided among heirs or dispersed among a variety of unrelated individuals through the sale of rights.[15] The estates belonging to the aristocratic feudal ranks of northern Europe were themselves experiencing a similar proliferation as fiefs and seigneuries became fragmented through donations, infeudation, and inheritance,[16] thereby allowing *parsonniers* or partners to share control of lands[17] and banal rights[18] at an increasing rate. In Lombardy and Tuscany between the tenth and twelfth centuries, the division of individual possessions within single patrimonies produced an ever larger number of heirs whose properties were reorganized around fortified centers to create zones[19] that could frequently protect lineages from the encroachment of a reforming Church.[20] In northern and central-southern Italy, the process of *incastellamento* caused local consortia to build independent defensive strongholds to ward off the attacks of Hungarians, Arabs, or Normans.[21] When the lords of these areas put collectivities of free tenant farmers in charge of the construction of fortified centers, they stimulated the development of joint ownership by granting the associates rights of selling, exchanging, and donating their allotments.[22] Meanwhile, in the cities of of these territories, tower societies were split into numerous associates.[23] By the end of the twelfth century, moreover, it was common for members of aristocratic *consorteria* to combine their liquid assets and acquire shares in collective enterprises.[24] In maritime trade, shares were apportioned into parts, or *partes*, that were freely negotiable.[25]

Co-proprietorship of this sort is strikingly demonstrated in medieval industries. North of the Alps during the twelfth century, mining activity was controlled by corporations of artisans who, with a small working capital at their disposal, obtained from lords the right to look and dig for ores in the appropriate territories.[26] In the Alpine regions of Italy, concessionaires were almost always a cohesive group of "socii," "fratres," or "comunicatores" who divided profits according to their shares,[27] and at Ardesio in the beginning of the thirteenth century, villagers and tenants escaped the control of their lords by forming independent associations to direct the operations of extraction.[28] At the very same time, an increasing associative process among natives and German immigrants was found at the Tuscan silverworks of Massa Marittima,[29] while the "moie" or saltworks located in the *contado* of Volterra were fragmented into as many as a thousand shares because of hereditary subdivisions and partial alienations.[30] Across the Alps, the saltworks of Salins in the Franche-Comté were split into numerous parts. In the course of the thirteenth century, the pits and boilers known as the Grande Saunerie became owned by the *parsonniers* of the Burgundian nobility.[31] The works that made up the Puits à Muire were held by noblemen, clergymen, and commoners by means of shares whose basic unit was the *mansus*,[32] the employment of which came about, if not as a direct result of the land divisions of an earlier period, then certainly from a definite familiarity with the process.[33]

Along with these developments, jointly owned mills expanded at an increasing rate in all areas of Europe. In the ninth century, the collective ownership of mills became prevalent in Christian Spain.[34] From the tenth into the twelfth centuries, the region of Poitou contained watermills whose ownership was allotted by halves, thirds, fourths, and sixths.[35] Around 1060, a consortium of six peasants sold half of its mill to the monastery of S. Aubin at Angers; the Domesday Book of 1086 includes English mills split into shares of one-sixth.[36] During the course of the twelfth century, peasants divided the owner-ship of mills located in the counties of Champagne and Hainault,[37] and in England peasant freeholders cooperatively owned a watermill at Wigston Magna while outside of Canterbury at the end of the century the proprietorship of windmills represented commercial enterprises jointly financed by several partners.[38] During the thirteenth century, consortial mills became established at the cities of Douai and Cologne with eight and ten shares respectively.[39] Throughout southern France, such mills were widespread, in some cases, as in Bas Languedoc, being divided into as many as sixteen parts.[40] At Toulouse during the late twelfth century, the development of landed undershot mills to replace the more cumbersome floating mills brought to light the large number of co-proprietors involved in the undertaking.[41] In 1277, the Florentine consortial mill at Ognissanti was composed of sixty parts.[42] A notarial entry of 1283 indicates that "several" shareholders were included in the ownership of the mill at Empoli as a certain Palmeruccio di Ginco pur-chased one-half of a sixteenth part of the establishment.[43] It would cer-tainly appear that at this time the *ottavo* had yet to be adopted.

II

There can be no doubt, therefore, that co-proprietorship was a ubiqui-tous phenomenon for medieval Europe. However, in all cases, whether they involved the ownership of land, *castelli,* cargoes, mines, or mills, the proliferation of shares caused distinct problems of management. While attempting to gain control of the "moie" of its *contado* through rights of preemption, the commune of Volterra had to deal with the greed of numerous parties that wished to retain the privilege of freely selling their shares; those involved included churchmen, lay citizens from Siena and Florence as well as from Volterra itself, and representa-tives of the German emperor Frederick II.[44] The evenly divided *partes* of shipowners and merchants became less manageable upon the division of any of them through sales, thereby leading to a cumbersome distrib-ution of increasingly smaller fractional units.[45] The proliferation of the co-seigneurs of the rural *castelli* frequently led to the extinction of these fortifications.[46] During the last years of the thirteenth century when Florence attempted to reestablish the *castello* of Casaglia by the consignment of plots of land to fifty families, the project failed because of the unexpected confusion caused by the manipulation of shares.[47] For their part, the associations that possessed the urban towers of northern and central Italy had to resort to pacts and regulatory statutes to lessen the internal discord brought about by the propagation of allotments.[48]

The immediate chaos produced by the disintegration of the *mansus* can be demonstrated by numerous examples,[49] but it is best illustrated by referring to the lands of the territory of Cecima found in the Bobbiese Apennines southwest of Piacenza. In this highland region where economic development was delayed in comparison with the rest of the continent, representatives of the bishop of Pavia discovered as late as 1409 a large number of dependent *mansi* differing in size and use and each possessing several household heads who created a confused pattern of rights and obligations. To resolve the matter, the episcopal representatives simply collected the required returns from the lands *ad personam* rather than *ad mansum*.[50] Such an ad hoc determination was similar to earlier judgments regarding the decomposition of the *mansus* that gave rise to a new holding called the *hereditas* in northern France,[51] to the tenures *à cens* and *à champart* in the French counties further south,[52] and to the hereditary leases known as *libellus* and *tenimentum* that held dependent peasants to lands in Italy.[53]

Another expedient for solving the problem of the inordinate fragmentation of properties was to use certain fractions routinely produced by the division as units of account. Through this process, the half *mansus* and quarter *mansus* became common entities during the twelfth century. In Lorraine and the Namurois of Belgium, the *quartier* was still conceded in return for a payment of rent during the course of the thirteenth century.[54] At the same time, the German *mansus,* known as the Hufe, was divided into the *Halbehufe* and the *Viertelhufe,* while the English equivalent of the *mansus,* the hide, was replaced by the *virgata,* or quarter hide, and the *bovata,* or an eighth of a hide.[55] In mining districts the number of shares into which galleries and workshops were apportioned had to be restricted for the sake of control. The silverworks at Massa Marittima and those of Villa di Chiesa on the island of Sardinia had their shares limited with the incorporation of the *trenta,* or thirtieth, to designate each unit.[56] During the fourteenth century, shares at the Sienese mines of Roccastrada could not exceed seventeen.[57] Meanwhile, at Salins one of the plants of the Grande Saunerie, known as the Chauderette, came into the hands of a number of unrelated shareholders or *rentiers.* In order to avoid the confusion into which the consortial ownership of the Puits à Muire had fallen, the associates of the Chauderette had every quantity of saltwater coming to the boilers divided into sixty-four quarters with each quarter, derived from the *mansus,* being further subdivided for ease of apportionment.[58]

The parts, or *partes,* of cargo ships created great enough perplexity that the *locum,* a concrete entity expressing a fixed, determined value, was introduced to facilitate the distribution of profits. It was divided into carats, each worth one-twenty-fourth, and half carats, worth one-forty-eighth apiece.[59]

With respect to this use of specific fractions as measures of value, Germain Sicard has argued that the *uchau* of the mills of Toulouse came into existence by a process of familiarization ("accoutumance") among the inhabitants of the city and its immediate surroundings. The documents of Toulouse show that in 1221 an eighth of a mill was sold. Thereafter, a variety of fractional parts were negotiated with the eighth being the most frequently held share.[60] At what particular point the *uchau* became a definite unit of account cannot be determined, but certainly it had attained this status with the initial attempts in 1369 to regulate the activity of the shareholders by the formation of the two societies of Bazacle and Château-Narbonnais.[61]

It would appear that, while Sicard's concept of familiarization is unmistakably plausible, it lacks dimension, especially since the development of the *ottavo* as a determined share was taking place simultaneously at Empoli in Tuscan Italy. As we have seen, the mill at Empoli was not using the *ottavo* in 1283. By 1 April 1352, it definitely was. At that time, two *ottavi* of the three runs at Empoli were sold for forty gold florins. That the two *ottavi* were units of account rather than simple fractions is shown by the notary's qualification: "that is, of the forty-eight parts, two *ottavi. "*[62] As to where the influence of one establishment on the other lies, we are left in somewhat of a quandary since further information is lacking regarding the relationship between the two areas. Germain Sicard claims that the organization of the mills at Toulouse was similar to other forms of medieval joint ownership because it had Roman law as its common source. Otherwise, the associative activities on the middle Garonne were independent developments as were all other cooperative efforts found in industry and trade throughout medieval Europe.[63] Since the *ottavo* was employed as a unit of account at Empoli, this point of view would have to be changed, whatever questions might remain. Both establishments were responding to changes occurring in the European social fabric between the twelfth and fifteenth centuries. Their common use of the eighth as a standard measure of value sought to solve a European institutional problem brought about by an ever increasing fragmentation of shares within familial, commercial, and industrial associations. Roman law, in this case, was meaningless.[64]

III

Like higher governmental authorities, the industrial associations had administrative bodies and officials to limit their members' actions and to direct the economic affairs of their organizations. Consequently, this supervision, despite a diversity of elements, displayed common characteristics that give even more meaning to the institutional framework of these societies. Some of them were managed very simply. At Massa Marittima, each ditch or *fossa* belonging to a group of co-proprietors was directed by a *magister montis* whose judgments were determined by the majority of the *partiari*. If disputes became serious, they were referred to a board of three other *magistri* named by the commune of Massa Marittima.[65] Since the possession of the sixteen watermills at Douai was decidedly influenced by feudal ties, the *parsonniers,* or *sires,* maintained a bond of confidence between themselves and their millers, even if the latter sublet a particular establishment to a plurality of other workers. Immediate control came through the right of each *parsonnier* to visit a mill once a year and the appointment of a sergeant who divided shares of flour and, in general, policed the working of whatever mill was involved; ultimate authority rested, of course, with the city magistrates or *échevins.*[66]

Managerial affairs at Salins and Toulouse were more complicated. In what was certainly equivalent to a modern-day stockholders' meeting, the *rentiers* of the Puits à Muire gathered each year during the month of January in an assembly called the *répons.* Here they adjusted the value of their shares, named the lessees who would manage the production of their salt, and elected officials who represented them in a permanent council that met each week. Besides the *assommeurs,* who were chosen by the shareholders to regulate the actions of the lessees and to supervise expenditures, this administrative council was composed of two other bodies: the *officiers,* or superintendents, who directed the various stages of production and the *vendeurs,* delegates of the lessees who sold the manufactured salt at suitable prices. The Chauderette of the Grande Saunerie had a similar type of management. However, for administrative simplicity, the shareholders did not farm out the processing of their salt, thereby eliminating the need for the lessees and the *vendeurs*.[67]

As early as the twelfth century, if not before, those who held shares in the mills of Toulouse had a general assembly that acted as the fundamental governing body of the association as a whole.[68] Nevertheless, it was not until the very end of the thirteenth century, when this body began meeting once a year, that representives known as bailiffs and procurators were chosen. Although initially the functions of the representatives were united in one person, gradually the duties were separated, and more than one official was chosen each year. The bailiffs were the general superintendents of the mills in their charge with extensive powers limited only by their annual term of office; the procurators, on the other hand, were lawyers who would represent their associates before the Parlement de Paris. Soon another group of administrators, known as the counsellors, superseded the bailiffs. These counsellors, or general supervisors, appeared at the mills of Chateau-Narbonnais as early as 1292; by the end of the fourteenth century the bailiffs at Bazacle as well as Château-Narbonnais were unable to make important decisions without the presence and approval of at least four counsellors. The bailiffs had become mere assistants.[69]

IV

The notarial chartularies found in the state archives of Florence have been extremely fruitful regarding the internal governance of Florentine jointly-owned mills. Unlike the strict, bureaucratic control that had developed at the mills of Toulouse and the saltworks of the Puits à Muire, the management of the consortial mills of Florence was quite flexible. Undoubtedly, this freedom was generated by the strong tradition of collective judgment that was embedded in the Florentine countryside and rested on the tacit understanding of mutual trust engendered by the hazards of a subsistence economy.[70] Without the ratification of the other members of the association, shares (*partes, paghe, sedes*[71]) in these mills were sold,[72] bequeathed,[73] donated,[74] or exchanged for another property;[75] they were frequently used for dowries;[76] and when owners were in financial difficulties, the shares could be rented perpetually, whereby, after dispensing with their allotments for a determined price, the owners would lease them back to the sellers for a recurring charge over a fixed span of time.[77] Although shareholders *(consortes, consotii, partionarii, participes, portionales)* let their shares corporately to the miller(s) who operated their establishments,[78] they just as often leased them out separately.[79]

When these procedures involved portions of the shares themselves, they fostered confusion and could result in the distribution of allotments that was demonstrated in the mill on the Arno near Mantignano. Shares could split to such a degree that unknowingly they went beyond the total aggregate of determined parts, as we will see below (p.86). Nonetheless, because of the strength of the associative phenomenon, it appears that in the large majority of the cases order was maintained, even to the point of adopting a fractional unit of account to cover what seems to have been the commonest of the smallest shares, the thirty-second. The *trenta*, used by the societies at the mines of Massa Marittima and Villa di Chiesa, served this purpose admirably. This is illustrated by a contract concerning the repair of the consortial mill at Chiavaccio located on the Elsa near the Villa di Isola. In 1371, the consorts, in need of 1,281 *lire* to renovate the mill, borrowed from one of their partners, Corso di Curaduccio, an undisclosed sum of florins, perhaps enough to cover the expense. Corso, in turn, had a pact drawn up on 12 June of the same year, which stipulated that each shareholder would pay him back by 1 August according to the value of his or her share. These shares, including those of Corso, were thus carefully tabulated and amounted to five $\frac{1}{8}$ parts, three $\frac{1}{16}$ parts, and six $\frac{1}{30}$ parts.[80]

All of these units add up to 1.0125, which leaves a small remainder beyond the totality. However, if the $\frac{1}{30}$ parts are converted to $\frac{1}{32}$ shares, the aggregate equals 1. Pure symmetry would perhaps be enough to accept the latter interpretation, but there are two other reasons to demonstrate why this solution is the correct one. First of all, the *trenta* was used in exactly the same way at the mines of Villa di Chiesa. In fact, when Carlo Baudi di Vesme realized that these Sardinian mining companies were made up of thirty-two parts each worth $\frac{1}{30}$, he decided in his bewilderment that *trenta* was not derived from the Italian word for this number, but from the German infinitive *trennen*, meaning to divide.[81] He was, as such, unaware of the institutional framework of the medieval corporate structure that allowed for these apparent incongruities. The second reason for accepting this solution involves the Italian word *trentina*, meaning "about a thirtieth." As seen in Table 5, it too was used by the owners of Florentine consortial mills to depict this thirty-second, the commonest of the smallest shares.

There was, therefore, a definite sense of regularity within the supposedly random processes employed in the manipulation of shares. If remainders appeared beyond the totality of the determined parts, they represented mismanagement rather than inherent confusion; their existence, it seems, was not connected with any effort to create additional financial benefits.[82] Outside of the necessary bonds of cooperation, the basic cause for the success of these milling associations lay in the tradition of leadership provided by the baptismal churches *(pievi)*[83] and the Lombard/Carolingian *sistema curtense*.[84] These venerable institutions gave the corporations the means for effectively organizing themselves according to established precepts that compensated for the uninhibited transfer of shares.

The governing of mills held jointly finds its truest form in those owned by rural communes[85] whose members usually controlled ideal shares that became real quite readily[86] and whose leaders, the rectors, reflected the customary command of the *plebanus* over the *pieve*. In managing their hydraulic installations, the administration as a whole sometimes intervened on behalf of the commune to carry out transactions. This was the case when on 28 December 1376 the rector, the treasurer or *camerarius,* and the four consuls of Barberino di Mugello leased to another the commune's grain mill and fulling mill located on the Stura.[87] On other occasions, the *camerarius* or the consuls alone performed this task as well as other responsibilities related to the welfare of the mills belonging to the association.[88]

In most situations, however, the management of the mills was accomplished by special representatives chosen by the male members of the commune or *popolo*. At the bidding of the rectors, these members, or at least the prevailing majority of them, would assemble in the baptismal church and elect one or more of their associates to deal with whatever the circumstances demanded. On 19 October 1326, for example, 114 men of the commune of Pulicciano, located north of the Sieve in the Mugello, gathered in the *pieve* of S. Maria a Castello to chose Bartolo di Simone as their *sindicus* and *procurator* for not only leasing to another one of their mills on the Ensa, but also for collecting the remainder of the rent due from the previous miller.[89] On 7 July 1333, the rector and 279 male members of the commune of Linari, situated directly north of Poggibonsi far south of the Arno, congregated in their baptismal church to elect Bertone di Corso and ser Giovanni di ser Loderingo, both of Linari, as their "vexos et legiptimos procuratores, actores, fattores certos et speciales nuntios et legiptimos responsales" for selling half of their partially damaged mill placed beside the Drove.[90] If the leasing out and selling of communal mills were customary obligations for these officials, so too were the renting back of mills they had previously sold,[91] the repair of press houses used for manufacturing olive oil,[92] and the settlement of disputes regarding the proper distribution of of flour.[93] These representatives, moreover, were frequently selected as the millers and fullers who worked establishments that the communes either held jointly with additional parties or rented from another.[94]

Since the rural communes experienced a variety of problems, the *sindicus/procurator* did not deal exclusively with those concerning mills. Among the strictly consortial mills, there was, however, a representative who did. This official was the *castaldus* or *castaldio*. While the *sindicus* and *procurator* signify in name survivals of the late Roman judicial system, the *castaldus* has his origin as the chief administrator of the estates directly controlled by a Lombard king.[95] With the consolidation of these estates under Carolingian rule, the position of *castaldus* was strengthened to the point that its title could be used separately or concurrently with others to designate leadership in a number of institutions, particularly following the collapse of the Frankish state during the ninth and tenth centuries. Accordingly, we find the *castaldus* as an official in bishoprics,[96] baptismal churches,[97] monasteries,[98] hospitals,[99] clans,[100] and emerging guilds.[101] It was not unusual for him to go beyond the status of a simple agent and gain considerable wealth and distinction.[102] Nevertheless, his position as the principal overseer of a consortial mill gives him still another dimension.

The Valdelsa, incorporating such towns as Colle, Poggibonsi, Certaldo, and Castelfiorentino and ending at the Arno just west of Empoli, appears to be the area where the *castaldus* was most commonly found as a superintendent of consortial mills. Since the middle of this valley was, as one historian has put it, the "center of gravity" of the Tuscan network of roads,[103] it is not surprising to find such a figure reflecting the more advanced circumstances of the region. We discover that on 9 April 1367 the two *castaldiones* of the consortial *molendinum Bettinghi*, located on the Elsa at Tobbiana, chose two master millers to estimate the value of the mill's apparatus in order to bring a lease to its conclusion.[104] On 26 January 1371, three *participes* of the mill of Canneto, in behalf of themselves and the other members of the association, selected Iacopo di Bindaccio of Canneto, called Cencio, as their "generalem castaldum." For a six-month term, Cencio was responsible, in particular, for determining all the expenses that would be involved in the repair of this mill whose ownership was divided into twenty-four parts.[105] The popularity and importance of this position in the Valdelsa is shown when on 28 February 1338 the four consorts of a mill at Pulicciano elected themselves as *castaldi* to serve successive six-month terms so that the dam and solarium of their establishment could be properly refurbished.[106] But it is the history of the *molendinum de Rofiano* that puts the *castaldus* and his position as superintendent of jointly owned mills in even greater prominence, and it is to this unfolding of events that we must now turn.

V

The *molendinum de Rofiano* was located on the Elsa to the south of Monterappoli in the *popolo* of S. Andrea a Rofiniano.[107] Beside it ran the famed Via Francigena that allowed pilgrims of northern Europe to visit Rome;[108] the *molendinum de Rofiano* was thus seen, and perhaps used, by various groups of travelers outside of its immediate clientele from the assorted towns and hamlets that composed the commune of Monterappoli. The notarial chartularies, combined with the Catasto of 1427–30, make it possible to trace the development of this consortial mill from 1319 into the early fifteenth century. In particular, these sources show how the office of *castaldus* for this specific mill was transformed from a basically ad hoc function into a position of permanence and strength, which by the beginning of the fifteenth century was apparently losing some of its vitality. Unfortunately, the entries for this establishment are not continuous; in fact, they contain two gaps of approximately twenty-five and fifty-four years. Nonetheless, this interrupted string of documents does highlight notable features that give the surviving details substance and character.

On 1 August 1319, the *consortes, consotii seu partionales,* in imitation of their compatriots in the rural communes, gathered in the church of S. Giovanni in Monterappoli specifically as a *societas* to elect Chele di Lippo of the *popolo* of S. Lorenzo as their "sindicum procuratorem et castaldum, actorem factorem et nuntium specialem et superstantem" who, in coordination with another shareholder, Bato di Dono, would purchase wood and other materials for the reactivation of their mill during an unspecified period of time.[109] Six days later, Pasqua di Guintavalle of Monterappoli sold his sixteenth part to a fellow inhabitant, who, in turn, sold it to another resident for the same price of forty-two *lire*.[110] Since ensuing entries indicate that prior to the middle of the century the *molendinum* had a determined limit of sixteen shares, we can surmise that the consortial mill at Rofiniano had a total value of 672 *lire* or approximately 168 florins.

On 30 August 1321, Chele di Lippo together with his son Coppo and Maggio di Corso leased their $\frac{3}{16}$ of the mill to two brothers for a period of six years at 138¾ Florentine bushels of grain per annum. On the same day, Manuccio di Ciato and Bindo di Bertino, both of Rofiniano, followed suit for their shares of $\frac{1}{16}$ and $\frac{1}{32}$, each expecting an annual return of 27¾ and 13¾ plus ½ of another ¼ (i.e., 13.875) bushels respectively.[111] Here we get a glimpse of the arithmetic employed by these shareholders of the general area of Monterappoli (and elsewhere), who used as a quota 27¾ bushels of grain for a basic allotment of $\frac{1}{16}$. How this amount was decided upon in advance of the six-year period cannot be determined, outside of the estimations generated by previous harvests. Whatever their method might have been, it does demonstrate that the consorts expected 444 bushels of grain as their total annual yield, a handsome sum indeed.

The contracts of 30 August relate even more. We find that the *molendinum de Rofiano* actually comprised two mills, one of which was a suspension mill perched on stakes above its wide vertical waterwheel toward the middle of the Elsa and the other a landed undershot mill whose narrower vertical waterwheel, located beside the structure, received its power, like its mate, from below.[112] In addition, they specify that Chele di Lippo, the former temporary but all-purpose *castaldus*, would be the assessor of these runs, who at the end of the six-year lease would appraise the millstones and the other parts of the plant for the benefit of the shareholders and the millers, with the present notary presiding.

On 31 November 1321, five other consorts, two from Monterappoli and three from the neighboring town of Stigliano, incorporated the identical stipulations of the contracts of 30 August when they leased two sixteenth and three thirty-second shares to the two brothers who were already working the mill at Rofiniano.[113] Between 23 November 1322 and 31 January 1323, four shareholders recognized the receipt of their first year's rent,[114] while Simone di Pietro of Stigliano was properly paid the final portion of an overdue return stemming from a previous agreement[115] and Coppo di Chele was advanced one-third of a year's payment beyond his annual compensation—a sign that 1322 obviously had a productive harvest.[116]

In May, Chele di Lippo, his son Coppo, and Maggio di Corso appear once again. It is confirmed that their efforts in constructing a certain mill in the vicinity of "aliud molendinum vetus positum in popolo Sancti Andree ... supra Elsa" had been fulfilled under the auspices of the *plebanus*, or rector, of the baptismal church of S. Giovanni a Monterappoli.[117] Since there were no other mills in this area, the new edifice was undoubtedly the landed undershot mill mentioned above, which must have been completed by the trio prior to 7 August 1321, the date when the two mills are first disclosed.[118] The notarial entry of 13 May 1323 is thus indicative not only of the prevailing influence of the baptismal church in consortial/communal affairs, but also of the technological capabilities of medieval peasants, who are so often considered as lacking initiative in economic and social developments. It is as if the consortium were bent on giving Chele di Lippo his due when we find that on 16 February 1326 he was selected by the society as the *sindicus* and *procurator* who would appear before the appropriate Florentine officials to explain the improprieties of their miller with respect to the proper payment of taxes on the produce of the mill.[119]

On 15 April 1327, the two brothers of Maggio di Corso were confirmed as the guardians of his son Giovanni. The properties reported in this confirmation reveal that Maggio, who must have died between 17 September 1325 (the date of his will) and the redaction of the confirmation, was apparently a dealer in either oil or wine with enough wealth to advance six gold florins and 287 *lire* to five of his neighbors. The inventory of this respectable merchant also includes a sixteenth and two parts of another sixteenth in the *molendinum de Rofiano,* the establishment he helped to complete.[120] By 21 October 1352, a division of property demonstrates that this consortial mill had been reduced to twelve shares, more than likely as a result of the Black Death. Although it also indicates that Giovanni di Meglio, a Florentine, had joined the company,[121] a subsequent entry establishes that all members, including the heirs of Giovanni, were from the commune of Monterappoli. The ties of this consortium were thus definitely secured within the community, even if partners found new habitations far from home.

That subsequent entry, dated 28 March 1364, had as its primary objective the appointment of two *castaldi* for the specific task of leasing the mill to Lenzo di Vanne, a "master of mills" from Monterappoli, who would rent it for sixteen months at 186 Florentine bushels of grain and in the process build and perfect a new dam.[122] We see, therefore, that the runs of the *molendinum de Rofiano*, which produced an annual rent of 444 Florentine bushels of grain between 1321 and 1327, were not working to their full potential. The consorts were so alarmed that they had the notary of this document, ser Prospero di Marco Battaglieri of Monterappoli, travel immediately to Florence to receive the approval of the contract from ser Nerio di Chello, who possessed either an eighth or a sixteenth of this establishment that was now back to its original number of basic shares.[123] This entry of 31 March 1364 thus proves the existence of a serious problem that needed the prompt and necessary cooperation of all the partners. Could it be that ser Nerio was the only consort wealthy enough to foot the bill for the repairs, which amounted to seventy-five *lire*?

By 1373, the administration of the installation was known as the *castalderia molendini de Rofiano* with the representatives of the sixteen shares of the organization choosing Antonio di Stefano "ad procurandum, guberna[n]dum, regendum, reperandum et recuperandum dictum molendinum et bonos dicti molendini... ad unum annum." These qualifications certainly indicate that the *castaldus* now had general charge of the mill for a fixed term of one year. He was responsible, like the sergeant at the consortial mills at Douai, for policing the physical plant and for being aware of the proper distribution of shares, as in the immediate case of two shareholders, one of whom was ser Nerio di Chello, letting their sixteenth portions to seven other associates for five years at an annual rate of twelve Florentine bushels of grain.[124] These increased obligations of the *castaldus* at Rofiniano were by no means unique among the jointly owned mills of the Valdelsa. As we have seen, in 1371 Iacopo di Bindaccio of Canneto, called Cencio, was appointed "generalem castaldum" of the consortial mill of his area for a six-month term. On 16 March 1373, the settlement of a dispute regarding this very same mill was determined "tam vigore fattorie molendini de Canneto quam etiam aliqua iuris causa."[125] In the Valdelsa at the dawn of the last quarter of the fourteenth century, the *castalderia* or *fattoria* had thus gained the force of law.

Regrettably, that gap of some fifty-four years now appears in the records of the *molendinum de Rofiano*. Nonetheless, Table 5, which registers the shares of this establishment as garnered from the Catasto of 1427–30, demonstrates that the *castalderia* had weakened. The totality of shares equals 1.0833, thereby leaving a residue of ½₂. Perhaps, the widowed, forty-five-year-old Monna Niccolosa, who was reported to be "miserabile" or destitute (*v.n.*1), made an error in her entry: she declared a return of four bushels of grain for her professed share of ¼ of the mill. It is more likely that centralized control had become less operative at the *molendinum de Rofiano*, which at this time had an ideal overall profit of only 192 bushels per annum. Stronger, more efficient organization has to be found elsewhere.

A more rigorous administration for a consortial mill during the last quarter of the fourteenth and the first quarter of the fifteenth century is found at Empoli, located about six kilometers directly north of Monterappoli. On 28 July 1392, fourteen individuals representing thirty-four of the forty-eight *ottavi* of this mill on the Arno chose for one-year terms the two chief officials or *officiales* of the establishment, two assessors or *ragionerii*, who would review all rates and expenditures, and a salaried master miller or rector who, although a shareholder himself, would work on the mill or its dam when it was necessary.[126] Surviving notarial entries for 1394,[127] 1407,[128] 1432,[129] 1433[130] 1438,[131] and 1439[132] indicate that this institutional framework definitely continued and that the lax management shown at the *molendinum de Rofiano* was not typical of all the consortial mills in the Florentine countryside during the late Middle Ages. The title of *castaldus/castaldio* was not used as a means to identify the leaders of this Empolese *societas*. However, even though an urban influence may account for the presence of *ragionerii*,[133] the organization cannot be far removed from the collective representation we have seen in the mills of rural communes and consortia. Since it used the *ottavo* as a unit of account, it certainly was in touch with the cooperative developments found in the rest of Europe.

VI

Taking into consideration the annual return of 444 Florentine bushels of grain for the *molendinum de Rofiano*, there can be no doubt that the owners of consortial mills had profit as their end. While such a generalization is basically true, it cannot be judged categorically. The shareholders of the grain mills of Toulouse, where those of the Château-Narbonnais in particular came once every two months to receive their grain according to their needs, still had large yields beyond immediate requirements.[134] However, subsistence was the goal of the owners of consortial mills located in the recesses of the Apennines that dominate the northern and eastern boundaries of Tuscany. At Palazzuolo, for example, one *paga* returned one bushel of flour each year (*v* references in nos. 1, 2, 8, and 12 of Table 3). There were, however, fifty-two shares, and even more, in this consortial mill on the Senio (v Table 3, n. a). Edifices of this sort were thus fair game for distant or even local speculators who wished to take advantage of their insolvent brethren, particularly during the second half of the fourteenth century.

Such avidity may have been the motive of Renzo d'Ugolino of Castelpagano in Romagna when he purchased three of the forty-five shares of his hometown mill beside the Senio on 20 and 27 August and 12 April 1391.[135] It was definitely the intention of Matteo di Simone di Dolfo of Palazzuolo when by means of nine separate contracts drawn up between 14 December 1420 and 19 April 1421 he acquired ten "partes sive pagas" of the communal mill of Rapezzo located on the Santerno.[136] The total number of shares that Matteo could have bought is unknown, but the Catasto of 1427–30 shows that he purchased them all. At this time, the fifteen-year-old, recently married sister of the now deceased Matteo had full control of the damaged grain mill and fulling mill that she estimated was worth 85 florins.[137] Monna Brizia di Simone di Dolfo, presently living in Tosignano in Romagna, also owned 5 ½ shares of the consortial mill at Palazzuolo. Obviously, this acquisition too came as a result of her brother's covetous efforts (v Table 3, n. 5).

These developments bring us to an interesting phenomenon that was apparently upsetting the internal governance of these rural communes. Paolo Pirillo has recently suggested that the territorial expansion of the city of Florence in the course of the fourteenth century caused rural communes, such as those in the zone of Montegiovi to the northeast of the city, to close ranks as a means of protecting themselves against external and internal socio-economic pressures. The prime symptom of this reaction was the distinction made between those who had rights in the rural communes (the originarii) and those who did not, a development that ironically spurred the creation of new consortia among the inhabitants who were being rejected.[138]

The history of the joint ownership of mills in the territory of medieval Florence lends support to this important thesis. Surely, the purchases of Matteo di Simone di Dolfo illustrate the threat to communal solidarity. As early as 1325, nineteen individuals of the commune of Pulicciano in the Mugello, in the name of this collectivity but without the usual representation, "sold" their annual return of 31¼ Florentine bushels of flour for five years at a cost of forty-eight lire.[139] The establishment of this perpetual rent indicates that each member of the commune was fully aware of his share of the mill and that the ideal parts of a communal entity could materialize without difficulty. More importantly, it illustrates that within a collectivity groups could form that might have experienced difficulty due to activities unrelated to the commune in general and thus had to separate themselves from the principal body, which could not help but be suspicious of their actions.

A more telling example of the emerging protectionism found among the communes of the Florentine countryside during the fourteenth century is observed when, on 21 July 1342, the *popoli* of S. Michele a Monteluco and S. Sano in the hills of the Chianti let out their horizontal mill for three years in return for an annual rent of 360 Florentine bushels of grain. The contract states that every inhabitant of the two areas must grind their grain continuously at the communal mill. If they do not, they will be condemned by the communes and required to restore the charge that the miller has lost. Moreover, on the day the offender is discovered, the miller will begin a denunciation for a period of one month.[140] Here, then, is a fourteenth-century rural collectivity assuming the prerogative of an aristocratic lord by establishing its "banal" rights over an industrial site in order to eliminate any outside competition. It is an example that certainly helps to bolster the argument of Paolo Pirillo. In addition, it would appear that the presumption of the leaders of the *popoli* of S. Michele a Monteluco and S. Sano was not found in Tuscany alone. In France, where ownership or tenancy of industrial centers was becoming increasingly consortial during the fourteenth and fifteenth centuries,[141] the bonds holding together the rural communes were concomitantly tighter and more influential with respect to the claims of their masters.[142]

Although they did not need to protect themselves against competition, the owners of the consortial mill at Empoli most assuredly had profit as their end.[143] Here the earnings were dispersed in kind, but, as in the situation at Toulouse, at substantial gains. An account book of Simone di Piero del Guanto, a wool merchant at Florence, shows that in 1415—a relatively unproductive year—the mill at Empoli was expected to produce for the 48 *ottavi* 864 Florentine bushels of flour, or 36 bushels for Simone's 2 *ottavi*.[144] Simone's very accurate recordings between 14 January 1413 and 14 July 1414 demonstrate, nonetheless, how expenses, particularly for upstream Florentine shareholders, could eat into the returns. During this time, twenty-one allotments, or *dovise*, produced for Simone 3,096 pounds of flour, or approximately fifty-four bushels. The expenses for his agent, who received and transferred the flour, and for the officials of the mill and commune amounted to 1,835 pounds of flour, or approximately thirty-two bushels, an overhead of more than 50 percent.[145]

The desire for profit is best seen in those establishments that determined their gains in coin rather than flour. The account book of the heirs of ser Niccolò Manetti reveals that between 1394 and 1399 the shareholders of the consortial mill at Ognissanti were closely associated with the bank headed by Luigi Guicciardini. As indicated in Table 6, this bank, presumably after selling the flour produced by the mill at the Florentine grain market of Or San Michele, issued returns in cash during four different times of the year, if yields were adequate. Otherwise, they could be reduced to three times a year or only once, with expenditures for repairs being divided according to the value of the share.[146]

Rural communes also owned mills whose final transactions were in money rather than kind. In 1427, the communes of S. Giovanni Valdarno, Terranuova, and Montevarchi, forming a triangle through which the Arno flows some thirty to fifty kilometers southeast of Florence, all reported to the Catasto officials grain mills with healthy monetary returns. Terranuova, in particular, boasted that together its two grain mills and an accompanying fulling mill were worth 500 florins and indicated that in its piazza was an elevated loggia "dove si vende il grano."[147] In addition, the communes of Castel S. Niccolò, Raggiolo, and Ortignano in the Casentino, located to the northeast of Terranuova across the Pratomagno, possessed grain mills that they rented out on a strictly pecuniary basis. The commune of Castel S. Niccolò alone owned four grain mills that produced a combined annual total of 128 *lire* as well as a fulling mill that produced two *lire* per annum, an hydraulic device for grinding oak galls used in the preparation of leather that produced three *lire* per annum, and a *fabbrica* for crushing hay that produced a very lucrative twenty-five florins, or approximately 100 *lire* per annum.[148]

Unfortunately, the notarial chartularies written by the rural notaries fail to yield even a scrap of information about these installations on either side of the Apennine spur known as the Pratomagno. Since S. Giovanni Valdarno, Terranuova, and Montevarchi were essentially Florentine colonies,[149] the greater part of the profits derived from their hydraulic machines must have served the founding city. Although Castel S. Niccolò, Raggiolo, and Ortignano were numbered among the few towns that outwardly recognized Florentine domination,[150] we can only guess at how they administered the earnings of their mills. More than likely, the gains were used to alleviate the immediate financial difficulties involved with the maintenance of their edifices.[151] This leaves the ownership of the consortial mill at Ognissanti in a very privileged position. Each shareholder, being totally separated from the inner workings of the mill, was definitely a passive participant in the association. This characteristic equates the organization at Ognissanti with the joint-stock companies of the early modern period much more than is the case with the milling operations at Toulouse, Douai, and Empoli, or even the partnerships at Salins.[152] Its closest competitor would have to be the *maona* that emerged from the maritime activities of the Genoese throughout the Mediterranean.[153] The development of the consortium at Ognissanti is, of course, intimately related to all of these societies as it is to the associations found throughout Tuscany; one in particular cannot be removed for special consideration. Ultimately, however, the origins of this milling complex return to the consortial mill that was flourishing near the walls of Pistoia in 726.

VII

In sum, the co-proprietorship of industrial establishments during the Middle Ages has to be considered a European phenomenon significantly involved with the consequences of the breakup of the *mansus*. The consortial ownership of mills, dating back to a period prior to the full-fledged emergence of this disruption, is its oldest form. As time proceeded, however, it became increasingly involved in the progressive disintegration of properties and the efforts to control it, a situation that represents a community endeavor with a minimum of influence from the dictates of Roman law or other legal abstractions. It is true that each area of Europe responded to the dispersal of rights and the division of property according to its own social and economic patterns. Yet collaboration remained the common denominator for coalescence whether among aristocrats, merchants, or peasants.

Such collaboration, moreover, may have provided a means for the interchange of technological innovations. Mining and metallurgical techniques were adopted by the Italians through the immigration of Germans and the consequent formation of co-operative associations between the two nationalities. The origins of the Italian fulling mill, or *gualchiera*, could easily be found in a similar process, given the German roots of the word that depicts this hydraulic device.[154] Then, too, if the *ottavo* represents a reciprocation between two separate geographical areas, perhaps it is related to the transmittal of mill mechanisms from France to Tuscany. As we have seen, by the end of the twelfth century Toulouse had adopted the landed undershot waterwheel to run her grain mills on the shores of the Garonne. By the middle of the thirteenth century, Florence was using this contrivance for establishments located on her major rivers, while incorporating the "French" overshot mill for grinding grain on the streams of her hills and mountains. Soon thereafter, the gearing mechanism of these mills was combined with the horizontal waterwheel to create an entirely new apparatus whose immediate European destiny has yet to be determined.[155] These examples of technological transfer thus represent a process that can be equated with the growth of co-proprietorship within the European community. Medieval technology was as basic to the development of European society as the proliferation and control of shares that has led to our modern corporations.

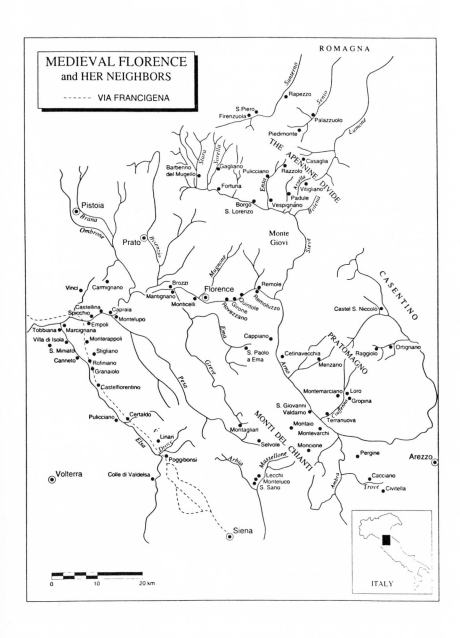

MEDIEVAL FLORENCE
and HER NEIGHBORS

------ VIA FRANCIGENA

Table 1.
The ownership of the newly constructed consortial mill on the Arno near Mantignano
according to the Florentine Catasto of 1427–30

Names of shareholders	Fractional parts	Total wealth[a]	Reference in Catasto
1. Nanni e Niccolò di Cristofano	⅛[b]	171	308,115ᵛ
2. Lorenzo d' Antonio d'Alessio Canacci	⅛	628	308,118ᵛ
3. Martino di Doldo e Iacopo e Zanobi di Giovanni	⅛	883	173,187ᵛ
4. Iacopo di Berto Canacci	1/12	1,453	76,329ʳ
5. Marco di Martino Canacci	1/12	558	76,347ᵛ
6. Stefano e Piero di Benvenuto	1/12	449	308,115ʳ
7. Bianco e Filippo di Benedetto	1/16	68	308,295ʳ
8. Giovanni di Marco	1/16[c]	53	173,214ʳ
9. Antonio di Marco	1/16[d]	125	173,215ᵛ
10. Ciulle di Cristofano	1/24[e]	91	308,104ᵛ
11. Guasparre di Benedetto	1/32[f]	38	308,287ᵛ
12. Giovanni di Benedetto	1/32	78	308,288ᵛ

Notes:
[a] Sums are given to the nearest florin. Numbers 4 and 5 were inhabitants of the city of Florence where the average total wealth per person was approximately 273 florins. The other shareholders lived in the countryside where the average total wealth per person throughout Tuscany amounted to roughly 14 florins. V Herlihy and Klapisch, *Les Toscans et leurs familles*, p. 243.

[b] "Anche le II parti d'uno ⅛ di molino in su detta pescaia," i.e. 1/16 for Nanni and Niccolò respectively.

[c] "Uno mezo otavo di mulino...."

[d] " ½ otavo di mulino...."

[e] Monna Gemma, an eighty-year-old widow of Giannino da Brozzi, owned ⅛ of the former mill (see Catasto 173, 219r), but she did not participate in the ownership of the new edifice. Ciulle must have purchased a third of her share ("⅛/⅛"), thus leaving 1/12 outstanding.

[f] Guasparre reported "Una quarta parte delle 32 parti d'uno mulino in su detta pescaia," but the officials reduced his share to 1/32 without any explanation. Perhaps, Guasparre was involved in an unsuccessful attempt to acquire the share of Monna Gemma.

Source: ASF, Catasto.

Table 2.
The ownership of the consortial mill at Ognissanti according to the
Florentine Catasto of 1427–30

Names of shareholders	Number of shares per 48 parts[a]	Total wealth[b]	Reference in Catasto
1. Convento d'Ognissanti	7 ⅚	(?)[c]	184,96[r]
2. Giovanni di Simone Vespucci	5	1,252	75,310[r]
3. Giovanni di Barduccio di Cherichino	3	31,316	64,79[r]
4. Cardinale Rucellai e Piero, suo figlio	2 ½	6,834	76,59[v]
5. Monna Caterina, donna fu di Matteo di Piero di Fastello Petriboni	2 ⅙	583	68,199[r]
6. Andrea di Giusto di Coverello	2	4,878	66,45[v]
7. Monna Zanobia, donna fu di Domenico di Niccolò Pollini	2	840	77,373[r]
8. Lotteringo d'Andrea di messer Ugo della Stufa	2	6,911	78,86[v]
9. Antonio di Luca da Filicaia e Bernardo di Bernardo, suo nipote	2[d]	1,962	80,65[v]
10. Toso d'Albizzo da Fortuna	1 ½	16,654	78,489[r]
11. Antonio di Bernardo di Ligo	1 ½₂	4,580	79,56[v]
12. Domenico di Buonsignore, *coreggiaio*	1 (?)[e]	543	64,256[r]
13. Santa Maria Nuova	1 (?)[e]	(?)[c]	64,256[r]
14. Maestro Leonardo di maestro Agiolo, *medico*	1 (?)[f]	7,795	67,107[r]
15. Compagnia del Bigallo e di Misericordia	1 (?)	(?)[c]	190,155[v]
16. Monastero di Santa Verdiana	1 (?)[g]	(?)[c]	184,5[r]
17. Messer Palla di messer Palla Strozzi	19,487	72,197[v]	
18. Tommaso di Ranieri Popolani	12,481	75,409[r]	
19. Baldasarre d'Arrigo di Simone, *agoraio*	1	3,464	76,31[v]
20. Niccolò Pollini e Domenico, suo figlio	1	5,426	76,148[v]
21. Piero di Mariotto della Morotta	1	502	76,164[v]
22. Messer Palla di Nofri Strozzi	1	162,926	76,171[r]
23. Giovanni di Bartolo, *sensale*	11	220	76,309[r]
24. Filippo e Taddeo di Zanobi Migliori	1	3,185	77,62[r]
25. Iacopo di ser Francesco Ciai	1	14,223	78,99[r]
26. Giuliano di ser Benedetto Ciai	1	5,924	78,120[v]
27. Iacopo di Bate di Giusto e fratelli	1	1,062	78,134[r]
28. Pierozzo di Sandro Bocchi	1	416	81,342[v]
29. Niccolaio e Alessandro e fratelli, figli d'Ugo degli Alessandri	⅙ [h]	24,077	80,74[r]

Notes:
[a] Numbers 2–3, 5, 9–11, 15, 18, 20, 27, and 28 declared that the establishment was made up of 48 parts. Number 6 stated that it was composed of 47 parts, and number 24 claimed 24 shares as the standard.

[b] Sums are given to the nearest florin. All household heads lived in the city of Florence. Cf. Table 1, note a.

[c] Since the returns of the clergy were essentially ignored by the Catasto officials who made the final tabulations, a true summation, comparable to the secular records, cannot be made for the wealth of any ecclesiastical institution. For the relationship of the Church to the Catasto, v Herlihy and Klapisch, *Les Toscans et leurs familles*, pp. 151–61.

[d] "Una e mezzo parte e una mezza delle 48 parti delle mulina d'Ongnisanti le quali isterzate in 3 anni passati."

[e] "E più dicie ch'a in chasa una sua chongiunta chon nome Mona Domenicha chen'e stata circha d'anni venti e la detta Mona Domenicha a per sua dota in sulle mulina d'Ognisanti circha florini 150 i quali sono mezzi di Santa Maria Nuova e mezzi suoi per uno lascio che fecie Franchesco Brunacci. Dice sene di rendita l'anno... *fiorini* 12. Tochagliene l'anno – *fiorini* 6." *V* below, note f.

[f] The shareholders received payments as many as four times a year (v Table 6). Their reported yields per share thus varied between *fiorini* 2, *soldi* 13, *danari* 4 and *fiorini* 8. Since Maestro Leonardo as well as the preceding two claimants gave only the value of their shares at *fiorini* 6 apiece, one share has been arbitrarily chosen for each.

[g] The monastery of Santa Verdiana and the preceding Compagnia di Bigallo each reported two shares in the establishment. However, these institutions each claimed a yield of *fiorini* 4. Since nine other participants declared a similar return, one share has been assigned respectively.

[h] The totality of shares equals 47½.

Source: ASF, Catasto.

Table 3.
The ownership of the consortial mill at Palazzuolo according to the
Florentine Catasto of 1427–30

Names of shareholders	Number of shares per 52 *paghe*[a]	Total wealth[b]	Reference in Catasto
1. Ser Filippo d'Antonio di Simone da Firenzuola	7[c]	2,155	77,78[v]
2. Giovanni di Paganino	7	279	326,198[r]
3. Antonio di Paganino di Santi	7	541	326,227[r]
4. Iacomino d'Antonio	6 ½	378	326,223[v]
5. Monna Brizia di Simone di Dolfo da Palazzuolo, abitante a Tosignano	5 ½[d]	295	326,214[v]
6. Modesto di ser Giovanni d' Ugolino	2	217	326,221[v]
7. Andrea di Bartolo[e]	1	81	326,200[r]
8. Iacomo di Gilio	1	24	326,208[v]
9. Poggino da Montebovaro	1	110	326,210[v]
10. Monna Francesca donna di Vignadi da Ciopeda	1	112	326,211[v]
11. Cenzio di Marsilio	1	127	326,212[r]
12. Bertozzo di Paganino	1	718	326,217[r]
13. Maggio di Guido	1	400	326,219[v]

Notes:

[a] There may have been more than 52 *paghe* acting as a limit. Number 3 claimed that there were "in tutto paghe cinquanta quatro." Number 13 reported "54 o più."

[b] Sums are given to the nearest florin. Number 1 was an inhabitant of the city of Florence. All other shareholders lived in the mountains. Cf. Table 1, note a.

[c] The wife of ser Filippo, Monna Zanobia, was specifically declared the owner of these shares in a special section for her property found within her husband's return.

[d] Among her liabilities or *incarici* (215[v]), Monna Brizia reported: "A Santo Stefano da Palazzuolo una pagha di mulino, fiorini due." This probably represented a donation to the baptismal church of the area. We must assume that it was a *paga* of the consortial mill at Palazzuolo.

[e] Many of the shareholders complained that the mill was broken down, or that they had received nothing from it for several years. Andrea declared that the mill "fu ghuasto per la ghuerra." This war was waged by Florence against the Milanese forces of Filippo Maria Visconti between 1423 and 1428. The confrontation, which took place principally in the mountains, would certainly help to explain why ten or more *paghe* are missing.

Source: ASF, Catasto.

Table 4.
The ownership of the consortial mill at Empoli according to the
Florentine Catasto of 1427–30.

Names of shareholders	Number of shares per 48 *ottavi*	Total wealth[a]	Reference in Catasto
1. Sinibaldo di Filippo da Carmignano, *ritagliatore*	8	2,283	69,235[r]
2. Leonardo di Guccio Brogiotti e Iacopo, suo nipote	6 ½	4,134	76,97[r]
3. Guccio e Ginevra d'Iacopo di ser Guccio Franceschi e monna Nidda, loro avola	5	1,512	79,239[r]
4. Lorenzo di Francesco di Buonsignore, *albergatore fuori di Porta d'Empoli*	4 ½	817	168,677[r]
5. Giovanni di Guiduccio da Spicchio	4	2,949	74,48[v]
6. Cipriano di Simone Guiducci da Spicchio	2 ½	1,647	81,73[v]
7. Pieve di S. Andrea a Empoli	2 ½	(?)[b]	184,538[r]
8. Compagnia dell' Ospedale di S. Andrea e di S. Giovanni a Empoli	1 ½	(?)[b]	184,548[r]
9. Compagnia di S. Lorenzo a Empoli	1 ½	(?)[b]	184,581[r]
10. Lippaccio e Francesco di Benedetto de' Bardi	1	19,434	64,57[r]
11. Compagnia della Croce a Empoli	1	(?)[b]	184,513[v]
12. Cappella di S. Giovanni Evangelista a Empoli	1	(?)[b]	184,538[r]
13. Cappella della Nativita di Nostra Donna a Empoli	1	(?)[b]	184,626[r]
14. Convento de' Frati di S. Agostino a Empoli	1	(?)[b]	184,680[v]
15. Cappella di S. Maria della Neve a Empoli	1	(?)[b]	184,760[r]
16. Francesco d'Andrea da Montelupo	1	306	168,342[v]
17. Biagio di Donato Pinucci	1	69	168,467[v]
18. Cristofano di Francesco, *pizzicagnolo in Empoli*	1	226	168,617[v]
19. Mazzeo d'Andrea, *maniscalco*	1	54	168,676[r]
20. Iacopo di Michele, *pellicciaio d'Empoli*	1	808	168,709[r]
21. Allivo di Giovanni di Lore da Empoli	½[c]	114	168,708[r]

Notes:

[a] Sums are given to the nearest florin. Numbers 1–3, 5–6, and 10 lived in the city of Florence. Number 17 resided in the commune of Pontorme within the jurisdiction of Empoli. Empoli, where all the other household heads and ecclesiastical institutions were located, was one of Tuscany's 15 notable towns whose inhabitants had an average

total wealth of approximately 32 florins. *V* Herlihy and Klapisch, *Les Toscans et leurs familles*, p. 243.
ᵇ *V* Table 2, note c.
ᶜ The totality of shares equals 47 ½.
Source: ASF, Catasto.

Table 5.
The ownership of the *Molendinum de Rofiano* according to the
Florentine Catasto of 1427–30

Names of shareholders	Fractional parts	Total wealth[a]	Reference in Catasto
1. Monna Niccolosa, donna fu di ser Zanobi di ser Bonaiuto	¼	16	66,355ʳ
2. Barone di Marco	⅛	261	96,793ᵛ
3. Niccolò d'Andrea Ciampelli	1/16	1,323	68,263ᵛ
4. Pietro di Dreasso	1/16	30	96,571ʳ
5. Monna Tommasa, donna di Domenico di Bartolomeo	1/16	100	96,588ʳ
6. Domenico di Bartolomeo	1/16	256	96,606ʳ
7. Pagolo di Pagolo	1/16	58	96,728ʳ
8. Piero e Pagno di Cecco	1/16	246	96,772ʳ
9. Meo, Rugada, Filippo, e Nanni d'Antonio	1/24 ᵇ	439	96,660ᵛ
10. Neri, Niccolò, e Bondo d'Andrea di Stefano	1/24 ᶜ	177	96,678ʳ
11. *Idem*	1/32 ᵈ	*idem*	*idem*
12. Stefano di Lencio	1/32 ᵉ	82	96,641ʳ
13. Compagnia dell'Ospedale del Crocisco a Monterappoli	1/32	(?)ᶠ	184,724ᵛ
14. Stefano di Tuccio	1/32	257	96,655ᵛ
15. Piero e Nanni di Piero	1/32	187	96,663ᵛ
16. Michele di Benuccio e Giovanni d' Antonio, suo nipote	1/32	356	97,109ʳ
17. Niccolo di Salvadore e fratelli da Granaiolo	1/32	320	97,110ʳ
18. Iacopo di Lencio e Guccio, suo figlio	1/32 ᵍ	104	96,681ʳ

Notes:
ᵃ Sums are given to the nearest florin. Numbers 1 and 3 lived in the city of Florence. All of the other shareholders were found in the countryside. Cf. Table 1, note a.
ᵇ "Anchora una terza ottava di mulino posta in detto popolo di Santo Andrea a Rofiano...."
ᶜ "Una terza ottava...."
ᵈ "...una meza sedicina...."
ᵉ "Anchora una meza sedicina di mulino posta a Rofiano nel fiume d'Elsa...."

^f V Table 2, note c.

^g Numbers 13, 14, and 15 had shares that were each called a *trentina*, which was equivalent to the *trenta* that specified a thirty-second part. Instead of a share, number 16 declared a return of 6 Florentine bushels of grain on an investment of 8 florins. Number 17 reported only his investment of 8 florins. Since both of these evaluations concur with the estimates of numbers 13, 14, and 15, numbers 16 and 17 have each been assigned a thirty-second share. Number 18 declared "una cierte parte" that had a yield of 5 Florentine bushels of grain on an investment of 7 florins. Because of the small difference, this evaluation has also been designated as a thirty-second part, thereby producing an aggregate of 1.0833.

Source: ASF, Catasto.

Table 6.

**Payments by the bank of Luigi Guicciardini to the heirs of ser
Niccolò Manetti for their share^a of the consortial mill at Ognissanti, 1394–99**

Date	Amount^b	Reference in account book^c
1394		
18 February	8*f*	2^r and 40^v
5 March	3*f* 28*s* 8*d*	2^r and 40^v
22 June	4*f*	4^r
10 November	4*f*	7^r and 47^v
1395^d		
6 February	4*f*	47^r and 65^r
27 May	1*f* 28*s* 8*d*	47^v and 65^v
16 November	2*f*	47^v and 65^v
1396		
24 January	3*f*	66^r
3 March	3*f* 8*s* 1*d*	48^r and 66^r
16 June	1*f* 4*s*	67^r
1397		
24 October^e	8*f*	69^r
1398		
17 March	8*f*	48^r and 68^r
19 April	3*f* 28*s*	48^r and 68^v
22 June	5*f* 9*s* 8*d*	48^r and 68^v
30 October	5*f* 9*s* 6*d*	48^v and 68^v
1399		
12 February	5*f* 9*s* 4*d*	48^v and 68^v

Notes:

^a The representative of the heirs did not report the number of their shares. Evidence found in the Florentine Catasto of 1427–30 shows that it was more than likely only one. V Table 2, n. f.

^b Sums are given *affiorino*, i.e., 1 *fiorino* = 29 soldi = 348 *denari*. Unless they were account-

ed for in the payments themselves, the costs of the establishment were not tabulated in the journal of the heirs. For the deduction of expenses according to the value of the share in 1427, *v* the information contained in the references of Table 2. If disbursements were registered, they are located here or in the shareholder's liabilities or *incarici.*

c The entries were recorded in a most chaotic fashion. Since in most cases they were repeated in a different section of the journal, a true sequence has been determined according to the scheme here detailed.

d On 14 January 1395, the heirs received 16*s* 6*d* for four Florentine bushels of leftover grain sold by the bank. Through the sale of four bushels of surplus flour on 4 March of the same year, they received 20*s* 3*d.* V 47ʳ and 65ʳ as well as 47ʳ and 65ʳ.

e Giovanni Targioni Tozzetti, *Alimurgia o sia modo di render meno gravi le carestie* I (Florence, 1767), p. 53, reports that in 1396 harvests in the territory of Siena were "sorrowful." It is quite possible that this was the case for the other areas of Tuscany upon which Florence depended for her grain. Such a dearth would help to explain the low payment of 16 June 1396 and the lack of further remuneration until 24 October 1397. V Giuliano Pinto, *Il libro del biadaiolo: Carestie e annona a Firenze dalla metà del '200 al 1348* (Florence, 1978), pp. 73–75, for the regions of Tuscany best suited for the cultivation of cereal.

Source: ASF, Conventi Soppressi, 90 (S. Verdiana), no. 144.

NOTES

1. David Herlihy and Christiane Klapisch, *Les Toscans et leurs familles: Une étude du catasto florentine de 1427* (Paris, 1978), pp. 17–106.
2. V e.g. Archivio di Stato di Firenze (hereafter ASF), Catasto (hereafter Cat.) 77, fols. 92v and 329r (the grain mill at Vespignano owned by Iacopo and Bartolomeo di Niccolò Malegonelle and their uncle Polito d'Iacopo Malegonelle); 68, fols. 5v and 86v (the grain mill at Cetinavecchia owned by Antonio di Niccolò di Michele di Vanni Castellani and Giovanni di Michele di Vanni Castellani); and 80, fols. 421r and 512v (the grain mill at Rovezzano owned by Piero di Filippo di Piero degli Albizzi and Luca di Pagolo di Piero degli Albizzi). A more complex structure of shares is found in the Albizzi ownership of fulling mills at Girone, Quintole, Rovezzano, and Remole. V Hidetoshi Hoshino, "Note sulle gualchiere degli Albizzi a Firenze nel basso medioevo," *Ricerche storiche* 14 (1984), 269–90. It should be pointed out, however, that ASF, Cat. 80, fol. 74r, has Niccolaio and Alessandro d'Ugo degli Alessandri as the partners of the Albizzi for 24 of the 60 shares of the company. Cf. ibid., fols. 28v, 34v, 136r, 341r; 48v, 117r; and 141v, 204r, 513r, 531r. For the internal organization of aristocratic Florentine families, *v* Francis William Kent, *Household and Lineage in Renaissance Florence: The Family Life of the Capponi, Ginori and Rucellai* (Princeton, 1977), pp. 25–43.
3. ASF, Cat. 76, fol. 329v, "in cholonne insu Arno" and fol. 347r, "in Arno insu pali." There is nothing to indicate the identity of the new edifice. Presumably, it was a landed undershot mill. For details concerning the types of mills used in the territory of medieval Florence, *v* John Muendel, "The 'French' Mill in Medieval Tuscany," *Journal of Medieval History* 10 (1984), 215–47.
4. It is possible that difficulties in apportioning flour did not exist if the miller or any member of the consortium was familiar with the commercial arithmetic taught in

the *scuole d'abbaco*. Perhaps problems of addition, subtraction, multiplication, and division were tackled in schools found in the towns and rural centers of the territory of medieval Florence. For the *scuole d'abbaco* in the city of Florence, *v* Richard A. Goldthwaite, "Schools and Teachers of Commercial Arithmetic in Renaissance Florence," *Journal of European Economic History* 1 (1972), 418–33. For literacy and education in the Tuscan countryside during the Middle Ages, *v* Duccio Balestracci, *La zappa e la retorica: Memorie familiari di un contadino toscano del Quattrocento* (Florence, 1984), pp. 15–31.

5. Florence Edler, *Glossary of Medieval Terms of Business: Italian Series, 1200–1600* (Cambridge, Mass., 1934; repr. Millwood, New York, 1970), p. 199. For the use of the *paga* in Genoa, *v* Jacques Heers, *Gênes au XVe siècle: Activité économique et problèmes sociaux,* in *Affaires et gens d'affaires* 24 (Paris, 1961), pp. 162–72.

6. Germain Sicard, *Aux origines des sociétés anonymes: Les moulins de Toulouse au moyen âge,* in *Affaires et gens d'affaires* 5 (Paris, 1953), p. 237.

7. Franco Niccolai, "I consorzi nobiliari ed il comune nell' alta e media Italia," *Rivista storica del diritto italiano* XIII (1940), 116–19; Marc Bloch, "The Rise of Dependent Cultivation and Seignorial Institutions," *Cambridge Economic History of Europe* I², (Cambridge, Eng., 1966), pp. 235–38 and 276–83; Georges Duby, *Rural Economy and Country Life in the Medieval West,* trans. Cynthia Postan (Columbia, S.C., 1968), pp. 5–11 and 28–58; Massimo Montanari, *L'alimentazione contadina nell'alto medioevo* (Naples, 1979), pp. 79–82 and 88–103; and Chris Wickham, *Early Medieval Italy: Central Power and Local Society* (London, 1981), pp. 121– 22. For peasant solidarity during the Roman Empire, *v* Henriette d'Escurac-Doisy, "Notes sur le phénomène associatif dans le monde paysan à l'époque du Haut-Empire," *Antiquités africaines* 1 (1967), 59–71.

8. Chris Wickham, *Studi sulla società degli Appennini nell' alto medioevo: Contadini, signori e insediamento nel territorio di Valva (Sulmona)* (Bologna, 1982), pp. 25–39 Cf. Giovanni Tabacco, *I liberi del re nell' Italia carolingia e postcarolingia* (Spoleto, 1966), pp. 113–39.

9. Niccolai, "I consorzi nobiliari," pp. 124–25.

10. *Codice diplomatico longobardo* I, ed. Luigi Schiaparelli in *Fonti per la storia d'Italia* 62 (Rome, 1929), pp. 130–32. For the career of Gaidualdo and his association with the *terra* and *porta Gaialdatica* of Pistoia, *v* Luigi Chiappelli, "L'età longobarda e Pistoia," *Archivio storico italiano* 79 (1921), 247 and 269–70.

11. Marcel Thévenin, "Études sur la propriété au moyen âge: La 'propriété' et la 'justice' des moulins et fours," *Revue historique* 31 (1886), 244–47. Paul Viollet, "La communauté des moulins et des fours au moyen âge (à l'occasion d'un récent article de M. Thévenin)," *Revue historique* 32 (1887), 86–99, argues, contrary to Thévenin, that communal mills made their appearance during the Middle Ages, perhaps as early as the barbarian era. Without referring to the debate between these two scholars, Marc Bloch, "The Advent and Triumph of the Watermill," in his *Land and Work in Mediaeval Europe,* trans. J. E. Anderson (Berkeley, 1967), p. 151, finds himself in the camp of Thévenin.

12. Pierre Toubert, *Les structures du Latium médiéval: Le Latium meridional et la Sabine du IXe siècle à la fin du XIIe siècle* 1 (Rome, 1973), p. 460, n. 3.

13. Marc Bloch, *French Rural History: An Essay on its Basic Characteristics,* trans. Janet Sondheimer (London, 1966), pp. 79–80 and idem, "Advent and Triumph," p. 151.

14. David Herlihy, "The Carolingian *Mansus,*" *Economic History Review,* 2nd series, 13 (1960), 83–85.

15. Duby, *Rural Economy,* pp. 28–33 and 116–18. Cf. Giovanni Cherubini, *Agricoltura e società rurale nel medioevo* (Florence, 1972), pp. 38–46.

16. Charles-Edmond Perrin, *Recherches sur la seigneurie rurale en Lorraine d'après les plus anciens censiers (IXe-XIIe siècles)* (Paris, 1935; repr. Geneva, 1977), pp. 634–38; Léopold Genicot, *L'économie rurale namuroise au bas moyen âge (1199–1429)* I (Louvain, 1943), pp. 36–91; and Guy Fourquin, *Les campagnes de la région parisienne à la fin du moyen âge: Du milieu du XIIIe siècle au début du XVIe siècle* (Paris, 1970), pp. 119–21.

17. Fourquin, *Les campagnes de la région parisienne,* pp. 121–26 and Maurice Berthe, *Le comté de Bigorre: Un milieu rural au bas moyen âge* (Paris, 1976), pp. 114–17.

18. Henri Sée, *Les classes rurales et le régime domanial en France au moyen âge* (Paris, 1901; repr. Geneva, 1980), p. 410, n. 3 and Léo Verriest, *Le régime seigneurial dans le comté de Hainaut du XIe siècle a la Révolution* (Louvain, 1916–17; repr. 1956), pp. 277–79.

19. Cinzio Violante, "Le strutture familiari, parentali e consortili delle aristocrazie in Toscana durante i secoli X–XII," *I ceti dirigenti in Toscana nell'età precomunale* (Pisa, 1981), pp. 24–27.

20. David Herlihy, *Medieval Households* (Cambridge, Mass., 1985), pp. 86–89.

21. Aldo A. Settia, *Castelli e villaggi nell'Italia padana: Popolamento, potere e sicurezza fra IX e XIII secolo* (Naples, 1984), pp. 166–67 and Wickham, *Studi sulla società degli Appennini,* pp. 69 and 85–86.

22. Gina Fasoli, "Castelli e signorie rurali," *Settimane di Studio del Centro Italiano di Studi sull' alto medioevo* 13 (Spoleto, 1966), 553–59; Gabriella Rossetti, "La discussione sul tema: Le istituzioni del contado," in Fasoli, "Castelli e signorie rurali," pp. 597–99; Toubert, *Les structures du Latium médiéval* 1, pp. 321–25 and 711–34; and Wickham, "The *terra* of San Vincenzo al Volturno in the 8th to 12th centuries: The Historical Framework," *San Vincenzo al Volturno: The Archaeology, Art and Territory of an Early Medieval Monastery,* eds. Richard Hodges and John Mitchell (Oxford, 1985), pp. 239–40 and 246–47.

23. Giovanni Gozzadini, *Delle torri gentilizie di Bologna e delle famiglie alle quali prima appartennero* (Bologna, 1875; repr. 1965); Pietro Santini, "Società delle torri in Firenze," *Archivio storico italiano,* 20 (1887), 25–58 and 178–204; Niccolai, "I consorzi nobiliari," pp. 138–47, 293–318, and 323–42; Manlio Bellomo, *Profili della famiglia italiana nell'età dei comuni* (Catania, 1966); and Jacques Heers, *Family Clans in the Middle Ages: A Study of Political Social Structures in Urban Areas,* trans. Barry Herbert (Amsterdam, 1976), pp. 174–201.

24. Niccolai, "I consorzi nobiliari," pp. 318–20 and Kathryn L. Reyerson, *Business, Banking, and Finance in Medieval Montpellier* (Toronto, 1985), pp. 26–29 and 35–39.

25. Antonio Scialoja, "Partes navis–loca navis," in his *Saggi di storia del diritto marittimo* (Rome, 1946), pp. 19–20 and Niccolai, "I consorzi nobiliari," pp. 320–23.

26. John U. Nef, "Mining and Metallurgy in Medieval Civilization," *Cambridge Economic History of Europe* II² (Cambridge, Eng., 1987), pp. 712–15 and 740–41.

27. Gioacchino Volpe, "Montieri: Costituzione politica, struttura sociale ed attivita economica d'una terra mineraria toscana nel XIII secolo," *Vierteljahrschrift für Sozial- und Wirtschaftsgeschichte* VI (1908), 368–69. Cf. Sicard, *Aux origines des sociétés anonymes,* pp. 335–36.

28. François Menant, "Pour une histoire médiévale de l'entreprise minière en Lombardie," *Annales: E.S.C.* 42 (1987), 786–87.

29. Volpe, "Montieri," pp. 370–73.

30. Ibid., pp. 376–78. For a description of the area and the techniques used for extraction, v Emanuele Repetti, *Dizionario geografico fisico storico della Toscana* 3 (Florence, 1839; repr. Rome, 1969), pp. 244–46. An excellent comprehensive survey of the history of the salt industry is Robert P. Multhauf, *Neptune's Gift: A History of Common Salt* (Baltimore, 1978).

31. Max Prinet, *L'industrie du sel en Franche-Comté avant la conquête francaise* (Besancon, 1900), 56–58. For the *parsonniers* involved in the exploitation of Burgundian mines yielding metallic ores, v Philippe Braunstein and O. Chapelot, "Mine et métallurgie en Bourgogne à la fin du moyen-âge: Première esquisse," *Mines, carrières et métallurgie dans la France médiévale*, eds. Paul Benoit and Philippe Braunstein (Paris, 1983), p. 35. Similar associations with the same purpose were found in Savoy and Languedoc-Roussillon. For the former area, v Paul Benoit and Philippe Braunstein, "Les comptes miniers d'Hurtières en Savoie (1338–1350)," *Mines, carrières et métallurgie*, pp. 184–85 and for the latter Charles Bonami, "Dans la haute vallée de l'Orb: Les mines de Ceilhes-et-Rocozels au moyen âge," *Mines et mineurs en Languedoc-Roussillon et régions voisines de l'antiquité à nos jours* (Montpellier, 1977), p. 96 and Claudie Amado, "La seigneurie des mines en pays de Béziers et en Razès: Analyse de trois documents de la second moitié du XIIe siècle," *Mines et mineurs en Languedoc-Roussillon*, pp. 132 and 137–38.

32. Prinet, *L'industrie du sel*, pp. 58–66 and 77–80. In n. 3 on p. 62, Prinet reports that in 1196, when Gaucher of Salins gave a "demi-meix" to the abbey of Rosières, it was designated in this fashion: "tantum de muria quantum medietas unius mansi refundere consuevit."

33. The association of industrial establishments with *mansi* was not unusual. Thomas Evergates, *Feudal Society in the Bailliage of Troyes under the Counts of Champagne, 1152–1284* (Baltimore, 1975), p. 24, relates that in 1158 Count Henry I, in the terminology of the document, freed from their obligations "six *hospites* and their families living on the six *manses* of the oven."

34. Thomas F. Glick, *Islamic and Christian Spain in the Early Middle Ages: Comparative Perspectives on Social and Cultural Formation* (Princeton, 1979), pp. 146–48.

35. Prosper Boissonnade, *Essai sur l'organisation du travail en Poitou depuis le XIe siècle jusqu'à la Révolution* I (Paris, 1900), p. 117.

36. Sée, *Les classes rurales*, p. 420 and Richard Holt, *The Mills of Medieval England* (Oxford, 1988), p. 107.

37. Thévenin, "Études sur la propriété au moyen âge," p. 257 and Gérard Sivéry, *Structures agraires et vie rurale dans le Hainaut à la fin du moyen âge*, I (Lille, 1977), pp. 277–80.

38. Edward J. Kealey, *Harvesting the Air: Windmill Pioneers in Twelfth-Century England* (Berkeley, 1987), pp. 78–79, 168–69, and 200. I concur with Holt, *The Mills of Medieval England*, p. 171, in identifying the mill at Wigston Magna as being run by water rather than wind.

39. Georges Espinas, *La vie urbaine de Douai au moyen âge* II (Paris, 1913), p. 444 and Otto von Gierke, *Das deutsche Genossenschaftsrecht* I (Berlin, 1868; repr. Grax, 1954), pp. 969–70.

40. Sicard, *Aux origines des sociétés anonymes*, pp. 162-65.

41. Ibid., pp. 69–72 and 148–54. For the identification of "landed" mills as undershot v Muendel, "The 'French' Mill," pp. 225–28. Cf. Jean Gimpel, *The Medieval Machine: The Industrial Revolution of the Middle Ages* (New York, 1976), p. 17.

42. Gian-Francesco Pagnini, *Della decima e di varie altre gravezze imposte dal comune di Firenze, della moneta e della mercatura de' Fiorentini fino al secolo XVI* II (Lisbon–Lucca, 1765–66), pp. 310–12.

43. ASF, Notarile antecosimiano (hereafter Not.), L99, fol. 27r, 14 January 1283.

44. Volpe, "Montieri," pp. 376–79.

45. Scialoja, "Partes navis," pp. 21–22.

46. Toubert, *Les structures du Latium médiéval* 1, p. 361, n. 1 and ibid., 2, pp. 1176–78.

47. Paolo Pirillo, "Uno caso di pianificazione territoriale nel contado di Firenze (secc. XIII–XIV)," *Studi e ricerche* (Università di Firenze. Istituto di storia) 1 (1981), 179–200.

48. Santini, "Società delle torri," pp. 35–37, 43, 46–58, and 178–90. Cf. Heers, *Family Clans in the Middle Ages,* pp. 194–98 and Duccio Balestracci and Gabriella Piccinni, *Siena nel Trecento: Assetto urbano e strutture edilizie* (Florence, 1977), pp. 131–33 and 135.

49. V, for example, Perrin, *Recherches sur la seigneurie rurale,* pp. 638–42.

50. Carlo M. Cipolla, "Per la storia della crisi del sistema curtense in Italia. Lo sfaldamento del manso nell'Appennino bobbiese," *Bullettino dell'Istituto Storico Italiano per il medio evo e Archivio muratoriano* 62 (1950), 289–98.

51. François Louis Ganshof and Adriaan Verhulst, "Medieval Agrarian Society in its Prime: France, the Low Countries, and Western Germany," *Cambridge Economic History of Europe* ² p. 319.

52. Fourquin, *Les campagnes de la région parisienne,* pp. 174–80.

53. P. J. Jones, "An Italian Estate, 900–1200," *Economic History Review,* 2nd series, 7 (1954–55), 23–26; Paolo Cammarosano, *La famiglia dei Berardenghi: Contributo alla storia della società senese nei secoli XI–XIII* (Spoleto, 1974), pp. 46–47; and Duane J. Osheim, *An Italian Lordship: The Bishopric of Lucca in the Late Middle Ages* (Berkeley, 1977), pp. 98–99.

54. Perrin, *Recherches sur la seigneurie rurale,* pp. 643–50 and Genicot, *L'économie rurale namuroise* I, pp. 227–28 and 232–34.

55. Cherubini, *Agricoltura e società rurale,* p. 48.

56. Niccolò Rodolico, "Massa Marittima e il suo statuto minerario," in his *Saggi di storia medievale e moderna* (Florence, 1963), pp. 97-98 and Carlo Baudi di Vesme, "Dell' industria delle argentiere nel territorio di Villa di Chiesa (Iglesias) in Sardigna nei primi tempi della dominazione aragonese," *Monumenta historiae patriae* 17 (Turin, 1877), col. CV.

57. Volpe, "Montieri," pp. 395–96. For the short-lived interest of the Sienese in the mines of Volterra, Grosseto, and Massa Marittima, v William M. Bowsky, *The Finance of the Commune of Siena, 1287–1355* (Oxford, 1970), pp. 63–65 and his *A Medieval Italian Commune: Siena under the Nine, 1287–1355* (Berkeley, 1981), pp. 218–19.

58. Prinet, *L'industrie du sel,* pp. 81–84. In n. 2 on p. 49, Prinet relates that on 23 June 1283 a canon of S. Anatoile sold a portion of the annual income "supra medietatem cujusdam quarterii de manso de la Chauderete, quam nunc tenet dominus Bauduinus dictus Engarranz, miles salinensis, et supra totam partem suam dicti mansi, siti Salinis, in Burgo heredum nobilis viri Johannis quondam comitis Burgundie et domini Salinarum."

59. Scialoja, "Partes navis," pp. 23–63. Cf. Robert-Henri Bautier, *The Economic Development of Medieval Europe,* trans. Heather Karolyi (London, 1971), p. 160.

60. Sicard, *Aux origines des sociétés anonymes,* pp. 237–38.

61. Ibid., p. 180.

62. ASF, Not., N65, fol. 128r-v.

63. Sicard, *Aux origines des sociétés anonymes,* pp. 172, 323, 335, and 340.

64. Cf. Susan Reynolds, *Kingdoms and Communities in Western Europe, 900–1300* (New York, 1984), pp. 152–54 and 215–16, who argues that, although it lacked regulation, collective judgment was highly influencial in the formation of medieval legal principles, much more than is usually recognized because of the exaggerated importance given to Roman law.

65. "Ordinamenta super arte fossarum rameriae et argentariae civitatis Massae," ed. Francesco Bonaini, *Archivio storico italiano,* appendice VIII, no. 27 (1850), pp. 646–47, 669–71, and 675–76. Cf. Sicard, *Aux origines des sociétés anonymes,* p. 335.

66. Espinas, *La vie urbaine de Douai* II, pp. 470–94 and 498–99.

67. Prinet, *L'industrie du sel,* pp. 144–55.

68. Sicard, *Aux origines des sociétés anonymes,* pp. 268-73.

69. Ibid., pp. 201–12.

70. Duane J. Osheim, "Countrymen and the Law in Late-Medieval Tuscany," *Speculum* 64 (1989), 317–37, demonstrates the implicit cooperation of Tuscan peasants who defended their neighbors against the presumptions of the Lucchese Curia dei Foretani, a small-claims court established by the elite who owned land in the countryside.

71. I have come upon *sedes* only once, but they nevertheless seem important. *V* ASF, Not., B2804, fol. 44r, 26 October 1323 (a consortial mill at Marcignana in the vicinity of San Miniato), "videlicet de otto sedibus aut partibus eiusdem molendini unam pro indivisa."

72. The examples are numerous. *V,* for instance, above, n. 43.

73. ASF, Not., F481, fol. 9r–v, 20 November 1334 ("medietas pro indiviso unius molendini... positam in popolo plebis Sancti Casiani de Padule"); G317, no pagination (hereafter n.p.), 22 June 1348 ("de triginta duabus partibus unam partem molendinorum positorum in flumine Arni... in portu de Montelupo"); idem, 29 June 1348 ("de otto partibus unam partem molendinorum positorum in flumine Arni ... in portu Sancti Pieri comunis Montislupi et Caprare.... Item ... de sedecim partibus unam partem dictorum molendinorum positorum in dicto portu"); and T434, n.p., 14 August 1404 (the annual rent for a "certam partem" of the consortial mill at Empoli to be given "pauperibus Christi et miserabilibus personis").

74. Ibid., P243, n.p., 25 May 1350 ("quartam partem pro indiviso unius molendini... positi in popolo Sancti Pauli ad Emam"); I58, fol. 46v, 9 August 1340 ("octavam partem pro indiviso domus in qua sunt molendina de Anghareccia ... posita ... in comuni Certaldi in loco dicto Al Anghareccia iusta flumen Else"); T462, fols. 84v–85r, 28 January 1347 ("tres partes de octo partibus cuius molendini positas in flumine Arni loco dicto A Portu de Ratto"); and P364, fol. 18v, 27 January 1377 ("medietatem pro indiviso unius ottave unius molendini positi in comuni Montislupi loco dicto A Saminiatello").

75. Ibid., B2779, n.p., 1 October 1313 (24 *lire* plus "dimidietatem pro indiviso cuiusdam petii terre et cuiusdam molendini et hedificii et rerum positarum in flumine Soserle" for "duos petios terrarum rerum possessionum et bonarum positarum in loco et ad locum [qui] esse dicitur Petrogano popoli Sancti Alexandri") and M559, fol. 120v, 30 July 1384 (the appointment of an agent "ad permutandum unum octavum molendini positi in flumine Else loco dicto Tobbiana quod dicitur Il Molino de Malandrino" together with half of a house located in the district outside the gate of S. Miniato).

76. Ibid., S764, fol. 2r, 15 May 1316 (half of a French mill located "in flumine Grevis and pedem chastellaris de Montelliari" as part of the payment for a dowry worth 190 *lire);* B2806, n.p., 6 March 1334 (an eighth part of the mill "de Capocavallo" located on the Elsa at Tubbiana as part of a dowry); P966, fol. 87r–v, 16 April 1371 (the restoration of a dowry by selling "vigesimam quartam partem molendini de Canneto ... positi in flumine Else et popolo Sancti Giorgii de Canneto" for 18 florins); and A131, fols. 62r-63r, 23 November 1394 (the acquisition by a widow of a house, five pieces of land, and "unam dimidiam octavam unius molendini positi in rivo plebis" of S. Blasio de Castellina for a dowry worth 265 *lire).*

77. Ibid., B2781, n.p., 12 November 1314 ("dimedietatem pro indiviso cuiusdam molendini ... positam in fossato sive flumine Soserle"). Cf. idem, 16 March 1318. *V* also ibid., 092, fol. 11r, 4 May 1325.

78. *V,* in particular, ibid., G830, filza 1, fol. 65r, 1 February 1296 (the 3 shareholders of the 8 parts of 2 suspension mills located on the Arno in the popolo of S. Lorenzo a Cappiano lease their establishments to a miller and his son for 3 years at 1,224 bushels, 34 bushels being paid each month); C480, fol. 117r–v, 5 August 1327 (the 4 shareholders of the 10 parts of a floating mill and a landed undershot mill placed in the Arno at the "Portus Thome" in the *popolo* of S. Piero a Monticelli rent the former to a miller for 1 year at 246 bushels paid weekly pro rata and the latter to a fellow shareholder, who possesses ⅒ of the complex, for 1 year at 192 bushels paid weekly pro rata); and I42, filza 2, fols. 4v–5r, 10 January 1329 (the 7 shareholders of the 20 parts of 3 undershot mills located beside the Arno at "Lo Porto ala Toma" in the *popolo* of S. Piero a Monticelli lease their runs to a miller for 1 year at 552 bushels of flour paid weekly pro rata at the homes of each partner). Cf. idem, fols. 18v–19r, 2 July 1329 (5 of the 7 shareholders just mentioned divide the ownership of 2 new undershot mills built beside the Arno at "Lo Porto ala Toma ... versus hospitale [m] Sancti Bartoli de Mungnone" into 20 parts and rent the edifices to a miller for 1 year at 444 bushels of flour paid weekly pro rata at the homes of the partners).

79. The examples are many. *V,* for instance, ibid., 093, fol. 146r, 26 November 1341 (the monastery of S. Paolo a Razzolo rents ¾ of the horizontal mill on the Ensa at Camagro in the commune of Pulicciano to a miller for 5 years at an annual return of 13 ½ bushels of flour) and N65, fol. 129r, 2 April 1352 (ser Francesco di Vita leases "duos ottavos" of the consortial mill at Empoli to a miller for 1 year at 20 bushels of flour).

80. Ibid., P566, insert, 12 June 1371.

81. Baudi di Vesme, "Dell'industria delle argentiere," cols. CV–CVIII.

82. Cipolla, "Per la storia della crisi," pp. 294–95, suggests that in the Bobbiese Apennines extra participation in the sharing of *mansi* that went beyond the aggregate represented manorial supplements (for example, fowl and eggs), grazing rights, or nothing at all. Christine E. Meek, "Public Policy and Private Profit: Tax Farming in Fourteenth-Century Lucca," in *The Other Tuscany* (Kalamazoo, Mich., forthcoming), has shown that in Lucca the shares of guarantors for the retail wine tax of 1351 and 1352 went beyond the total sum in order to spread the risk and to compensate for possible deficits. Since mills were frequently repaired, extra resources such as these would have helped, but none have been found for this study. My thanks to Prof. Meek for sending me a copy of her paper prior to its publication by the Medieval Institute.

83. Catherine E. Boyd, *Tithes and Parishes in Medieval Italy: The Historical Roots of a Modern*

Problem (Ithaca, 1952), pp. 53–62. Cf. Andrea Castagnetti, *L'organizzazione del territorio rurale nel medioevo: Circoscrizioni ecclesiastiche e civili nella "Langobardia" e nella "Romania"* (Turin, 1979), pp. 7–42 and 255–61 and Chris Wickham, *The Mountains and the City: The Tuscan Appennines in the Early Middle Ages* (New York, 1988), p. 173. *V* George Dameron, "Episcopal Lordship in the Diocese of Florence and the Origins of the Commune of San Casciano Val di Pesa, 1230–1247," *Journal of Medieval History* 12 (1986), p. 147, for an example of the strength of the traditional tie between the baptismal church and the local community in Tuscany.

84. Bruno Andreolli and Massimo Montanari, *L'azienda curtense in Italia: Proprietà della terra e lavoro contadino nei secoli VIII–XI* (Bologna, 1983), pp. 45–54 and 161–73.

85. Osheim, *An Italian Lordship,* pp. 58–66 and 122–23 and Odile Redon, *Uomini e comunità del contado senese nel Duecento* (Siena, 1982), pp. 97–223. For the possibility of earlier manifestations of the rural commune, *v* Wickham, *Early Medieval Italy,* pp. 98–99.

86. When mills found in the returns of the Catasto of 1427–30 are compared with the grain mills and fulling mills included in the Florentine tax records of 1425–27, identical edifices of a particular area can be classified as either communal or consortial. *V* John Muendel, "The Distribution of Mills in the Florentine Countryside during the Late Middle Ages," *Pathways to Medieval Peasants,* ed. J. A. Raftis (Toronto, 1981), p. 97.

87. ASF, Not., F520, filza 1, no. 45, fol. 95r–v.

88. Ibid., N70, fol. 125v, 11 December 1347 (the *camerarius* of the commune of Cacciano "et negotiorum gestor dicti comunis" lets the "molendinum de Sancto Georgio in pede coste Cacciani" to a fellow inhabitant for one year at 60 bushels of grain); idem, fol. 148v, 28 September 1348 (the two consuls of Cacciano lease the "molendinum de Piano" to 2 brothers for one year at 32 bushels of grain); and 092, fol. 11v, 6 May 1325 ("Iohanna filia olim Ghezzi dela Casa ... fecit finem ... Tramontino olim Manzi nunc camerario comunis Puliciani recipienti pro se et dicto comuni et hominibus et universitati dicti comunis de omni edificio et melioramento" that was completed "in dicto molendino Riprofatte de Riprofatta" at a cost of 66 *lire* 5 *soldi*).

89. Ibid., 092, fol. 39r–v, 19 October 1326 (his responsibilities involved the "molendinum Riprofatte" of n. 88 above). Cf. ibid., V342, n.p., 21 August 1274 (4 *sindici* of the commune of Montemarciano declare that they have received from the *plebanus* of the baptismal church of Gropina not only the 216 bushels of grain for the past year's rent of the communal mill on the Ciuffenna, but also an advance of 144 bushels of grain for the following year's rent due on 1 April 1275); U52, fols. 93v–94r, 10 January 1329 (the *sindicus* and *procurator* of the *popolo* of Selvola leases to a fellow inhabitant the mill of the *popolo* "in fossato dicto Aristefoli" for one year at 28 bushels of grain, with the additional responsibility of rebuilding the house of the mill at a cost of 40 *soldi*); N75, filza 6, fol. 16r, 1 January 1347 (in this abbreviated entry, the "sindicus comunis Moncionis comitatus domini comitis Guidonis de Battifolle... pro dicto comuni locavit ad affictum Guccio olim Corsi" the mill of the said commune); N70, fol. 117v, 11 September 1347 (the *sindicus* and 2 "consiliarii" of the commune of Cacciano lease out the "molendinum de Piano in curia dicti Cacciani in strata que itur Civitellam" for one year at 45 bushels of grain); and F520, filza 1, no. 48, fol. 101r–v, 2 February 1377 (the men of the commune of Gagliano select two *sindici* "ad locandum et deflorandum molendinum dicti comunis in popolo Sancti Stefani de Reczano in dicto comuni in flumine de Forcella loco dicto Al Teggiano" among other duties to be performed in behalf of the commune).

90. Ibid., I47, fols. 2v–6r, 7 July 1333. Cf. ibid., L234, fol. 26r, 14 July 1342 (the men of the commune of Monteluco a Lecchi "fecerunt ... verum et legiptimum sindicum et procuratorem actorem factorem et etiam numptium specialem Ruzolum Duccii dicti loci ... ad affictandum molendinum dicti comunis positum nel Massollone").

91. Ibid., S765, fol. 66r, 18 April 1340 (among other obligations, the 3 *sindici* and *procuratores* of the commune of Montaglieri are elected "ad vendendum mulendinum eorum et molendinum recipere ad fittum et infrantorium olivarum exercere et facere fare").

92. Ibid.

93. Ibid., G465, filza 2, fol. 203v, 21 September 1397 (the commune of Piedimonte selects 2 inhabitants as *sindici* and *procuratores* for the allotment of flour produced at the communal mill "in loco dicto La Spiglia in aquimine fluminis Sennis").

94. Ibid., V342, n.p., 8 May 1269 ("Lorese olim Turetocti de Loro per se suosque heredes in perpetuo iure livellario et ad fictum locavit ... Orlando olim Regolliosi de Loro ... recepienti et stipulanti vice et nomine dicti comunis Lori quam sindico et procuratore dicti comunis et hominum comunis prefati medietatem pro indiviso molendini de Meciarino quod est positum in curia Lori in dicto vocabulo Meciarini" for an annual rent of 8 bushels of grain); N70, fol. 11r, 4 May 1337 ("Ego Nerus notarius predictus tanquam vicarius camerarius et negotiorum gestor monasterii Verginis vice et nomine dicti monasterii ... locavit ... Milanetto Mascaruccii et Gioio consulibus comunis Verginis ... molendinum dicti monasterii" for 50 bushels of grain during an unspecified period of time); M437, n.p., 2 December 1338 (a canon of the baptismal church of S. Maria a Poggibonsi leases the grain mills and fulling mills of the church "ad annos quinque proxime venturos Piero olim Conselli de Podiobonizzio qui se dixit sindicum ... hominium et personarum universitatis dicti comunis" for an annual rent of 408 bushels of grain); and N75, filza 5, fol. 124r, 3 April 1346 ("Presbyter Peruzus rector ecclesie Sancti Marci de Pogi comunis Moncionis jurisdictionis domini comitis Guidonis de Battifolle vice et nomine ecclesie locavit ad affictum Petro olim ser Brandini sindico et procuratori comunis Moncionis predicti" the mill of the said church and commune for unspecified terms).

95. Gian Piero Bognetti, "Il gastaldato longobardo e i giudicati di Adaloaldo, Arioaldo e Pertarido nella lite fra Parma e Piacenza," in his *L'età longobarda*, I (Milan, 1966), pp. 268–70.

96. Volpe, "Montieri," pp. 366–67; Osheim, *An Italian Lordship*, pp. 38–41; and Wickham, *The Mountains and the City*, pp. 189–90.

97. ASF, Not., V342, n.p., 21 August 1274 (the 4 *sindici* of the commune of Montemarciano receive 144 bushels of grain "a dicto plebano et castaldo" of the baptismal church of Gropina) and B2782, n.p., 8 January 1319 ("Lapuccius Petri tamquam procurator et castaldio ... in plebe Sancti Stephany in Botena pro domino Gentile plebano in plebe predicta").

98. Cammarosano, *La famiglia dei Berardenghi*, pp. 290, n. 49 and 312 and P. J. Jones, "A Tuscan Monastic Lordship in the Later Middle Ages: Camaldoli," *Journal of Ecclesiastical History* 5 (1954), pp. 171, 173, 175, and 179. For an excellent portrait of the *castaldio* Pietro di Giovanni of the Casentino, who is known to have thrived between 1025 and 1050, *v* Wickham, *The Mountains and the City*, pp. 242–44.

99. Cammarosano, *La famiglia dei Berardenghi*, pp. 276, n. 9 and 277, n. 11.

100. Ibid., pp. 180 and 211, n. 178.

101. Pier Silverio Leicht, *Operai, artigiani, agricoltori* in *Italia dal secolo VI al XVI* (Milan, 1946), pp. 107–108 and Roberto Zago, *I Nicolotti: Storia di una comunità di pescatori a Venezia nell'età moderna* (Padua, 1982), pp. 8 and 58–60.

102. Wickham, *Studi sulla società degli Appennini*, pp. 64–67 (the Sansoneschi family originating with the *castaldo* Sansone) and E. Balda, "Una corte rurale nel territorio di Asti nel medioevo: Quarto d'Asti e l'amministrazione del capitolo canonicale," *Bollettino storico-bibliografico subalpino* 70 (1972), 96–100 (the *castaldo* Giacomo Berruto).

103. Claudio Meli, "La Valdelsa: Lotta economico-militare e dinamica degli insediamenti nel baricentro viario della Toscana," *Città, contado e feudi nell'urbanistica medievale*, ed. Enrico Guidoni (Rome, 1974), pp. 37–62.

104. ASF, Not., P566, fol. 47r–v.

105. Ibid., B966, fol. 85r.

106. Ibid., I58, fol. 10r–v.

107. Repetti, *Dizionario geografico* 3, p. 494, refers to this *popolo* as located at *Rofiniano*. All of the archival sources I have examined regarding this area have the designation *Rofiano* or *Rufiano*.

108. ASF, Not., D150, n.p., 7 August 1319, "a primo strata Romea" and G106, filza 3, fol. 44v, 15 April 1327, "a primo strata publica." For the history of the Via Romea or Francigena, *v* Meli, "La Valdelsa," pp. 37–62.

109. ASF, Not., G106, filza 1, fol. 7v.

110. *V* above, n. 108.

111. ASF, Not., D150, n.p.

112. The contracts do not contain such an elaborate description. Chele, Coppo, and Maggio let out ⁵⁄₁₆ "duorum molendinorum, unius penzoli, alterius orbi." For the technological identification of these mills, *v* Muendel, "The 'French' Mill," pp. 222–28 and his "Medieval Urban Renewal: The Communal Mills of the City of Florence, 1351–1382," *Journal of Urban History,* 17 (1991), p. 383, n. 16.

113. ASF, Not., D150, n.p.

114. Ibid., 23 November 1322 (Chele di Lippo and Maggio di Corso); G106, filza 2, fol. 55r, 17 December 1322 (Ciambene di Pelegrino); and D150, n.p., 31 January 1323 (Gallo di Davino).

115. Ibid., G106, filza 1, fol. 86v, 12 December 1322.

116. Ibid., D150, n.p., 31 January 1323.

117. Ibid., 13 May 1323. Coppo, who has reinstated the *plebanus* with an eighth part of the new mill in the name of his father and Maggio, must have been primarily responsible for the workmanship.

118. *V* above, ns. 108 and 110. The sale involves a "sextamdecimam partem pro indiviso duorum molendinorum positam in popolo Sancti Andree de Rofiano comunis Monterappoli [[s] iuxta et super flumen Else." The contract of 1 August 1319 (*v* above, n. 109) refers to the "ipsum molendinum sive molendina," but this expression is either formulaic or refers to the runs of the original mill.

119. ASF, Not., G106, filza 2, fol. 84r–v.

120. Ibid., filza 3, fol. 44r–v. Beyond these shares, the following property belonged to Maggio: three vats ("tres vegetes"), one with a capacity of 32 barrels or approximately 1,458 liters, another with a capacity of 28 barrels or approximately 1,276 liters, and another with a capacity of 18 barrels or approximately 820 liters; another vessel ("unum tinum") with a capacity of 20 barrels or approximately 912 liters; a wooden footstool ("unum soppedanum de lingno"); and two pieces of land and a house in

the *popolo* of S. Giovanni a Monterappoli. For the advocation of different trades by a single individual, *v* John Muendel, "The Millers, of Pistoia, 1200–1430," *Journal of European Economic History* 6 (1977), p. 396 and his "The Mountain Men of the Casentino during the Late Middle Ages," *Science and Technology in Medieval Society*, ed. Pamela O. Long (New York, 1985), p. 38. It is possible that, if Maggio was an olive-oil salesman, he could have sold his product to the milling concerns of the Valdelsa as a lubricant to overcome friction created particularly by journals turning in the blocks of suspension mills and landed undershot mills. Olive oil was common in the area as indicated by the joint ownership of a *fattoio* in the *popolo* of S. Giovanni a Monterappoli. *V* ASF Not., G106, filza 2, fol. 47r, 18 March 1322. For the use of olive oil as a lubricant in the mills of the Valdelsa, *v* ibid., R150, n.p., 14 August 1305 (a jointly owned suspension mill at Catignano); G106, filza 3, fol. 34v, 10 February 1327 (an ecclesiastical undershot mill beside the Elsa at Certaldo); and I58, fol. 11r, 28 February 1338 (the consortial undershot mill next to the Elsa at Pulicciano). For the employment of olive oil in the communal mills of the city of Florence, *v* Muendel, "The Internal Functions of a 14th-Century Florentine Flour Factory," *Technology and Culture* 32 (1991), pp. 512–14.

121. ASF, Not., P382, n.p.
122. Ibid., B966, fols. 24v–25r.
123. Ibid., fol. 25r, 31 March 1364.
124. Ibid., fols. 106v–108r, 3 October 1373.
125. Ibid., fol. 100r–v.
126. Ibid., Al31, insert 1, fol. 56r–v.
127. Ibid., insert 2, fol. 34r–v, 21 June (election); fol. 36r–v, 27 July (parties are registered for a dispute with the *officiales*); and fol. 51v, 23 October (settlement of 15 florins in another suit that lacks details, but involves one of the *officiales*).
128. Ibid., T433, n.p., 27 December (election).
129. Ibid., n.p., 22 April (election).
130. Ibid., T435, insert 4: "Fogli mancanti o senza date," n.p. Although this entry lacks the year in which it was written, it involves Sinibaldo di Filippo di Simone da Carmignano, a Florentine citizen who was selected as an official on 22 April 1432 (v above, n. 129). Realizing that Sinibaldo could have been reelected in another year, I have nonetheless chosen 1433 for this 4 February entry that has him renting the runs at Empoli to two millers for five years at an annual rate of 912 Florentine bushels of flour.
131. Ibid., T433, n.p., 4 January. This entry is a separate, badly damaged folio with at least two inches of its left side torn or eaten away. It nevertheless reveals that as many as 12 consorts elected Cipriano di Simone di Guiduccio to one of the offices.
132. Ibid., T435, document 93, 4 September (election).
133. For the incorporation of a *ragionerius* into the administration of the communal mills of the city of Florence during the late fourteenth century, *v* Muendel, "The Internal Functions," p. 508.
134. Sicard, *Aux origines des sociétés anonymes*, pp. 259–62 and 283.
135. ASF, Not., G465, filza 1, fols. 2r, 2r–v, and 19v–20r.
136. Ibid., G465, filza 3, fol. 142v, 14 December (2 parts); fol. 154v, 11 January (1); fol. 155v, 25 January (1); fol. 155r–v, 25 January (1); fol. 155v, 15 February (1); fol. 157v, 8 March (1); fol. 162v, 19 April (1); fols. 162v–63r, 19 April (1); and fol. 163r, 19 April (1).
137. ASF, Cat. 326, fol. 214v. Cf. ibid., Cat. 77, fol. 78r and 178, fol. 490r for a mill in the

popolo of S. Piero a Santerno ²³⁄₂₅ of which is owned by ser Filippo d'Antonio di Simone da Firenzuola, who is registered in the city of Florence, and ²⁄₂₅ by Lando di Cecco, a local inhabitant.

138. Paolo Pirillo, "I beni comuni nelle campagne fiorentine basso medievali: Evidenze documentaire ed ipotesi di ricerca," *Mélanges de l'école français de Rome. Moyen âge, temps moderne* 99 (1987), 622–43.

139. *V* Above, n. 77.

140. ASF, Not., L234, fol. 26r–v. When Matteo di Simone di Dolfo da Palazzuolo purchased the shares in the communal mill of Rapezzo *v* above, n. 136), he established in each contract a clause stipulating that the seller(s) could not build another mill nor grind their grain anywhere else within the district. It would appear that he was capitalizing on the protectionism originally decreed by the commune. Other rural communes were less rigid. When the *sindicus* of the *villa* or *popolo* of Selvole in the Chianti rented its mill to another on 10 January 1329, he specified that the members of the *villa* could go to another establishment if after three days the miller had not ground the grain they had brought to the mill. If they proceeded in any other manner, they were required to reimburse the miller with his fee. *V* ibid., U52, fol. 93v.

141. Robert Boutruche, *La crise d'une société: Seigneurs et paysans du Bordelais pendant la Guerre de Cent Ans* (Paris, 1947, repr. 1963), pp. 115 and 118–22 and Pierre Charbonnier, *Un autre France: La seigneurie rurale en Basse Auvergne du XIVe au XVIe siècle,* I (Clermont-Ferrand, 1980), pp. 258–59.

142. Boutruche, *La crise d'une société,* pp. 122–28. Cf. Fourquin, *Les campagnes de la région parisienne,* p. 190 and Robert Fossier in Jean Chapelot and Robert Fossier, *The Village and House in the Middle Ages,* trans. Henry Cleere (Berkeley, 1985), pp. 149–50. For the earlier manifestations of the growth of privileged peasant communities, *v* Evergates, *Feudal Society in the Bailliage of Troyes,* pp. 136–53. Cf. William Chester Jordan, *From Servitude to Freedom: Manumission in the Sénonais in the Thirteenth Century* (Philadelphia, 1986), pp. 81–99.

143. For the sale of half and whole *ottave* in the late fourteenth and early fifteenth centuries, *v* ASF., Not., Al31, insert 2, fols. 11v–12r, 22 February 1394 and fol. 40v, 30 August 1394 as well as T434, n.p., 2 April 1405, 15 March 1406, and 17 November 1406.

144. ASF. Conventi soppressi, 79 (S. Ambrogio), no. 213, fol. 123v. My thanks to Prof. Richard Goldthwaite of Johns Hopkins University, who indicated the whereabouts of this source in addition to the one I utilized in Table 6.

145. ASF, Conv. soppr., 79 (S. Ambrogio), no. 213, fol. 125r.

146. I have not uncovered information for the specific make-up of the administration at the mill of Ognissanti. For the relationship between the runs of Ognissanti and those controlled by the urban commune further upstream, *v* Muendel, "Medieval Urban Renewal," pp. 363–89.

147. ASF, Cat. 181, fol. 336v (Terranuova, 52 florins for the said installations); 315, fol. 261r (S. Giovanni Valdarno, 200 *lire* for 1 grain mill,; and 315, fol. 716r (Montevarchi, 56 florins for 1 grain mill). The small commune of Montaio, found about 7 kilometers to the west of Montevarchi, had 2 grain mills that produced annually 54 *lire,* and the *popolo* of S. Donato a Menzano, placed approximately 10 kilometers north of S. Giovanni, possessed a "bad-weather" mill with 1 run that returned a respectable 5 florins. *V* ibid., 315, fol. 448r and 326, fol. 665r. Were they simply mimicking their neighbors by converting their returns into cash?

148. Ibid., 181, fols. 442v–43r (Castel S. Niccolò); 180, fol. 686v (Raggiolo, 40 *lire* for 1 grain mill); and 179, fol. 175v (Ortignano, 50 *lire* for 1 grain mill).

149. David Friedman, *Florentine New Towns: Urban Design in the Late Middle Ages* (Cambridge, Mass., 1988), pp. 6–7 and 167–73.

150. Herlihy and Klapisch, *Les Toscans et leurs familles*, pp. 139–40.

151. The commune of Ortignano was actually utilizing earnings from perpetual rents to convert its grain mill into a *fabbrica*. V ASF, Cat. 179, fol. 175v; 68, fol. 227v; and, particularly, 179, fol. 225r. Cf. Muendel, "The Distribution of Mills," p. 105.

152. *Vendeurs*, who sold processed salt at suitable prices at the Puits à Muire, were not established at the Chauderette because it caused too much administrative confusion for the *rentiers*. The latter were thus actively involved in the management of the company. It would seem that those at the Puits à Muire were close enough to the activities of their association to be more than touched by its daily affairs.

153. For the individualistic, yet familial basis of Genoese businesses *a carati*, v Heers, *Family Clans in the Middle Ages*, pp. 219–22. The difficulty of accepting limited liability in Sienese firms is thoroughly discussed by Edward D. English, *Enterprise and Liability in Sienese Banking, 1230–1350* (Cambridge, Mass., 1988), pp. 55–113. Thomas W. Blomquist, "Commercial Association in Thirteenth-Century Lucca," *Business History Review* 45 (1971), 157–78, indicates that the partnership *ad partem lucri* in which the investor had a liability limited to the amount of his investment appeared at Lucca during the thirteenth century. Cf. Armando Sapori, "Le compagnie mercantili toscane del Dugento e dei primi del Trecento: La responsabilità dei compagni verso i terzi," in his *Studi di storia economica (secoli XIII–XIV–XV)* II (Florence, 1955), pp. 765–807 and "Dalla 'compagnia' alla 'holding'," *Studi di storia economica*, III (Florence, 1967), pp. 121–33.

154. Volpe, "Montieri," pp. 370–73.

155. Muendel, "The 'French' Mill," pp. 215–47.

SECULAR CANONESSES AS ANTECEDENT OF THE BEGUINES IN THE LOW COUNTRIES: AN INTRODUCTION TO SOME OLDER VIEWS

Joanna E. Ziegler

Holy Cross College
Worcester, Mass.

Secular Canonesses as Antecedent of the Beguines in the Low Countries: An Introduction to Some Older Views

Few topics of historical research have been quite so affected by recent contributions as the beguines, if one measures impact by sudden interest. Once comprised of but a mere handful of dedicated enthusiasts who read Dutch and were often fiercely passionate about mysticism, beguine scholars now represent a remarkably broad cross-section of the disciplines. Students of varying degrees of scholarly preparation are also studying the beguines today, now that the beguines have become routine business in undergraduate courses and are continually being nourished by the unceasing production of tradebook texts on the subject. Nowhere are these changes clearer than in North America—the newest and nowadays most frequent national contributor to the beguine scholarship industry.

The situation was quite different in 1954 when Ernest McDonnell published his seminal findings on the beguines in a book entitled, *The Beguines and Beghards in Medieval Culture, with Special Emphasis on the Belgian Scene.*[1] In those days, for an American to study late medieval urban religious history (the social context of the beguines), let alone to focus on women's part in that history, was unconventional, to say the least. In the mid-1950s McDonnell's focus was decidedly not on political or religious institutional history—the type of research most common among American academicians practicing medieval history at that time. It is remarkable, then, to consider that by 1980, just one generation after McDonnell, the situation has changed entirely. The beguines are now warmly received into the mainstream of American historical research.

With interest came disciplinary diversity, which arguably has had the greater impact. Gender studies, anthropology, literary criticism, and feminism employ different methods than traditional historical inquiry did, for they are seeking different ends. The beguine bibliography has therefore, and rather suddenly, undergone radical diversification. The contribution of recent writing to beguine historiography therefore constitutes an intriguing situation, for the beguines are not a "new" topic of historical inquiry; they are "new" only to North American academics, and especially to the feminist branch of its practitioners.

Questions about beguine models and influence are an interesting case in point. Of all the issues that beguine writings touch on— mysticism, devotional art, clerical supervision, local institutional definition, comparative history of institutions, among others—none has proven still quite so vexing, or simply unanswerable, as that of the beguines' antecedents. Which, if any, religious organization (or organizations) provided the model for these communities of lay holy women? And where, geographically, was it located? Contrary to perceptions of American scholarship today, recent interest in the beguines has not suddenly spawned this question anew. Since the middle decades of the nineteenth century, German and Belgian scholars frequently speculated about the possible prototypes for the beguines, a point to be returned to shortly.[2] The pages that follow explore this particular aspect of beguine history by retrieving for reconsideration the theories that propose the institution of the secular canonesses as primary antecedent of the beguines. "Modern" analytical history of the narrowest focus has robbed us of the truly forceful parallels and comparisons which the older schools of thought explored. This essay is not intended, however, to prove the older theories. Its purpose rather is to emphasize the value of earlier discussions of the origins of the beguines and to underscore the central importance of local sources written in Dutch.

For several reasons, the theory proposing the secular canonesses as antecedent appears to have been eclipsed by mid-twentieth century North American historical scholarship as well as by current feminist writing. First, McDonnell, who has been singularly influential on recent writings, did not endorse it. He was more interested in accounting for the social forces behind the emergence of the beguines at the end of the twelfth century than he was concerned with identifying their institutional prototypes. Other scholars interested in that approach increasingly identified those forces, as McDonnell had, with the *vita apostolica*—a partly societal, partly spiritual phenomenon that accompanied twelfth-century monastic reforms.[3] Generally, this view held that those reforms, in combination with social upheaval in urban areas, had spread to the laity who, in turn, began to seek alternate ways of imitating Christ and the apostles than by joining monasteries and becoming clergy in perpetuity. The beguine movement thus came to be seen as a significant manifestation of the *vita apostolica*.

McDonnell's shadow was not alone, however, in casting the secular canoness theory into darkness. Since the last decade or so, the discipline of history has undergone changes that have seriously affected the ways people study the beguines, and especially the kinds of sources they use. Secondary writings, McDonnell's being preeminent among them, have tended to be tapped more frequently for information about the beguines than archival sources. This holds especially true for the feminist constituent of beguine authors.[4] With the exclusion of archival research a complementary practice has arisen—an increasing reliance on Anglo-Germanic, secondary writings. This practice means that the literature written in Dutch, and highly informed by archival research, is now almost totally absent from most American bibliographies of the beguines. The point is worth considering further.[5]

While the absence in recent bibliographies of references in Dutch is understandable (for so few Americans know how to read the language), it is puzzling nonetheless. Beguines in the southern Low Countries (present Belgium) were the earliest flower of the movement, and became its hardiest stem. The women whom every scholar associates with the "heroic" age of beguine history—Marie d'Oignies, Hadewych of Brabant, Christina Mirabilis, and Beatrijs of Nazareth—were born and lived in communities in the southern Low Countries. The movement was most widespread in that area; it outlived all examples from elsewhere, by a truly exceptional amount of time. It is only in our own century that the beguine movement is drawing to a close in Belgium, where it has been a viable choice of life for women for more than seven centuries. The local literature, as might well be expected from this remarkably continuous history, constitutes the largest, and arguably most important, contribution to that history. Those studies at least since the Second World War have been largely written in Dutch—a language that, no less than Latin, McDonnell obviously considered a responsibility to read fluently.

The present study is grounded in both the local archival sources and the secondary literature written in Dutch. Both illuminate a very different set of historical conditions than Anglo–Germanic, secondary writings or their recent derivatives do. Knowing these texts and documents has placed me in an appropriate position to contribute something different to recent discussions of the beguines and to suggest other ways to approach their history. In my 1987 article, "The *Curtis* Beguinages in the Southern Low Countries: Interpretation and Historiography," I focused, for example, on the way that older, especially Belgian, scholarship distinguished Low Country from Rhenish beguines in their social status, in the longevity of the Low Country movement, and in the scale and types of their housing settlements, among other things.[6] That essay also explored some of the reasons why the distinction has been neglected by more recent authors, who in resting their interpretation on Anglo–Germanic scholarship have either blurred the fundamental differences among Continental beguines or missed them altogether.

The present essay explores this ongoing problem in beguine historiography by taking up a specific issue, this time from the theoretical perspective of the beguines' antecedents. It looks at this issue, in the first place, to introduce venerable writing into the fresh ground of our present efforts: the older sources may be familiar to Dutch and Belgian scholars but they are known not at all by us. Dormant for nearly half a century now, these sources need to be looked at again for, whether provable or not, they offer a theory that may help solve the problem of antecedents. This has been a particularly challenging piece of the beguine puzzle to locate with certainty. Returning to the older sources sheds light on one especially key part of the puzzle that has long fascinated, and often confounded, scholars—Jacques de Vitry's ardent promotion of women founders of the beguine movement. Although recognized as central, Jacques de Vitry and his motives still constitute something of a major scholarly conundrum. As will be suggested shortly however, we may view Jacques' endorsement as his response to the secular canonesses, whose exclusive recruitment practices prohibited non-noble women (like the women who became beguines) from entering their community. Jacques's reaction to the canonesses, when combined with the older hypotheses about them as antecedents, indicates new reasons to reconsider the relations between these two distinctive groups of women.

Although it will receive more precise attention below, a general definition of what secular canonesses and beguines were may be helpful at the outset. Generally speaking, both institutions should be viewed against women's monastic life. Women living in monasteries, or nuns, were members of regular orders and were obliged to live according to contrary sets of regulations. From early Christian times there were widows and virgins who chose the celibate life, observed certain standards of conduct and lived in the paternal home doing acts of charity and piety. It was not until the eighth century, however, that the term, *canonicae,* canonesses, appears in the Latin West to designate some of them, and their institution only became organized by the Council of Aachen in 816, which provided them with a rule. The institution was largely confined to the Germanic lands, for canonesses elsewhere after the twelfth century belonged to various regular orders, such as the Augustinians, Gilbertines in England, Norbertines, and Premonstratensians.[7] In the Germanic lands, however, canonesses gradually abandoned the rule and secularized, meaning that they did not submit themselves to regular discipline and reform, but rather developed their own peculiar observances, customs, and privileges. The women members remained aristocratic, owned private property, and were at liberty to leave the community at any point.

The beguines are no less difficult to define in terms of institutional religious status than canonesses. And their origins are equally difficult to establish chronologically. One thing is certain. Beguines did not emerge until approximately the end of the twelfth century or beginning of the thirteenth. At that time, they formed into *ad hoc* groups or else lived alone under the parental roof doing works of piety and charity. This remained the case in the Rhineland until such groups were persecuted in the fourteenth century, dying out in that region altogether shortly thereafter. In the southern Low Countries, beguines exhibited a more organized life, almost from the start.[8] Large housing settlements were founded in the thirteenth century to group together the women in the towns. These settlements, enclosed by walls and moats, and containing all necessary residential and institutional buildings are known as *curtis* beguinages.[9] Widows and virgins became beguines and could live in the community without taking vows of poverty. Their life as beguines was revokable. Also like the canonesses, beguines did not have a single rule and therefore did not submit themselves to the regular observances of the orders. Although the majority of the women came from lower social stations than the aristocratic canonesses, beguines, too, were permitted to own private property and to maintain a high degree of contact with the secular world. Neither institution held the status of an order at any point in its history.

Until the mid-twentieth century, scholars frequently drew comparisons between the secular canonesses and the beguines. The following examples will serve to demonstrate the point. In 1624, Franciscus Zypaeus, canon at Antwerp Cathedral, published his *Iuris pontificii enarratio* in which he compared the secular canonesses and the beguines[10]; in 1700, the canon lawyer and professor at the University of Leuven, Zegerus-Bernardus Van Espen equated the religious status of the two institutions[11]; in 1837, associations were again pointed out in the Belgian Catholic periodical published in Liège, the *Journal historique et littéraire*[12]; but it was Karl Heinrich Schäfer in his monumental study of 1907, *Die Kanonissenstifter im deutschen Mittelalter*, who developed the comparison most comprehensively.[13] All these scholars agree that the secular canonesses and the beguines were similar in their institutional definition; and the governing term on which they based this comparison is *quasi-regular*.

When drawing their comparison, the authors cited above do not say that the secular canonesses and the beguines are *extra-regular*, as has become the common term in contemporary discourse. Rather they say that they are *quasi*, half or semi-regular. This is important. When used by institutional church historians, the prefix *quasi* should be interpreted to mean that both groups maintained fundamental features of regular observance while at the same time exercising exceptions to the regular life: specifically, women were permitted to enter the profession of secular canoness or beguine without having to profess perpetual vows and they were given the right to maintain and dispose of their own property. They also reserved the liberty to return to society if they chose to do so. Early historians have also found striking the fact that, in addition to their comparable *quasi-regular* status, both groups emerged within the same geographical area. Both institutions originated and were confined to the Germanic lands, the area known in the mid-thirteenth century as *Allemania* or *Teutonia*, the lower Rhine and present Belgium. In light of these institutional and geographical comparisons, certain scholars went so far as to suggest that some degree of formal interaction had occurred between the two groups.[14]

By the mid-twentieth century, however, the conditions of discussion had changed. A comparison between the secular canonesses and the beguines was no longer considered tenable or informative, let alone intriguing. In 1958 the *Lexikon für Theologie und Kirche* claimed that "uncanonical" consecrated virgins (women living alone or in groups such as the beguines) do not fall under the concept of canoness.[15] There is no further explanation offered: beguines are uncanonical, therefore they are not canonesses. Ernest McDonnell discarded the notion equally forcefully, but he was more direct about his reasons for doing so. Although he did not identify them by name in the text, McDonnell squarely addressed Zypaeus's and Van Espen's arguments nonetheless:

> To maintain with *older commentators* that the canonesses and beguines were identical ... would overlook the fact that the communities claiming Gertrude and Begga as founders remained essentially aristocratic, whereas the beguines came principally from the middle and lower classes. The first belonged to the feudal era, the second to an urban civilization.[16]

McDonnell's position deserves to be set within the larger context of developing scholarship, especially as his position marks what will become a characteristic shift in the perspective of church historical scholars, generally, and beguine scholars, specifically. Putting the matter more simply, after World War II the approach to history writing changed radically. Scholars looked askance at vast, broad, and sweeping comparisons such as Schäfer made between Greek temple virgins, Merovingian canonesses, and Low Country beguines.[17] Historical analysis rather emphasized much more of an "everything in its own time and place" approach to the past than Schäfer and his generation had taken. Scholars considered as problematic, even irresponsible (judging from which writing they excluded from their bibliographies), generalizations of the sort that enabled scholars to view secular canonesses and beguines as an ensemble.

The mid-twentieth-century approach preferred to view the canonesses not as a fixed historical monolith but as an evolving institution whose specific institutional profile was modified by specific time and place.[18] For beguine historiography this more cautious contextual and chronological approach is also at work in the documentary analyses, especially as such analyses pertain to establishing institutional and social definitions.

What has proven most important to discussions of beguine antecedents, and particularly to the practice of excluding the secular canonesses therefrom, are interpretations of the canonesses based in analyses of the early documents. Those analyses established for the canonesses, in strident contrast to the beguines, the existence of a legal institutional status. The Council of Aachen held in 816[19] provided a definitive title for secular canonesses, *canonicae*, and a rule, the *Institutio Sanctimonialium*.[20] The existence of the rule for canonesses proved central to the historiography of beguine antecedents for this reason: the beguines never received a title or a rule. Scholars viewed this as a key fact. If one group possessed a rule and the other did not, their institutional character was interpreted as incompatible. Comparisons between beguines and secular canonesses were therewith terminated. This position is developed thereafter according to fixed chronological and denotative classifications for the secular canonesses and the beguines. Interpretation proceeds from an analysis of the institutions of the Church as defined by official councils and passed down by written law rather than by examining actual practice as evidenced in the archives. Similarly, McDonnell established distinction between the two institutions according to social classifications of wealth, property, and social rank. And, he employed rather strict chronological divisions—the canonesses come from feudal times, whereas the beguines come from the later medieval period.

It is not difficult to see why the more systematic and scientifically cautious historical analytic, enacted in precisely controllable frameworks of time and place, found distasteful Schäfer's impressionistic and grand historical eye, looking across the centuries and often caring little about the landscape in which it paused for information. The new history had no place for a–historical (i.e., chronologically dislocated) comparisons. No wonder, then, that the younger generation of history writers considered negligible the intellectual profit to be gained by comparing the secular canonesses (who originated in the ninth century) with the Low Country beguines (who originated in the late twelfth). This accounts partly, therefore, for why the interest in making these comparisons passed from acceptable scholarly discourse into a kind of near oblivion. To call for its reintroduction, as is being done here, requires that the mid-century objections be answered, at least in part.

The first point to be introduced concerns the Church institutional problem—the existence of a rule for secular canonesses. It is wise to proceed cautiously when interpreting the rule. After the Carolingian period the canonesses abandoned the prescriptions mandated by the rule (the *Institutio*) of 816—the vow of perpetual chastity and perpetual profession. The medieval historian Georges Despy, McDonnell's highly regarded Belgian contemporary, demonstrates in a series of articles which focus on the southern Low Countries that although the twelfth century addressed their abuses, the canonesses had already rejected the vow of poverty and commitment to stability for quite some time before that.[21] For example, in 1139 the Second Lateran Council condemned the canonesses for living in their own houses and directed them to have a common refectory and dormitory.[22] And the synod at Reims in 1148 again mandated them, to no avail, to abandon their privately derived income or *prebends*[23] and take up regular observance.[24] Historians have termed these conditions regarding private property, living quarters and life style—which are wholly opposed to regular or monastic life—as "secularization." Despy proposes an early date for this conversion.[25]

Yet even without turning to secondary interpretation, close reading of the *Institutio*, the rule for canonesses promulgated in 816, suggests that by the ninth century regulations regarding property (poverty) and stability (chastity) had already been left somewhat equivocal. This is what the *Institutio* of 816 has to say regarding property:

> Canon 9: *How Those Who Enter Monasteries Shall Deal with Their Property:*
> "... If she does not want to give her goods to the church—the abbess and the other nuns each retaining theirs—she shall entrust them by an official act to a relative or to a reliable friend, who will defend the goods in matters of secular law. So in this system the nuns shall decide and dispose of their own goods...."[26]

Additionally, although the *Institutio* implies that women should remain inside the "monastery" until their death, there are numerous references indicating that the rule permitted them to come and go with some frequency into the secular world.[27] Contact with the world outside increased in the eleventh century to the point that canonesses could leave the chapter permanently by choice. In other words, the confusion perceived in the eleventh century about the canonesses' abuses had been incipiently present *from the start* at Aachen in 816—particularly those abuses that concerned the right to have private property and the appropriateness of maintaining a quasi–secular life. Thus the argument that cites the existence of the canonical rule for canonesses and uses it to isolate them from the beguines—who also owned property, maintained secular activities, and could return to society at any point—is faulty, when the historical facts are seen in addition to the abstract prescriptions of Church law.

The secular canonesses have also been rejected as models because their social position and economic status was higher than beguines. This point needs to be reexamined, too. McDonnell argues that the communities of canonesses were essentially made up of aristocrats, whereas the beguines were not.[28] This is true. McDonnell was correct in claiming that the secular canonesses remained aristocratic while the beguines came principally, if not exclusively, from the lower and middle social stations. McDonnell's facts are not incorrect; it is how he interprets them that needs to be reconsidered here.

McDonnell concludes from the evidence of different social status that the two groups acted exclusively of one another. Despy proposes, however, rather that interaction had occurred between them. From his analysis of a group of mid-thirteenth-century papal documents issued by Innocent IV in 1245 and by Honorius IV in 1285 and from a group of related texts, Despy contends that the chapters of the secular canonesses in the Low Countries were redefending their right to exclude all but nobles by birth. They did so by securing papal approval and confirmation of their statutes, where restricted recruitment was plainly stated.[29] Despy makes the point that these chapters did not *become* noble in the thirteenth century but *were defending their right to remain noble.*[30] Pope Honorius IV tried to prevent such practices of exclusiveness, albeit unsuccessfully.[31] Despy suggests—and this is the crucial point—that the canonesses were responding to the demands for entry generated by women from the new nobility, women whose nobility was not inherited but resulted instead from the acquisition of *(franc-) fiefs.*[32]

McDonnell's interpretation that divergent economic status difference necessarily signals exclusiveness or rigid isolation of one social group from the other may now, in light of Despy's findings, be modified. What rather seems to have been the case, following Despy, was that precisely because of their separate and mutually exclusive social status, the two social groups of women comprising canonesses and beguines came into conflict with one another. But, this historical condition is perhaps better interpreted as interdependence rather than exclusiveness. This interpretation can therefore help to elucidate the specific social conditions that were operative in the crucial early phases of the emergence of the Low Country beguines.

Jacques de Vitry, zealous champion of the beguines in the Low Countries, complained—indeed he deplored—in his *History of the West* that in Hainaut, Brabant, and certain German provinces religious communities only accepted daughters of knights and nobles and that they preferred worldly nobility to the nobility of religion and conduct.[33] Jacques's understanding of the situation corresponds closely to Despy's. Reading the *History of the West* side by side with Jacques's other work of major importance to beguine history, the *Life of Marie d'Oignies,* one learns that Jacques was already fully aware of the consequences of the canonesses' recruitment policy on the beguine movement which was burgeoning in the Germanic provinces at the same time as that policy was rigidifying.[34] That policy is the same one discussed by Despy: giving entry to noblewomen only.

In his biography of Marie d'Oignies, Jacques was at pains to stress two characteristics in particular: Marie's *noble* lineage and her *complete rejection* of worldly goods and pleasures. Importantly, Marie was active in Nivelles (in present Belgium), which contained one of the oldest and most aristocratic chapters of secular canonesses in the West.[35] In light of Despy's findings it becomes possible to reinterpret Jacques's discontent with recruitment practices for women's religious communities in Hainaut, Brabant, and certain German provinces. It appears that Jacques was aiming his remarks at the exclusive policies of chapters of secular canonesses, which should very well have accepted women who wanted an active, charitable religious vocation but wanted to do so without having to become nuns or who were unable to do so for social or economic reasons.

The demographic conditions behind women wanting a non-monastic religious vocation, such as those seeking entry to chapters and beguinages, are still somewhat obscure. Walter Simons recently reinterpreted the problem by demonstrating that the demand for entry may have stemmed not only from a surplus of women in urbanized regions in the Low Countries, as scholars in the past have thought, but that the demand also arose from an influx of women from the countryside.[36] Other scholars have suggested that women in the southern Low Countries were denied the monastic habit because of insufficient dowries or because they could not tolerate the strictness of regular observance.[37] Such claims, whatever the specific social motivations and conditions, suggest that the women seeking entry to monasteries came mostly from the middle and lower rungs of society. The *only other available option*—joining a chapter of secular canonesses—was denied them as Jacques bitterly complained about an entrance policy specifically excluding non-noble women.

Authorities in the southern Low Countries did ultimately develop an alternative—and non-regular (ie., non-monastic)—institution to service and house women of non-noble birth and non–hereditary noble status. That alternative was the great *curtis* beguinage.[38] During the fourteenth century *curtis* beguinages flourished in the urban centers of the southern Low Countries, where as many as seventy arose. *Curtis* beguinages have been continuously in use in Belgium to the present day. From the formative phase in the thirteenth century, the routines of beguine communities dictated the need for specific building types: chapel, hospital, detached houses for wealthy beguines, and convents for poorer beguines. These communal service buildings and private living quarters were most often grouped around a court-yard (Dutch. *hof*). Some beguinages (Dutch. *begijnhoven*) became inde-pendent parishes with their own pastor and cemetery; many were wealthy enough to own grazing fields and mills. Beguinages could be quite large, housing as few as thirty and as many as eight hundred to one thousand women.[39] The entire architectural complex was enclosed by a wall or a moat. This architectural complex—a comprehensive reli-gious and residential settlement—is a *curtis* beguinage, unique to the towns of the southern Low Countries, where it was devised.

This extraordinary architectural and institutional solution was patterned closely on the long accepted model of chapters for secular canonesses. In Nivelles, to introduce a particularly salient demonstra-tion, the chapter's abbess was considered guardian and protectress of the beguinage and its hospital, at the moment of the latter's founding in the thirteenth century.[40] Like the canonesses, the beguines adopted characteristics of both monastic and non-monastic life. As an example of the former, both secular canonesses and beguines vested in one woman discipline in matters of the flesh and spirit. Although both groups lacked centralization typical of monastic houses, they nonethe-less abided by local statutes, read routinely and collectively at chapter meetings. The divine offices were sung in common and members were strongly encouraged to participate. Provisions were operative for public penance and demonstrations of contrition. Enclosure was a vital con-cern; individual communities were secured by walls and moats, there to ensure strict supervision and to regulate contact with the world outside. Charity, next to obedience, was the highest virtue. Both the secular canonesses and the beguines gave personnel, time, and funding to their hospitals as well as to the moral instruction of young girls.

Canonesses and beguines departed from the cloistered monastic life in significant and similar ways: individual members of both groups maintained the right to possess personal property (the canonesses, the right to dispose of hereditary goods and the beguines, the right to support themselves by income from manual labor or trade), the right to live in their own houses and maintain servants, and the right to re-enter society, to marry, or to rejoin family. Both groups offered a collective, enclosed life as an architectural setting, and enforced routine of work and prayer and as a collective, supportive atmosphere. At the same time both institutions allowed their walls to be a more open and therefore a more permeable boundary, physically as well as statutorily, than was the case for cloisters of the regular female orders. In these ways both groups maintained a balance between monastic and secular prerogatives, prerogatives that in the thirteenth century were normally seen to be antithetical forms of female religious life.

From the comparisons raised here, it would appear that the early commentators had detected special characteristics in the Low Country beguines. Although their field of vision may today seem too broad chronologically, it was precisely that field that induced them to see that in the medieval period there were no institutions for women comparable to the secular canonesses and beguines—certainly not nuns or third orders and certainly not those individualistic women, also called beguines, who lived alone or in small groups, especially in the Rhineland, and who were suppressed by the Council of Vienne in 1311–12, the very point at which the secular canonesses and the *curtis* beguines opened a new and successful phase of their history.[41]

By exploring the theories of the early commentators some suggestive issues come to the fore. Church and society found it convenient, perhaps even necessary, to let women in the southern Low Countries live together in comprehensively organized social and religious communities outside regular observance. Although in other parts of the western medieval world women were strenuously prohibited from doing so, authorities in the Germanic lands permitted women to group in tightly supervised, enclosed settings and at the same time allowed them to keep personal property and to revoke their membership. This is puzzling since such permissiveness flew in the face of official definitions of acceptable religious communal life. Property, whether it is defined as immovable (land, inheritance) or liquid income, was apparently a key factor. Secular canonesses and beguines maintained the right to keep their property. This was one of the fundamental characteristics of their religious institutional status—their *quasi-regular* status, which they shared. Further research may reveal that, when viewed as an ensemble, the secular canonesses and beguines reflect property policies that are strictly relative to inheritance laws for women and the legal status of women in the Germanic lands.[42] David Nicholas recently contended, for instance, that "'Flemish' Flanders, an area of strong Frankish settlement, had allowed widows full disposition over the dowries given by their husbands. French customs tended to restrict this practice from the twelfth century.... but Flemish community property law continued to give widows exceptionally extensive rights over their husbands' estates."[43] Wives were not liable, Nicholas adds, for their husband's debts incurred without their participation.[44] Exploring our two groups of women may, as well, be pointing to other evidence of a gender-specific economy and particular legal customs in that part of the western European world.

Both institutions, secular canonesses and beguines, permitted vows to be temporary. This, too, likely points to purely local, social conditions.[45] There seems to have been a need in the Germanic lands—why else would it have been permitted—for women to cross into and out of the enclosed boundaries freely. Both groups maintained a high degree of contact with the secular world by nursing, visiting family, and similar activities. It is quite possible, therefore, that local authorities there faced special conditions besetting their women inhabitants.[46] A model of semi-enclosure was developed early in the Germanic lands for the secular canonesses and was reinstituted later for the beguines. Semi-enclosure contained the architectural feature of monastic enclosure in its walls and moats, as well as in the communal activities that were required to take place inside them. At the same time, enclosure was not total as it was in monastic settings, for women in the groups discussed here could leave the enclosure and enter the secular world much more routinely than nuns could. Thus this particular model of semi-enclosure, or semi-claustration, appears to have exercised a great deal of influence on the institutional forms that women's religious communities adopted in the Low Countries—a model that was maintained well into the modern period. Lastly, the prevailing attitude toward property and temporary vows suggests that officials permitted both the secular canonesses and the beguines an uncommonly high degree of personal autonomy. It is true that the secular canonesses and the beguines were not the first or only examples in the history of Christianity where consecrated virgins lived together in "the midst of the world."[47] But in the medieval West, they constitute the singular examples of women's communities devised to resist the Church's concerted efforts to place them into monastic habits and keep them there.

By reviving the observations of the early commentators, who were the first to note a reciprocal relationship between the secular canonesses and beguines, it becomes clear that the two groups potentially cast considerable light upon each other and, with further research, may point out the essential bases of semi-religiosity that scholars still hope to discover in the data. Those bases appear strongly rooted in economic and social conditions particular to the Germanic territories. The preceding discussion suggests, however, that our understanding of the territorial context needs to be accompanied by greater flexibility in our approach to the chronology. By framing an analysis of the two women's groups according to strict periodization or legislated definitions, scholars have compromised the benefits of doing geographically-limited, contextual history. This essay suggests that the conditions that gave rise to the beguines in the thirteenth century may have been present in the region long before then, at least since the eleventh century, when the secularization of the institution of the secular canoness had clearly taken place.

Notes

I wish to thank Lorraine Attreed, Diane Bell, and Walter Simons for reading this essay at various points in its development. An anonymous reader provided perceptive comments which helped to shape the argument greatly. To Kermit Champa and Judith Tolnick I owe, as always, gratitude for their editorial assistance and support.

1. Ernest W. McDonnell, *The Beguines and Beghards in Medieval Culture, with Special Emphasis on the Belgian Scene* (New Brunswick, 1954).

2. For an introduction to German and Belgian scholarship seeking prototypes for the beguines, *v* J. E. Ziegler, "The *Curtis* Beguinages in the Southern Low Countries: Interpretation and Historiography," *Bulletin van het Belgisch Historisch Instituut te Rome/Bulletin de l'Institut Historique Belge de Rome* 57 (1987), 31–70, esp. 37–50.

3. Ernest W. McDonnell, "The *Vita Apostolica*: Diversity or Dissent," *Church History* 24 (1955), 15-31; M.-D. Chenu, *Nature, Man and Society in the Twelfth Century* (Chicago, 1968), pp. 202–69; André Vauchez, "La pauvreté volontaire au Moyen Âge," *Annales E.S.C.* 25 (1970), 1566–73; Lester K. Little, *Religious Poverty and the Profit Economy in Medieval Europe* (Ithaca, 1978), pp. 71–169; and Ludo Milis, "Kerkelijk en gods-dienstig leven circa 1070-1384," *Algemene Geschiedenis der Nederlanden* (Haarlem, 1982), III, pp. 165–211.

4. For an exception to the pattern of dependence on secondary sources and on Anglo-Germanic bibliography, *v* Walter Simons, "The Beguine Movement in the Southern Low Countries: A Reassessment," *Bulletin van het Belgisch Historisch Instituut te Rome/Bulletin de l'Institut Historique Belge de Rome* 59 (1989), 63–105.

5. For a review of the rise to prominence of the Anglo-Germanic bibliography within beguine historiography, *v* my "*Curtis* Beguinages." Dependence on Anglo-Germanic scholarship has been especially characteristic of North American feminist scholarship, most recently, e.g., in Carol Neel, "The Origins of the Beguines," *Signs* 14/2 (1989), 321–41, where the author argues that beguine antecedents can be found in the Premonstratensian *conversae*. Neel overlooked Alcantara Mens' indispensable study, *Oorsprong en betekenis van de Nederlandse begijnen- en begardenbeweging.*

Vergelijkende studie: XIIde–XIIIde eeuw (Antwerp, 1947), which explores her thesis, in Dutch, quite extensively.

6. Ziegler, *"Curtis* Beguinages" (*v* n.2).

7. Mary Pia Heinrich, C.D.P., "Historical Survey of the Institution of Canonesses," *Crosier Heritage* 10 (January 1987), 1–14.

8. Simons, (*v* n.4), esp. pp. 84–87.

9. Ziegler, pp. 64–70; Simons pp. 67–68, 84–99.

10. Franciscus Zypaeus, *Iuris pontificii novi analytica enarratio* (Cologne, 1624), esp. pp. 302–306.

11. Zegerus-Bernardus Van Espen, *Jus ecclesiasticum universum* (Cologne, 1777), esp. pp. 349–60, entitled "De quasi-regularibus."

12. "Chapitres des chanoinesses," *Journal historique et littéraire* 37 (1837), pp. 11–18, 57–63, 111–15.

13. K. Heinrich Schäfer, *Die Kanonissenstifter im deutschen Mittelalter,* Kirchenrechtliche Abhandlungen, *XLIII–XLIV* (Stuttgart, 1907), esp. pp. 255 and 255, n. 3.

14. *V* notes 10–13 above; Schäfer (*v* n.13), p. 11; P. Torquebiau, "Chanoinesses," *Dictionnaire de droit canonique* (Paris, 1942), III, cols. 488–530; and P. Schmitz, "Bénédictines," *Dictionnaire d'histoire et de géographie ecclésiastiques* (Paris, 1934), VII, cols. 1211–12.

15. M. Schmid, "Kanonissen," *Lexikon für Theologie und Kirche,* ed. M. Buchberger (Freiburg im Breisgau, 1960), *v* cols. 1288–89.

16. McDonnell, *Beguines and Beghards,* 63 (italics mine).

17. Schäfer (*v* n. 13).

18. For bibliography on the secular canonesses in addition to that cited in the notes above, *v* J. Sencie, "L'Origine et le dévoloppement des chapitres nobles en Belgique," *Annuaire de l'Université de Louvain* 55 (1891), 186–95; P. Wenzel, *Drei Frauenstifter der Diözese Lüttich nach ihre ständischen Zusammensetzung bis zum XV. Jahrhundert,* Inaugural dissertation (Bonn, 1909); H. Leclercq, "Chanoinesses," *Dictionnaire d'archéologie chrétienne et de liturgie* (Paris, 1914), III, pt. 1, pp. 248–56; E. de Moreau, S. J., *Histoire de l'Eglise en Belgique* (Brussels, 1945(1), I, pp. 176–81; N. Backmund, "Canonesses," *New Catholic Encyclopedia* (New York, 1967), III, pp. 53–54; M. Parisse, "Les chanoinesses dans l'Empire Germanique (IXe-XIe siècles), *Francia* 6 (1978), 107–26. For an excellent introduction, *v* Suzanne Fonay Wemple, *Women in Frankish Society: Marriage and the Cloister 500 to 900* (Philadelphia, 1981), pp. 168–74; and Heinrich, "Historical Survey," pp. 1–14.

19. The most comprehensive and precisely documented treatment of the Aachen Council of 816 is by J. F. A. M. van Waesberghe, *De Akense regels voor canonici en canon-icae uit 816* (Assen, 1967), esp. pp. 306–76 for the *Institutio Sanctimonialium* (notes, 492–521). There is a chapter-by-chapter summary in English, pp. 378–82. The rule I have consulted is published in Latin as *Institutio Sanctimonialium Aquisgranensis,* ed. A. Werminghoff, *Monumenta Germaniae Historica,* Legum Sectio III, *Concilia II* (Hanover and Leipzig, 1908), pp. 421–56. Referred to hereafter as *Concilia II.* The *Institutio* is also published in J. D. Mansi, *Sacrorum Conciliorum Nova et Amplissima Collectio* (Venice, 1776), XIV, cols. 294ff. and J.-P. Migne, *Patrologia Latina* (Paris, 1851), CV, cols. 835–976.

20. *Concilia II,* pp. 421–56.

21. Georges Despy, "Note sur deux actes pontificaux inédits du XIIIme siècle, concer-nant le statut des chanoinesses séculières," *Handelingen van de Koninklijke Commissie*

voor Geschiedenis 115 (1950), 427–41; idem, "Note sur le sens de capitulum," *Bulletin du Cange (Archivum Latinitatis Medii Aevi)* 20 (1950), 245–54; and idem, "Les chapîtres de chanoinesses nobles en Belgique au Moyen Âge," *XXXVIe Congrès de la Fédération Archéologique et Historique de Belgique* (Ghent, 1955), pp. 169–79.

22. For canon 25 of the Council of Lateran (1139), *v Corpus juris canonici,* ed. A. Richter and A. Friedberg (Leipzig, 1879), I, col. 836: "Perniciosam et detestabilem quarumdam consuetudinem mulierum (que licet neque secundum regulam B. Benedicti, neque Basilii, aut Augustini uiuant, sanctimoniales tamen uulgo censeri desiderant) aboleri decreuimus. Cum enim, iuxta regulam degentes in cenobiis, tam in ecclesia quam in refectorio atque dormitorio communiter esse debeant... simili modo prohibemus, ne sanctimoniales simul cum canonicis et monachis in ecclesia in uno choro conueniant ad psallendum." (The latter prohibition is especially interesting from the history of west choir architecture.)

23. The terminology alone is not enough to pinpoint the schedule of the evolution towards the abandonment of the vow of property. For instance, Georges Despy has especially cautioned scholars on the use of *prebend,* that it will eventually come to mean the portion of goods assigned to the individual, although it did not mean that at first. He also says that the appearance of prebends, or any other regime of personal property, shows the abandonment of the vow of poverty. Moreover, this secularization—abandonment of the vow of chastity and poverty—is infrequently accompanied by the term *capitulum,* as opposed to *conventus, coenobium, sanctimoniales, sorores,* or *virgines.* Despy argues that the term *capitulum* and its opposing terms are still employed after secularization; they appear *post factum* and therefore Despy disagrees with the procedure of using them to date the appearance of secularization ("Note sur le sens de capitulum," pp. 245, 246, n. 2).

24. Importantly, had the canonesses taken up the prescriptions of Lateran II and Reims 1148, they would by definition have become nuns. For canon 4 of the Council of *Reims* (1148), *v* Mansi, *Sacrorum conciliorum* (Venice, 1776), XXI, cols. 714–15: "... ut sanctimoniales & mulieres, quae canonicae nominantur, & irregulariter vivunt, iuxta beatorum Benedicti & Augustini rationem, vitam suam in melius corrigant & emendent ... & relictis praebendis, & aliis propriis, earum necessitatibus de communi provideant ... Prohibemus etiam, ne in earumdem collegiis aliqua quae irregulariter victura fuerit, recipiatur."

25. Despy, "Note sur le sens de capitulum," pp. 245, 246, n. 2.

26. *Concilia II,* 444–45.

27. *Concilia II,* 450. For a different interpretation of the canonesses' contact with the outside world and the chronology, *v* Wemple, *Women in Frankish Society,* p. 172.

28. McDonnell, p. 63.

29. Ibid.

30. Despy, "Les chapitres de chanoinesses nobles," p. 176.

31. Ibid., pp. 245–54; documentation, pp. 439–41.

32. The role of the new nobility deserves elaboration, especially its relation to the religious orders. This topic is unfortunately beyond the scope of this study. For discussion of the possibilities of access to nobility in the Low Countries, *v* J. M. van Winter, "Adel, ministerialiteit en ridderschap 11de–14de eeuw," *Algemene Geschiedenis der Nederlanden,* II (Haarlem, 1982); and P. De Win, "Queeste naar de rechtspositie van de edelman in de Bourgondische Nederlanden," *Tijdschrift voor Rechtsgeschiedenis/The Legal History Review* 53 (1985), 223–74.

33. Jacobus de Vitriaco, *Historia Occidentalis*, ed. Johan Frederick Hinnebusch (Freiburg im Breisgau, 1972), esp. pp. 156–58 ("De irregularite secularum canonicarum").

34. There is an English translation of Marie d'Oignies' life in, Jacques de Vitry, *The Life of Marie d'Oignies*, trans. Margot H. King (Saskatchewan: Peregrina Publishing Co., 1986). For the Latin text, *v De Maria Oigniacensi in Namurcensi Belgii Dioecesi*, ed. D. Papebroec, in *Acta Sanctorum* Junii 5 (Paris, 1867), (June 23), pp. 542–72.

35. Hinnebusch noted that de Vitry might have been referring to the Nivelles chapter in his discussion of the canonesses.

36. Simons, "The Beguine Movement" (*v* n. 4).

37. In addition to Simons, for a discussion of the demographic factors, *v* L. J. R. Milis, "Het begijnenwezen, uiting van een middeleeuwse maatschappij in de kering," *Toespraken gehouden bij de Begijnhoffeesten* (Breda, 1980), and idem, "Kerkelijk en gods-dienstig leven circa 1070–1384." Additionally, in 1246 Bishop Robert of Thoroute addressed precisely the matter of social standing in the prologue to his *Body of General Statutes for the Beguines in the Diocese of Liège*, written by Jacques Pantaleon, the future Pope Urban IV. It says there that "therefore so many of you virgins and women, who have been unable to find access to obedience, or were able to do so without being able to bear the strictness of the Orders, have wisely and prudently chosen this way." This document is reproduced in L. J. M. Philippen, *De begijnhoven* (Antwerp, 1918)—appendix. On 14 May, 1328 the delegates of the bishop of Tournai reported that the countesses of Flanders and Hainaut had founded beguinages "taking into account that the aforesaid county abounds in women who, because of their own condition and that of their friends, were shut out from a decent marriage, and *that daughters of honest men, both of the nobility and of the middle classes, if they wanted to live in chastity, could not easily gain admittance to religious convents*, owing to their multitude or to the poverty of their parents ..." (italics mine). This document is reproduced in Jean Béthune, *Cartulaire du béguinage Sainte Elisabeth à Gand* (Bruges, 1883) and in Paul Fredericq, *Corpus documentorum inquisitionis haereticae pravitatis Neerlandicae* (Ghent and The Hague, 1889–1906), I, p. 176ff.

38. I introduce evidence and bibliography to support the hypothesis that southern Low Countries beguinages were devised according to a monastic model in my article, "The *Curtis* Beguinages." This material is elaborated in my forthcoming book, *Sculpture of Compassion*. *V* also Simons, (*v*. n. 4 "The Beguine Movement").

39. Simons, (*v* n. 4), pp. 78–84.

40. R. Hanon de Louvet, "L'origine nivelloise de l'institution béguinale d'une Reine de France Marie de Brabant et la légende de la béguine de Nivelles," *Annales de la Société archéologique et folklorique de Nivelles et du Brabant Wallon* 17 (1952), 5–78.

41. Ziegler, (*v* n. 2), esp. pp. 51–60.

42. For a discussion of property and inheritance systems in the county of Flanders and suggestions regarding their exceptional quality, *v* David Nicholas, "Of Poverty and Primacy: Demand, Liquidity, and the Flemish Economic Miracle, 1050–1200," *The American Historical Review* 96/1 (February 1991), 37, esp. pp. 37–41. For further read-ing on inheritance customs in the county of Flanders, *v* David Nicholas, *The Domestic Life of a Medieval City. Women, Children, and the Family in Fourteenth-Century Ghent* (Lincoln and London, 1985), pp. 10–12 and 188–98; and Philippe Godding, *Le droit privé dans les Pays-Bas méridionaux du 12ᵉ au 18ᵉ siècle* (Brussels, 1987), pp. 77–81 and 259–413.

43. Nicholas, "Of Poverty and Primacy," p. 37.

44. Ibid.
45. Researching local conditions in the county of Flanders, Nicholas ("Of Poverty and Primacy," pp. 17–41) has postulated the conditions for Flanders' rise to economic preeminence as having occured in the twelfth century, and that its unique urban situation is based on a particular economy. His reconsideration of the span of the chronology is important and bears implications for the present study.
46. More comparative work is needed to demonstrate whether nursing and care of the sick may also contain evidence that certain social conditions were particular to the Germanic countries. For recent research on the hospitalsisters and -brothers in the southern Low Countries, *v* G. Maréchal, "Armen- en ziekenzorg in de Zuidelijke Nederlanden," in *Algemene Geschiedenis der Nederlanden*, II (Haarlem, 1982), pp. 268–80, with bibliography on p. 514.
47. The multitude of terms applied to women not observing an approved rule demonstrates that the situation was as confusing for contemporaries as it is for us. More research is needed on the "consecrated virgin" who is not a nun—*canonicae, sanctimoniales, mulieres religiosae, mulieres Deo devotae, ancillae Dei, ancillae Christi*. Among the issues before the historian of the beguines are the myriad terms applied to these women in the early stages of the movement's development, many of which have also been applied to the canonesses. *V* nn. 12, 14, 15, and 18 above. The clearest account of the chronology and application of the terms for virgins is in the *Dictionnaire de droit canonique* (Paris, 1942); *Dictionnaire d'histoire et de géographie ecclésiastiques* (Paris, 1934); and *Lexikon für Theologie und Kirche* (Freiburg im Breisgau, 1960).

LITERACY AND *LITTERATURA*

Mark Vessey
University of British Columbia

BRITISH HISTORY: AN IRISH PERSPECTIVE

Brendan Smith
University College, Dublin

Review Essay

LITERACY AND *LITTERATURA*,
A.D. 200–800

Brian Stock, *Listening for the Text: On the Uses of the Past*. Baltimore: Johns Hopkins
University Press, 1990. Pp. x, 197.
William V. Harris, *Ancient Literacy*. Cambridge, Mass.: Harvard University Press, 1989. Pp.
xv, 383.
Rosamond McKitterick, *The Carolingians and the Written Word*. Cambridge: Cambridge
University Press, 1989. Pp xvi, 290.
Rosamond McKitterick, editor, *The Uses of Literacy in Early Mediaeval Europe*. Cambridge:
Cambridge University Press, 1990. Pp. xvi, 345.
Ernst Robert Curtius, *European Literature and the Latin Middle Ages*, trans. Willard R. Trask,
with a New Afterword by Peter Godman. Princeton: Princeton University Press, 1990. Pp.
xv, 718.

I.

When modern study of the cultural role and significance of literacy
began in the early 1960s, its main focus was on writing as new technology. The periods and cultures which it privileged were those in which
new writing systems were invented (notably ancient Greece) or where
literate practices could be seen penetrating for the first time (so-called
"traditional" societies at the instant of their modernization). The
researchers themselves were typically either classicists or anthropologists, sometimes both at once. Predictably, emphasis on literate origins—on transition from "primary" orality to some sort of literacy, however restricted—tended to deflect attention from cultures which had
long known the use of writing, such as that of Europe in the Middle
Ages. In time this bias became less pronounced. As anthropologists
learnt to distinguish different types of literacy and the various forms of
interaction between oral and literate modes of thought and communi-

cation, historians were encouraged to return to the problems posed, or passed over, in older studies of literacy in the Middle Ages. (For a review of some recent scholarship see D. H. Green, "Orality and Reading: The State of Research in Medieval Studies," *Speculum* 65 (1990): 267–80.)

The distinctive qualities of this new interest in medieval literacy are already evident in Michael T. Clanchy's *From Memory to Written Record: England 1066–1307* (London, 1979). Although the title of Clanchy's book, chosen to recall H. J. Chaytor's *From Script to Print* (1945), still evoked the twin concepts of origin and primary transition, his presentation relied surprisingly little on them, emphasizing instead the pre-Conquest antecedents of post-Conquest English literacy and the "symbiosis" of oral and literate modes in the later period. According to Clanchy, the shift "from memory to written record" in the eleventh and twelfth centuries could equally well be seen as a shift "from sacred script to practical literacy", as a realignment of existing literate habits rather than as a fundamental innovation. A comparably revisionist perspective commands Brian Stock's *The Implications of Literacy: Written Language and Models of Interpretation in the Eleventh and Twelfth Centuries* (Princeton, 1983). Stock's study complemented Clanchy's in three major respects, being based on continental rather than insular sources, oriented towards "literary" as opposed to documentary uses of writing, and more theoretically ambitious. Again the title is allusive, referring not to the "consequences" of literacy (the phrase coined by Jack Goody and Ian Watt in their pioneering paper of 1963) but to its "implications." The change reflected Stock's desire to free the historian from a narrowly diachronic model of oral-literate transition. His aim was to "de-emphasize the problem of (literate) origins" and so open the way for a historiography that would take account of all kinds of relation between the (real and imaginary) written and other modes of discourse, including the multiple discourses of action. By adopting a more synchronic approach to literacy, he was able to offer a unified view of a wide range of seemingly disparate social and intellectual phenomena, at the same time elaborating a theoretical construct (of the "textual community" as a social group organized around the shared understanding of a text) of impressive explanatory power.

In both these works, it now appears, the "problem of (literate) origins" was simultaneously transposed and deferred. Stock, like Clanchy, claimed a large measure of novelty for the phenomena described in *The Implications of Literacy*. He spoke not just of a "rebirth of literacy" in the eleventh and twelfth centuries, but of a "new type of interdependence" between the written and the oral, of "unprecedented parallels between literature and life". He also stated that it would be useful to know where the individual components of this "new" oral-literate culture had come from. Such knowledge—which might confirm or invalidate Clanchy's hypothesis of an underlying continuity between "sacred" and "practical" literacy in the middle ages—was to be sought in the records of earlier western European culture. Between the appearance of alphabetic script in ancient Greece and the emergence in the medieval West of a distinctive oral-literate culture (Stock) or proto-modern practical literacy (Clanchy) stretched two millenia of reading, writing, and the use of texts. What kinds of literacy prevailed in the (later) Roman Empire, in the "barbarian" kingdoms, or at the time of the Carolingian "renaissance"? How did older ideas and practices contribute to the literate culture of the eleventh and twelfth centuries? How are they related to "modern" literacy? In the course of the 1980s a number of historians in Europe and North America were drawn to consider these questions. The first four books under review offer an important sample of their work. Together with other studies of classical, late antique, and medieval literacy recently published or announced, they register strong seismic activity in a type of research that is rapidly transforming our historical landscape. It is too early to draw new maps, but it is possible to take some bearings.

II.

Brian Stock's *Listening for the Text: On the Uses of the Past* gathers material from a series of papers on literacy, historiography, and the Middle Ages, published separately or written for conferences between 1974 and 1987. The whole is considerably more than the sum of its parts. Rather than retain the order of original composition, Stock has rearranged and in some cases rewritten the individual papers, stitching them together with his latest thoughts to make eight chapters with an introduction. There is an irony in this method. One of the author's principal concerns, in this book as in its predecessor, is with the way in which we write the past, creating history as text. But writing can also unmake history, and in rewriting these papers Stock has partly effaced the record of his own scholarly progress. In order to understand how the positions presented here were reached, the reader must undo his carefully constructed text. Two early pieces, "Romantic Attitudes and

Academic Medievalism" (Chapter Three) and "Literary Discourse and the Social Historian" (Chapter Four), were first printed in *New Literary History* in 1974 and 1977 respectively; the latter now appears substantially modified. Both papers focus on what Stock regards as the unrealized potential for merger between the historical and literary disciplines, considered as one aspect of a general failure by modern scholars to explore the interdisciplinary or "comparative" option in medieval studies. The first paper champions Eric Auerbach as a philologist committed to the "sociology of literature", and ends with a grim (and intentionally comic?) vision of the contemporary medieval historian forced to choose between "getting on with his work" and succumbing to the quasi-religious attractions of semiotics or poststructuralism (p. 74). The second juxtaposes modern approaches to history and literature, to conclude despondently: *"It is not possible to historicize literary discussions,* nor does it seem likely that historical ones will treat texts as anything but repositories of fact" (p. 91, my italics). This sentence, not in the 1977 article, reads oddly in a time of resurgent historicism in literary studies, the more so as there are clear affinities between Stock's aspirations for a new literary history and the work of many "new historical" critics. Stock's pessimism regarding the prospects for a historicized study of literature is matched by his dissatisfaction with the current practice of medieval history, in particular with the kind of text-blind empiricism that he considers characteristic of much of it. Social historians, he believes, have not yet taken seriously the philosophical distinction between objective and subjective meaning, and thus have failed to realize (with Max Weber) that "social reality is an intermingling of reality and perception" (p. 86) and that every kind of cultural expression, including the literary text, must be seen as an "arbitrary imposition onto reality of a new conjunction of object, subject, and meaning" (p. 88). This emphasis on the text as individual social "event" recalls the main theme of *The Implications of Literacy,* the gestation of which is marked by a gap of several years in the dates of papers reissued in the present volume. Weber's name was not prominent in the earlier work, largely no doubt because, as Stock remarks in the introduction to a piece entitled "Max Weber, Western Rationality, and the Middle Ages" (Chapter Six), he "said little about orality and literacy" (p. 113). In this essay Stock sets out to correct Weber's view of the origins of western rationality by drawing attention to a number of medieval advances in critical thought, all of which, he suggests, are somehow connected with the rise of literacy. The argument depends heavily on Jack Goody's *The*

Domestication of the Savage Mind (1977). However, in adapting Goody's thesis of a link between literacy and rationality to the medieval situation, Stock is led to formulate three important hypotheses: (1) that the rationality of the twelfth century was founded on the literate achievements of the Carolingian "renaissance" and, in a lesser degree, of earlier periods; (2) that the developed literacy of the Middle Ages was characterized by a high level of interplay between oral/aural and written norms; (3) that the distinctively oral-literate quality of that literacy was, at least in part, a product of early Christian attitudes to scripture. The first point was anticipated, the second already well made, in *The Implications of Literacy*. Further reflections on the emergence of medieval oral-literate culture are to be found in a paper on "Medieval Literacy, Linguistic Theory, and Social Organization" (Chapter Two), first published in 1984, which also contains a reference to "the rebirth of textual communities" (p. 37) in the eleventh century. This is a revealing phrase, since it implies that it was not just literacy as a set of skills but a particular mode of literate activity that was revived at that time. The assumption is a natural one in the context of the present collection, which is much concerned with precedents; indeed Stock's urging of the third claim listed above, regarding the role of early Christian tradition in the formation of medieval literate culture, marks perhaps the most important single development in *Listening for the Text* of the positions outlined in *The Implications of Literacy*.

The ideal of a rapprochement between historical and literary approaches to texts—which, no less than the preoccupation with "the uses of the past," provides a unifying theme for *Listening for the Text*—helps to organize two pieces from the mid-1980s: "History, Literature, Textuality" (Chapter One) and "Language and Culture: Saussure, Ricoeur, and Foucault" (Chapter Five). In the former, Stock identifies "textuality" as the common ground of several recent attempts to explore the relations between literature and history, and argues convincingly that the exploration of textuality itself should begin with "the period in which Europe became a society that used texts on a large scale" (p. 18)—i.e., the period treated in *The Implications of Literacy*. A less adventurous or more complacent scholar might have left the matter there. Stock, however, goes on to assert the need for a "basic chronology of medieval literacy" that will allow for such major influences as "Greek and Roman education," "Jewish scripturalism as transformed by early Christians," and "Germanic languages and institutions" (p. 19). The importance of the first two factors is underlined by his statement that after A.D. 1000 "the spoken and written were drawn into closer interdependence than they had been *at any time since the end of the ancient world*" (p. 20, my italics). The adverbial phrase is potentially ambiguous: it is not clear whether "the end of the ancient world" is to be taken literally as a moment dividing antiquity from the middle ages, or as shorthand for a terminal phase of ancient culture with a distinctive literacy of its own. The latter interpretation is perhaps the more likely, for it is quickly apparent that the author of *Listening for the Text* has a special interest in late antiquity—or the "later ancient world" as he prefers to call it. Although there is no universally accepted definition of late antiquity, it is usually taken to encompass the years A.D. 200–600. Sooner or later, the historian of western literacy is bound to traverse this period. It was during these centuries that the ideology and institutions of Graeco-Roman literary *paideia* were cast into the forms that they would hold for most of the Middle Ages; then, too, that Judaeo-Christian scripturalism, under the pressure of secular literary culture, acquired its enduring character. Stock saves consideration of such matters for later essays, devoting the rest of this one (pp. 21–29) to an exposition of his concept of the "textual community."

The concept of the textual community is also invoked in the essay on Saussure, Ricoeur, and Foucault, most constructively at the point where Stock offers an adaptation of Ricoeur's theory of discourse, designed to integrate historical as well as literary aspects of experience. The first three stages in Stock's proposed four-stage scheme are: (1) "text production", (2) "the use of potential, actual, recalled, and imagined texts to organize experience", and (3) "the enactment of texts as living narratives and the organization of life according to their implicit rules" (p. 104). The products of this process are, on the one hand, the literary work (as defined by Ricoeur) and, on the other, the textual community (as defined by Stock). Stock does not insist on his expanded Ricoeurian model of discourse—it is merely one episode in the continuous theoretical dialogue of his book—but as a statement of his ideas on the "interpenetration of written structures with reality" (p. 108) it has the advantage of being at once clearer and of more general application than any model proposed in *The Implications of Literacy*. Taken in conjunction with the call for a "basic chronology of literacy," it suggests the possibility of extending the literary and historical study of textual communities to the immediate prehistory of medieval (and modern) western textuality, into the period of early Christianity and of the later Roman empire.

That possibility is raised formally in Chapter Seven, "Textual Communities: Judaism, Christianity, and the Definitional Probem", based on a paper given in 1986. Here Stock reminds us that his idea of the textual community was originally intended "to fill a theoretical gap in the conception of Church and sect as outlined by Ernst Troeltsch and...Max Weber." Neither Troeltsch nor Weber, he argues, took sufficient account of "the fact that what one believes is shaped by the means of communication by which the content is transmitted" (p. 157). In the terms suggested by Stock's final chapter, entitled "Tradition and Modernity," both attempted to divorce the *traditum* of belief from the process of its *traditio*, forgetting or failing to appreciate that such transmission is "not neutral [but] rooted in politics and institutions" and thus partly determines the message it conveys (p. 162). The concept of the textual community was meant to provide a way of studying the processes of *traditio* in societies which knew the use of writing, even where literate skills were confined to a single person or to a small circle within a community (as was generally the case in the Middle Ages). Since, by definition, textual communities exist wherever the interpretation of a text serves to organize the experience of a group, the application of this concept to the study of early Christian communities and their use of scripture was always likely to suggest itself. (In view of the persistent failure of early Christian philology, before and since the time of Adolf von Harnack, to produce an integrated model of the processes of literary and religious tradition, one might say that a place had been reserved for it.) Stock's particular interest in Chapter Seven is with the relation of the earliest Christian scripturalism to rival Jewish modes of attention to the sacred text. Yet it is clear that the techniques of literary and historical analysis used in *The Implications of Literacy* could also be extended to the study of text-centered movements within early Christianity, or indeed to areas of interference between "pagan" and Christian approaches to the written word during the late Roman period. To be effective in these fields, the medievalist's methods will need some modification. "In antiquity," Stock observes, "conditions were different [from those in the Middle Ages]. Above all, *in a society in which literacy was routine,* more attention must be paid to reception and reader reconstruction, to intertextuality, and to oral discourse within well-worn rhetorical channels. One must also deal with canon and authority" (p. 151, my italics). From this we may infer, using a distinction made elsewhere by Stock (pp. 147–48), that the social-historical or "contextual" approach to literacy which he advocates ought to be matched by a cor-

responding literary-historical or "compositional" initiative on the part
of specialists in early Christian and late antique literature: only when
the two approaches are combined should we expect to understand
both how texts made communities and why those communities made
the texts they did.

The introduction to *Listening for the Text* (entitled "Orality,
Literacy, and the Sense of the Past") should be read last as well as first,
since it outlines a thesis about the formation of medieval and early
modern attitudes to language, literature, and textuality that goes well
beyond the conclusions of the other essays. It is a thesis which, while
generally applicable to "the period of Western history...between the
late ancient world and the thirteenth century" (p. 2), assigns special
importance to the period between the second and eighth centuries A.D.
Taking for granted that "the ancient [Graeco-Roman] world was by and
large a literate society" (p. 3), Stock argues (1) that the coming of
Christianity led to a new emphasis on the spoken word in opposition to
Jewish literalism and Roman literary culture, and (2) that the religious
conversion of the Germanic peoples completed the transformation of
Christianity into a scriptural religion in which "literacy meant legitima-
cy." As he puts it: "in the passage from Hellenistic Roman and Jewish
antiquity to the Christian Middle Ages, the oral did not simply replace
the written. Nor did the literate orality of the gospels and the primary
orality of the Germanic tribesmen merge. By an inversion of symbols,
one type of scripturalism [i.e., the Christian] succeeded another [i.e.,
the Hellenistic Jewish and/or Hellenistic Roman] (p.4)." If the logic
and sequence of these developments in western literacy here remain
somewhat vague, the conclusion that Stock wishes to draw does not. In
his view, the late ancient world "discovered" an idea of the text which
included both "visible and aural forms of language," thus establishing a
"legal, institutional, and societal framework for the interdependence of
oral and written traditions" (p.4). It also discovered our idea of "literature." These innovations mark the beginning of "a new chapter in relations between texts, verbal or written, and nascent European societies"
(p. 11).

The impression left by *Listening for the Text* is of a bold case
incompletely stated and of exciting work in progress. It would be unfair
at this point to pronounce either for or against Stock's thesis of the late
antique roots (or proximate origins) of modern western textuality.
Whatever its final merits, his statement of the case is certain to bring a
new kind of scrutiny to bear on a phase of European culture that par-

ticularly invites interdisciplinary treatment. Those who are attracted by the general shape of Stock's arguments will have to address some large questions. How safe are his assumptions about the extent and character of literacy in the late ancient world? What changes in Roman attitudes towards spoken and written language should be allowed for in the centuries that separate the Julio-Claudian emperors from Constantine or Theodosius the Great? How far was the Jewish scripturalism to which the early Christian church reacted itself determined by habits of thought fostered by the secular literary and legal culture of the Hellenistic and early imperial periods? By what stages did Christianity become a scriptural religion? How, exactly, did the Christian religion adapt or convert the literate manners of its late antique "pagan" environment? What forms did the encounter between Romano-Christian literacy and "barbarian" orality actually take? What sense (or difference) does it make to suppose that the men and women of late antiquity, or an elite group of them, discovered an idea of the text that included both visible and aural forms of language? Did they in fact discover such a thing? Some of these issues have already been taken up by scholars of religion and students of early Christian and late antique literature. Stock's readers may look forward to following his own research as it proceeds; meanwhile, they can turn to several other recent books on ancient and medieval literacy which help to sharpen the focus provided by his work.

III.

William V. Harris's *Ancient Literacy* is an essentially empirical study of the literacy of the Greeks and Romans "from the time when the former were first provably able to write a non-syllabic script, in the eighth century B.C., until the fifth century A.D." (viii). Harris writes as an historian whose reaction when "faced with claims such as those of [E. A] Havelock and (Jack) Goody [concerning the cultural effects of literacy] is ... a desire for detail" (p. 41). Before we can even begin to assess the effects of literacy on Greek and Roman culture, he asserts, we must establish some "elementary facts" (p. 42). How many people could read and write in the ancient Graceo-Roman world? Why did they use writing? How did levels of literacy vary between social classes, between the sexes, between town and country, from one period to the next? What determined the differences? In an attempt to answer these questions Harris combines the customary methods of the ancient historian with a judicious use of anthropological and sociological data derived from the study of other societies, "traditional" and modern. There is certainly no shortage of detail in his account. For each of the phases of ancient society successively considered, from the archaic Greek to the late Roman, we are given a full conspectus of the evidence relating to literacy (literary, documentary, epigraphic, and iconographic); an inventory of the functions or social contexts of writing (e.g., economic, legal, civic, magical, religious, commemorative, literary, epistolary); a survey of the materials and techniques, institutions, and ideologies that structured literate activity; and a breakdown by class, area, and gender of the literate and semi-literate population. Despite the attention given to the early Greek experience of the written word in the past thirty years, this is the first analytical study of the literate habits of the ancient world as a whole. For anyone concerned with the later or long-term history of western attitudes to writing and texts it will henceforth be an indispensable reference work.

The main tendency of the quantitative part of Harris's research is to correct downwards the optimistic estimates usually made of ancient literacy. On his calculation, literates in Greek or Roman society rarely exceeded 10% of the total population, the vast majority of these being male inhabitants of the cities. Even in fourth-century Athens or late republican Rome that figure was probably only doubled. During the Hellenistic period certain Greek cities may, as a result of philanthropic initiatives in education, have experienced literacy on an "early-modern" scale, "perhaps even at a level of 30–40% among the free-born men" (p. 329), but such achievements were exceptional. Harris supposes, perhaps with reason, that his conclusions will be unwelcome to some classical scholars. To the dispassionate reader of his book they seem well justified. "Each society," we are reminded, "achieves the level of literacy which its structure and ethos require and its technology permits" (p. 331). Lacking either the technology or the educational institutions which would eventually permit "mass literacy" in modern Europe, ancient Graeco-Roman society lacked above all the ideological commitment to a universal or quasi-universal diffusion of literate skills that Reformed Christianity or (more important, in Harris's view) industrialized production would later require. Even when an "ideology of citizen literacy" (p. 102) was entertained, as it was in the Greek cities from the mid-fourth century onwards, the legislation and social provision that would have been needed to make all citizens liter-

ate were never implemented. The Romans inherited the Greek enthusi-
asm for a *paideia* based on literacy but did little to make it accessible to
those without private means: the result, in both cases, was "the cultural
hegemony of a social class" (p. 333). Thus while literacy may indeed be
called "routine" (Stock's phrase) in ancient society, inasmuch as the
operations of that society depended on the literate skills of particular
individuals, it was demographically very restricted. Oral modes of interaction continued to play a significant role. The Greeks and Romans,
Harris notes in passing, "held on to oral procedures to a greater extent
than is commonly realized ... both in the sense that the literate
retained some non-literate ways of doing things and in the sense that
the majority stayed illiterate. Both political persuasion and the diffusion of literature [sic] remained oral to an important degree throughout antiquity" (p. 326).

Harris begins his last chapter, on "Literacy in Late Antiquity",
with a reference to Constantine's commissioning (c. 324) of fifty bibles
for use in the churches of Constantinople, as recorded in the *Vita
Constantini* of Eusebius of Caesarea. This action, he observes, "had no
kind of classical precedent, and it stemmed from an important cultural
change, the rise of a state-sponsored religion which relied heavily on
the written word. But at the same time the emperor's letter [to
Eusebius] hints at the continuity of ancient conditions, for he ordered
books which the faithful would for the most part hear read aloud, and
he expected that fifty volumes would cater for the needs of the capital
city" (p. 285). This is a momentous event for historians of western textuality interested in the line of inquiry indicated by Stock. Harris plausi-
bly relates the oral component of the oral-literate procedure implied by
Constantine's letter to ancient practices in the public "delivery" of
texts; presumably we are to think of literary recitation (discussed pp.
225–26) and of certain kinds of legal proclamation (pp. 164–65). It is
also worth noting that the emphasis on the written word is, in this case,
partly attributable to an emperor whose approach to religion was
markedly legalistic; the order for bibles coincided with the summoning
of a council that would fix in writing the Christian dogma of the Trinity
(the Nicene Creed, of which Harris surprisingly makes no mention).
The situation is evidently a complex one, and in that respect typical of
the conditions under which writing came to be used in the Christian
Empire. Whatever view we finally adopt of the late antique "idea of the
text," it must take account not just of the novelty (such as it was) of

Christian attitudes to the spoken or written word but also of the constant and not always predictable interaction of secular and religious norms.

Harris assumes that literacy declined in the late Roman Empire. "It is evident," he asserts, "that the level of literacy did in fact fall in the area of the classical Roman Empire between the second and the seventh centuries" (p. 285). So it may be, even if—as he freely admits—the proof of such a negative development is not easily presented. But it is also evident that the pattern of general decline was interrupted by periods of revival (notably in the fourth century) and that conditions varied widely from region to region, especially after the break-up of the western Empire. Regrettably for students of the Middle Ages, Harris's sense of the limits of "ancient" history keeps him from going much beyond the threshold of the fifth century. Thus he does not repeat the panoramic survey by provinces offered for the period of the early Empire, which the fifth-century situation evidently demands. In relation to the longer history of literacy and textuality, a cut-off point c. 400 appears somewhat arbitrary; here it produces some strange distortions and omissions. Harris discounts the possibility that two late third-century legal collections, the *Codex Gregorianus* and *Codex Hermogenianus,* could "represent the investing of...greater authority in the written word," on the grounds that they were merely private compilations (pp. 292–93), but makes no mention of the early fifth-century *Codex Theodosianus,* a governmental enterprise of massive scope and with important implications for attitudes to the *lex scripta*. His attempt (pp. 306–312) to demonstrate reduced opportunities for elementary education from the mainly fourth-century evidence of writers like Ausonius understandably runs into difficulties; a few pages later he cites some well-known remarks of Bishop Caesarius of Arles (d. 542) to confirm the general decline in literacy "after the barbarian invasions of the early fifth century" (p. 316), but without any discussion of the situation as it had developed in Gaul in the intervening period. In general, the author's control of his materials in this chapter seems less sure than in previous ones. Nevertheless, he has provocative things to say about the workings of late Roman bureaucracy (pp. 290–94: less "paperwork" than is commonly supposed) and gives a good critical summary of modern debate on the shift from roll to codex in late antique book production (pp. 294–97). Nor does he omit to consider "in what may seem disproportionate detail" (p. 298) the functions of the written word among the Christians.

In order to round off his book on "ancient" literacy, Harris is obliged to insist on a terminal decline. Once the crisis of the third century is passed, however, there is no obvious place for him to stop. The low-point in subsequent western literacy has usually been placed in the seventh century, beyond the ancient historian's scope. Long before that, Christianity had worked fundamental changes in attitudes to writing and texts. "Ancient" literacy, it seems, neither ended nor declined. Instead, it gradually turned into something recognizably different. The final chapter of *Ancient Literacy* catches a part of this transformation, without being able to contain or describe it. Why did literacy decline in the later Roman empire, Harris asks. Unable to give due weight to the political and economic factors operative from the fifth century onwards, he is left to ponder the role of the Christian religion. He cautiously concludes that "its effect on literacy *as it is understood in this book* was very probably negative" (p. 321, my italics: the main discussion of Christianity and literacy appears at pp. 298–306). This conclusion rests on three interrelated premises: (1) Christian suspicion of pagan literary culture discouraged literacy; (2) the Christians of late antiquity never developed an educational program of their own that could supply the place of a secular training in elementary letters; (3) despite their faith in scriptural teaching, church leaders in this period never took "the kind of practical measures in favour of (private or individual) reading which some Protestant churches took in later times" (p. 312). None of these arguments is persuasive. Professions of disdain for secular *litteratura* by Christian writers of the third and fourth centuries may indicate a change of attitude on the part of the well educated; they can hardly attest rejected or missed educational opportunities. (Harris's desire to use Augustine's *De doctrina christiana* as evidence of a practical disregard for literacy is perverse; in the prologue to this work the new bishop of Hippo makes it plain that he considers the religious instruction of the majority of Christians to be providentially dependent on the learned literate skills of their fellow believers.) True, churchmen of this period did not set up their own elementary schools. Why should they? They assumed that the sons of well-to-do Christian families would follow the normal course of late Roman education. The comparison with modern Protestantism is useful mainly as a corrective to a tendentious (albeit informative) monograph by A. von Harnack on private bible-reading in the early church, published in 1912. Given that the "ideology of citizen literacy" in the ancient world was, as Harris shows, in general too weak to inspire practical measures, the failure of Christian ideology to do so (except in certain monastic milieux) cannot reasonably be cited as a cause of decline in this area of civic life.

Although Harris's interest in implicating Christianity in the "decline of ancient literacy" does not keep him from noticing other aspects of the relation between *litteratura* and *scriptura* (see, for example, his remarks on *sortes Vergilianae* and *sortes apostolicae* [p. 303], both apparently late antique novelties), it can at times be seriously distracting. Thus he cites with approval Peter Brown's observation that "behind Augustine's vast output at Hippo, we can sense the pressure of the need to extend...religious literacy as widely as possible," only then to cast doubt on the validity of the concept of "religious literacy" on the grounds that it "run(s) up against the awkward fact that neither Augustine nor any other influential ecclesiastic ever even considered *the problem of mass illiteracy*" [pp. 320–21, my italics], as though such considerations were obviously relevant. The point to be made, surely, is that the very nature of this "religious literacy," including its desired extension, was determined by a variety of factors intrinsic and extrinsic to the Christian religion. The historian's task is to discern those factors and (by this means and others) define the literacy in question. The phenomenon described may indeed turn out to be something other than literacy "as it understood in [Harris's] book"—one would expect it to be the matter of at least another book (cf. Stock's work in progress). In any case, it deserves fuller scrutiny than Harris is able to provide. He himself recognizes that "the functions of reading underwent some change" in the conversion to Christian literacy, and that there was "an almost entirely new social location for the written word among the more professionally and the enthusiastically pious of the Christians" (321–22). These are important insights, all the more valuable for appearing at the term of an inquiry as wide ranging and thoroughly documented as *Ancient Literacy*.

IV.

Notions of decadence and decline, long prejudicial to the study of late Roman and early medieval Latin literature, have undoubtedly also obscured the history of literacy in the period. Even if we could quantify the literates in successive European populations over the period A.D. 200–800, and found them (as we might expect) notably less numerous than in classical Greece or late republican Rome, we should still not be able to say much of interest about the role of writing in their societies.

As the possession of an individual, literacy may perhaps be considered a simple commodity. As the attribute of a society, it is better conceived as an economy in which objects and skills have certain prices and particular relations hold: the stock in Text A or Scribal Habit B may rise or fall, but the local currency of letters is not convertible to that of any other time or place. While comparisons with preceding and succeeding epochs may help us to understand the workings of a given literate "economy," they cannot fix its value.

In her introduction to *The Carolingians and the Written Word*, Rosamond McKitterick reacts against "the preoccupation with the later middle ages of most recent studies of medieval literacy" and a concomitant exaggeration of the "orality" of early medieval society by scholars interested in promoting the literate achievements of the eleventh and twelfth centuries (pp. 1–3). Insofar as this mild polemic is directed against Stock, it risks missing a moving target. *Listening for the Text* (known to McKitterick as a work forthcoming under another title) can only provisionally be said to "concentrate on the eleventh century onwards" (p. 1, n.1.), and the assertion that *The Implications of Literacy* "begins too late and is too categorical about the irrelevance of the earlier period" *(The Uses of Literacy in Early Medieval Europe*, p. 3) is clearly unjust. Such claims are a normal part of the process by which a new historical subject is marked out; they do not have to imply incompatible conclusions. In fact, McKitterick's determination to see a "continuous pattern [in the social evolution of literacy] from late antiquity to the early Germanic kingdoms" (p.1) and her belief that "the roots of later medieval developments are to be sought in the centuries immediately succeeding the period of Roman rule" (p. 3) harmonize easily with the project announced in *Listening for the Text*.

Like Harris, McKitterick is anxious to ascertain the "elementary facts" of literacy, to distinguish the various functions of writing, and to "quantify" literate skills wherever possible—in this case without assigning percentages. She would revise upwards our estimates of Carolingian literacy, particularly among the laity (see especially Chapter Six: "The Literacy of the Laity"). Given the contrary tendency of *Ancient Literacy*, this may appear a naively optimistic aim. Yet it is likely that the overestimation of "classical" literacy to which Harris responds had as its corollary an underestimation of the literacy of subsequent "barbarian" societies. Besides, McKitterick has impressive evidence to present, and the cumulative force of her arguments is hard to resist. She is also interested in "qualitative" changes, arguing that "in the prodigious output of the written word at every level of Carolingian society we are observing essential phases in the development of a literate culture, with new ideals and definitions of education and knowledge dependent on a written tradition" (p. 3). The argument for those "new ideals and definitions" becomes more audible in the later stages of her book, while the earlier chapters substantiate the Carolingians' "prodigious output" of the written word in "pragmatic" (as opposed to "learned") contexts.

The first part of *The Carolingians and the Written Word* deals with the legal uses of writing. In this area, as in others, historians of medieval literacy have access to a body of documentary evidence of a type generally denied their ancient-historical counterparts. With that advantage, however, comes a responsibility to organize and interpret often intractable material. Not the least of the virtues of McKitterick's book, the work of a paleographer-historian, is the help it offers in this respect. Chapter Two ("Law and the Written Word") concentrates on the manuscript tradition of the *Lex Salica* as a striking instance of "the proliferation of texts of the laws in the Carolingian period", reflecting (in the author's opinion) a "growing understanding of the authority of the written word and an attempt to establish that authority in relation to legal procedure and judicial decisions" (p. 38). A table of more than eighty manuscripts of the *Lex Salica* (pp. 48–55) gives valuable indications of date and origin derived largely from palaeographical data, together with notes on the codicological context in which the text of the Law appears. On the basis of the latter, McKitterick is able to classify the manuscripts as law books (presumed to be for practical use), school texts about the law, or ecclesiastical legal collections. As she concedes, definite conclusions about the functions of these texts must await detailed study of the various collections. One would like to know more, for example, about the genesis and use of the ecclesiastical collections containing both secular and canon law (and not just those which include *Lex Salica*). McKitterick's own research, presented in this chapter and in several articles cited in the notes, will provide a powerful stimulus for future work in this area. Chapter Three ("A Literate Community: The Evidence of the Charters") exploits a store of eighth- and ninth-century legal documents from St. Gall in order to show how a monastery could coordinate the literate activity of the community to which it belonged, without holding a monopoly of literate skills. Here again, the author illuminates a large expanse of documentary material before drawing her own conclusions, and leaves the field open for others.

In Chapter Four ("The Production and Possession of Books: An Economic Dimension"), McKitterick turns from the reconstruction of literate practices in Carolingian society to a consideration of attitudes towards writing, books, and written knowledge in general. The Carolingians, she argues, possessed a special sense of the value of books, based on an appreciation of their combined material and spiritual worth. The information she provides on such matters as the cost of book production and decoration, the respect shown for particular texts, books as gifts, and books as symbols of wealth and status, amply supports this view—which no one who has seen any of the great codices from Carolingian scriptoria would dispute. There is, however, a larger claim implicit in the demonstration. "Historians of the later middle ages...take it for granted that books were valuable, that they were considered as treasure and that people also wanted books for their intellectual import." When, asks McKitterick, "did this first become the case *in barbarian Europe after the transformations of the fifth century?*" (p. 150, my italics). As long as the question is phrased in this way, the answer can only be: in the Carolingian period. But why draw a line between late Roman and "barbarian" Europe, unless the "transformations" of the fifth century can be supposed to have swept away all consciousness of the value of writing? McKitterick is well aware of the role of classical and late antique models in early medieval literary theory and practice, yet in her desire to enlarge the "Carolingian contribution" to western culture (p. 164) she seems momentarily to forget how much of it was made with materials from the past. At one point she quotes a poem of Hrabanus Maurus to show how Carolingian scholars "appear to have elevated all books into a special category" (pp. 150–51). The same poem is cited by E. R. Curtius in his study of "The Book as Symbol" *(European Literature and the Latin Middle Ages,* Chapter Sixteen). The terms of Curtius' conclusion—that in its attitude to books and writing "the Carolingian period shows us many things, but few new things" (p. 315)—reflect his determination to plot a path of classical continuity through the Middle Ages. Even so, the long perspective of his chapter may serve as a control on McKitterick's chronologically more limited discussion. Although the Carolingians did much to enhance the prestige of the book in medieval society, their ideology of writing depended in many particulars on the literary culture of (late) Graeco–Roman antiquity. The use they made of such inherited material remains, of course, within the province of the medieval historian. At least one medievalist, following the lead of Jacques Derrida, has recently used

Curtius's insights as the base on which to rear an ambitious theory of the medieval "idea of the book" (Jesse M. Gellrich, *The Idea of the Book in the Middle Ages: Language Theory, Mythology, and Fiction.* Ithaca and London: Cornell University Press, 1985). By replacing Hrabanus' tropes in their social and economic context, McKitterick suggests how much might be gained from a consistently historicized study of the book as symbol.

The heritage of late antiquity is explicitly recalled in McKitterick's penultimate chapter, "The Organization of Written Knowledge", which draws on catalogues of monastic libraries to document an emerging sense of the canon and categories of "Christian" literature (here properly understood to include classical texts copied and preserved by monks). Once reminded that books produced in monastic scriptoria "constitute the most eloquent witness to the Carolingians' conviction of the paramount importance of the written word," we are asked to consider how it was that monasteries came to play this role in literary culture, "when in the early years of the Christian church monks were not famed for either learning or scribal activity". (So much for Jerome or the Egyptian copyists commemorated by John Cassian!) The reader fresh from Harris's account of the debilitating effects of Christianity on ancient literacy might be forgiven for regarding this as an aporia. McKitterick, however, duly recognizes the significance of the learned tradition in late antique monasticism, especially in Gaul, and is able to cite the work of Clare Stancliffe and others showing that some "newly recruited members of the early monastic communities in Gaul carried over from their secular life their respect for their literary heritage [and] their assumption of its necessity" (p. 167). At the same time, she wants to see a marked change in the content of the literary heritage between late antiquity and the Carolingian period: "In place of the former preponderance of classical and pagan authors... there was now a Christian emphasis, and a growing body of new authors and new works to form a distinctive culture and intellectual tradition in its own right" (p. 168). It is not clear exactly where McKitterick locates this change, but I suspect that she is inclined to make it too late. Like her earlier chapters on the legal uses of writing, the discussion of Frankish library catalogues displays a wealth of information hitherto available only to specialists, if at all. Her main conclusions concerning the Carolingian "organization of written knowledge" are concentrated in a few pages towards the end of the chapter, under the heading: "The role of the *De viris illustribus,* the *De libris recipiendis* and other early medieval bibliographical guides" (pp. 200–205). Her argument is that the bio-bibliographical catalogues of Jerome, Gennadius, and Isidore, together with certain other works such as the pseudo-Gelasian *De libris recipiendis,* created "a habit of mind and a customary framework within which to organize knowledge" (p. 205). This is an interesting and highly plausible suggestion, even if the parallels between the literary models adduced and the catalogues analyzed are not always striking. Once again, however, we should beware of ascribing more to the Carolingians than is really their due. If the works of writers like Jerome, Gennadius, and Cassiodorus (to say nothing for the moment of pseudo-Gelasius, here speculatively assigned to "a north Frankish or north Burgundian centre at the turn of the seventh century" [p. 203]) could inspire the habits of mind which McKitterick detects, it is fair to assume that they themselves already possessed them in some measure. In other words, the work of defining and organizing a distinctively Christian "[literary] culture and intellectual tradition" should be seen as a process begun in late antiquity and zealously prosecuted by the Carolingians. Whether or not they became famous for their literate activity, those early Christian monks did in fact lay many of the foundations for the literacy of the Middle Ages.

    The Carolingians and the Written Word concludes with a summons to collaborative scholarship in keeping with the spirit of the book as a whole: "Not only have I concentrated on the Frankish kingdoms, and thus, perhaps, not given due weight to developments in Visigothic or Muslim Spain, Lombard, Byzantine or Papal Italy, Anglo-Saxon England, or elsewhere, I have also had to leave for treatment or fuller discussion another time, and by others, many more kinds of evidence and other contexts and manifestations of literacy, ideological as well as practical, in the Carolingian realm itself" (p. 271). Part of this burden is taken up in *The Uses of Literacy in Early Medieval Europe,* in which McKitterick has collected new papers by herself and ten other scholars on diverse aspects of literacy within and beyond the Frankish kingdoms. Like McKitterick's own book, the contributions to this volume are based on extensive new research. Since it is not possible to consider them severally here, a sentence from the editor's conclusion must suffice to convey the flavor of the collection: "Early medieval society as a whole, in whatever historical context one chooses to see it, was one in which literacy mattered, and where literacy had repercussions right down the social scale, from the king issuing directives, and the nobleman endowing a monastery with books, to the freed slave clinging to his new social status by means of a written charter" (p. 333). The message is clear: the literacy of the early Middle Ages can no longer be dismissed as a debased remnant of classical culture, nor should it be used merely as a foil for the glories of the eleventh and twelfth centuries. It is an integral part of European society in one of its formative phases, demanding serious attention by all who would understand either the epoch itself or its complex cultural legacy.

V

Having begun this review with a highly schematic account of historical research on literacy in the past three decades, I shall close it with two general observations on the present state of the subject as reflected in the books considered above.

My first point may be stated briefly, since it is already implicit in many of the preceding remarks. We need more studies, and more detailed studies, of the functions and ideology of writing in late antiquity, especially in the critical period between Diocletian's reorganization of the Roman Empire in the late third century and the collapse of Roman rule in the West in the late fifth. To stop c. 400 as Harris does in *Ancient Literacy,* or to start shortly afterwards as medieval historians are disposed to, is to risk obscuring important developments both in the secular administrative use of writing and in Christian attitudes to the written word. (McKitterick's introduction to *The Uses of Literacy in Early Medieval Europe* neatly poses this problem of chronological *termini.*) Most of the "elementary facts" of late antique literacy have still to be elucidated; until they have been, attempts at large-scale reconstruction must remain largely conjectural.

My second observation has to do with the disciplinary context of current research on early western literacy, especially with the involvement (or lack of involvement) in it of scholars of Latin literature. To judge from the books under review, most of the work in this area is being done by ancient and medieval historians. Stock is a partial exception to the rule, teaching both at the Pontifical Institute of Mediaeval Studies and at the Centre for Comparative Literature at the University of Toronto. Given the natural proximity of "literacy" to "literature" in both the Latin and English vocabularies of letters, and the multiple coincidences in all periods of practical and artistic recourse to writing, one might expect such crossing of the literary and historical disciplines to occur as a matter of course. Not so, apparently. It is true that students of early European vernacular literatures are now generally attentive to the issues of orality and literacy. By contrast, the science of late antique and early medieval Latin literature does not seem to have been touched in any significant way by modern historical research on literacy. Bearing in mind Stock's critique of the institutions of medievalism, we might regard this as just another instance of scholarly inertia. Even if we do (and even if it is), we should also suspect the influence of a factor peculiar to medieval literary studies.

The fusion of literary- and social-historical approaches to the literacy of late antiquity and the early Middle Ages has been seriously hindered by the vestigial *classicism* of most contemporary research on post-classical Latin literature. An example must suffice to make this point. The outstanding representative of classicizing medieval Latin philology is E. R. Curties, whose *European Literature and the Latin Middle Ages* (1953) rightly remains the *vade mecum* of every traveller in Gothic realms. For Curtius, "literature" preserved its original connection with *litteratura,* the cherished possession of those who "knew [Latin] grammar and poetry" (p. 42); it was the fruit of their study and imitation of the classical poets, begun at school. This classical and scholastic bias in the conception of literature informs the whole of his monumental work—a work which, as Peter Godman points out in a balanced and illuminating epilogue to its latest reprinting, is fundamentally unhistorical in outlook. Curtius presented the Latin Middle Ages "almost exclusively, in terms of language and literature, both of which are treated as if they self-evidently possessed such a degree of independence from actuality, that their historical context could be cursorily sketched and then safely ignored. Three factors predisposed [him] to take this position: his quest for timeless continuities; his assumption (complementary but unargued) of literature's autonomy; and his enmity to historical relativism" (Godman, pp. 644–45). Curtius's assumption of literature's autonomy is nowhere more evident than in the following sentences introducing a section on canon-formation, a topic recognized by Stock as central to any future study of late antique textual communities:

> The formation of a canon serves to safeguard a tradition. There is the literary tradition of the school, the juristic tradition of the state, and the religious tradition of the Church: these are the three medieval world powers, *studium, imperium, sacerdotium.* (p. 256)

In characteristically epigrammatic fashion, the author confines literary activity to the classroom of the late Roman *grammaticus* and his medieval successors. The scheme of the "three world powers" is a thirteenth-century invention with no obvious relevance to the processes of canon formation (H. Grundmann, *Archiv für Kulturgeschichte* 34 [1952], 5–21); Curtius uses it to divide the universe of writing—*lit(t)erae* in the broadest sense—into three distinct spheres, only one of which is supposed to concern the student of "literature." To the extent that such distinctions were observed by medieval *litterati,* that may seem a legitimate proceeding. But how far were they observed in the period before A.D. 800? And how helpful are they to modern scholars attempting to understand the forms taken by early medieval literate activity? Recent work on late antique and early medieval literacy suggests that there was no stable category of the "literary" at that time, that the cultural capital traditionally associated with "letters" in Roman society was (to revert to an economic analogy in preference to Curtius's political model) in the process of being variously reinvested. Curtius promised that readers of his book would find out "where the word *literature* comes from and what meaning it originally had" (p. ix). We now need, and are in a position, to know more than that. If the present generation of philologists and historians can discover what became of *litteratura* in late antiquity and the early Middle Ages, how the pattern of ancient literary studies and pursuits was adjusted to the changing requirements of individual, church, and state during those centuries, and what the long-term consequences of such institutional and ideological accommodations were, they will bring us a step closer to the "sociology of literature" that Curtius also promised (p. ix) but conspicuously failed to provide. To that enterprise—at once literary and historical—the latest studies of literacy constitute valuable prolegomena.

Mark Vessey
University of British Columbia

Review Essay

BRITISH HISTORY: AN IRISH PERSPECTIVE

Elizabeth Ewan, *Townlife in Fourteenth-Century Scotland,* Edinburgh: Edinburgh University Press, 1990. Pp. ix, 201,
David Walker, *Medieval Wales,* Cambridge: Cambridge University Press, 1990. Cambridge Medieval Textbooks. Pp. x, 235
R. R. Davies, *Domination and Conquest The experience of Ireland, Scotland and Wales 1100–1300.* Cambridge: Cambridge University Press, 1990. Pp. xvii, 134, cloth.
Robin Frame, *The Political Development of the British Isles 1100–1400,* Oxford, New York: Oxford University Press, 1990. Pp. x, 256.

'The power of the Irish over the Britons was great, and they had divided Britain between them into estates; ... and the Irish lived as much east of the sea as they did in Ireland, and their dwellings and royal fortresses were made there. Hence is Dind Tradui, ... that is, the triple rampart of Crimthann, king of Ireland and Britain as far as the English channel... And they were in that control for a long time, even after the coming of St Patrick to Ireland.'
(Cormac's Glossary, ninth century)[1]

"British history," as presented by Professor Davies and Dr. Frame is offered as a complementary, rather than an alternative, approach to the national histories of England, Ireland, Scotland, and Wales in the Middle Ages. It seeks to explain the domination of the British Isles by the Anglo-Normans and their successor, the English state, from the beginning of the twelfth century. Its purpose is two-fold; first to encourage English historians "to repossess the districts of medieval Britain over and within which English kings, magnates and settlers claimed or exercised a measure of authority," and second to highlight comparisons and contrasts between the different parts of the British Isles.[2] While acknowledging that as an area of historical study the British Isles is "highly artificial" it is argued that" the wider perspective has the advantage that it refreshes those parts of the past that "national" history does not reach".[3]

One topic which might benefit from a "British" approach is urban history. The spread of towns throughout the British Isles was one obvious and important result of Norman domination of the region. Elizabeth Ewan's book on fourteenth-century Scottish towns is an important contribution to a subject which has not received the attention it deserves. The "ordinary people of fourteenth-century Scotland," as Dr. Ewan calls them, have rarely attracted the attention of historians preoccupied with the aristocracy, the church and, of course, the Scottish monarchy[4]

Ewan's book offers a good summary of the archaeological work done to date on Scottish towns and she provides an interesting picture of the social and economic structure of fourteenth-century burghs. Her own interest is in the community of the burgh, a segment of Scottish society for whom the fourteenth century was of special significance, witnessing, as it did, their "coming of age, their full participation in the community of the realm."[5]

Unlike their English and continental counterparts, most Scottish burghs were not walled. It was royal policy from the time of David I to encourage the growth of burghs as trading centers and, again in contrast to England, markets were restricted to burghs while their monopolies of trade and cloth manufacture were maintained long after they had disappeared south of the border. The church played an important part in the life of the burgh with most burghs forming single parishes, and Scottish towns saw little of the tension with the nobility and the church that marked English and continental equivalents. Nobles had little land in the town, although there was some intermarriage with burgess families, while townsmen who held of nobles or the church were more answerable to burghal authorities in Scotland than was the case elsewhere.[6]

Central to the development of fourteenth-century Scottish towns were the wars with England. Archaeological evidence refutes the notion that war led to a decline in Scottish industry at this time. Scottish pottery, for instance, replaced the English variety which was no longer available.[7] By the 1330s almost all Scottish trade was in Scottish hands and the dependence on foreign shipping was reduced. Trade was conducted on behalf of the aristocracy and Crown by the townsmen, leading Ewan to conclude that "as promoters of trade ... they played a major role in the development of Scotland's nationhood from the fourteenth century."[8] Burgesses rose in society through service to the Crown and their part in paying David II's ransom brought them recognition as the third estate in 1357, although they had been sending representatives to parliament since 1326. Like the rest of Scottish society their loyalties had been divided in the time of Edward I, but by the middle of the fourteenth century they exhibited, in Barrow's words, "burghal solidarity in the patriotic cause."[9]

Hidden in the middle of the book, unmentioned in the table of contents, is a much-needed map showing the distribution of burghs in Scotland before 1430. Unfortunately, ecclesiastical burghs are not distinguished on this map. The system of notation also leaves something to be desired. A list of abbreviations is needed. *The Scottish Medieval Town*, eds. M. Lynch, G. Stell and R. M. Spearman (Edinburgh, 1988), for instance, is abbreviated to *Scottish Town* without the reader being alerted.[10]

Given the emphasis Ewan places on the importance of the wars with England in shaping the development of Scottish burghs in the fourteenth century, it is regrettable that she has virtually nothing to say about Ireland's contribution to those wars and about trade with Ireland in general. Western Scottish burghs from Tarbert in the north to Whithorn in the south must have been dependent on trade with Ulster and the involvement of Robert I (Robert Bruce) with Ireland certainly included trade—even if, as in 1326, this did take the form of extortion.[11]

By the fourteenth century towns in Scotland and Ireland probably had little in common in terms of the political problems they faced. Ireland was a frontier country and the racial divide there between the "two nations" was most virulent and long-lasting in the towns, as their anti-Irish legislation proves.[12] In this regard the Irish experience was more akin to that of Wales, particularly in the towns founded there after the English conquest of 1282–83, than to that of Scotland.[13]

Ewan deliberately steers clear of the debate on burghal origins in Scotland, but nevertheless hopes that her book "may help to underline the fact that towns were not some strange new-fangled institutions introduced by the feudalising David I under Norman influence, but rather a form of settlement which fitted easily into, and complemented, the largely rural pattern of medieval Scotland."[14] This is questionable, to say the least. Does the development of towns in Scotland not reflect the desire of the Scottish monarchy to bring their kingdom more into line with the French feudal world represented by Anglo-Norman England to the south? While this is not the place to enter a similar debate about Irish town origins, it is incontrovertible that after 1170 they were introduced under Anglo-Norman influence. It was the nature of this influence which made the difference; in Ireland towns were established by conquering foreigners, in Scotland they were introduced by a native monarchy.[15]

A study of Scottish towns in the fourteenth century in a British context, therefore, highlights their uniqueness and lack of similarity with counterparts in England, Ireland, and Wales. This, however, does not render invalid the exercise of examining them in this context. Scotland often fits in uneasily with what Davies and Frame have to say about the British Isles in the Middle Ages and following lines of investigation such as urban history tends to reinforce this unease.[16] Nevertheless, the increasing importance of the burgh in the politics of fourteenth-century Scotland reflects the success there of Anglo-Norman feudal fashions, which reinforces Davies's and Frame's case for a wider view to be taken. British history must be broad enough to accomodate both comparisons and contrasts and Ewan's book provides plenty of both from an Irish perspective.

The absence of a comparative aspect is the most obvious flaw in David Walker's book on medieval Wales. The appearance of a short history of Wales in the Middle Ages is to be welcomed, but Walker's book is disappointingly narrow in its approach. Welsh literary culture and the structure of the Welsh economy, for instance, do not fall within the scope of this study. Instead the emphasis is placed on "the clash of race and culture which is so characteristic of Wales".[17] The result is a study of the Norman penetration of Wales from the end of the eleventh century and its conquest and settlement by the English from the late thirteenth to the early sixteenth centuries. Within these confines the book succeeds well enough, although maps could have been provided to help illustrate such points as the carving out of a marcher lordship in the early twelfth century by Gilbert Fitz Richard de Clare and the political allegiances of Welsh lordships during the Wars of the Roses.[18]

Walker's picture of medieval Wales would have benefited from a perspective which did not concentrate exclusively on relations with England. The notion of a "Celtic church" may no longer be fashionable, but recent work has shown the merits of comparing the churches of Wales and Ireland in the reform era of the eleventh and twelfth centuries.[19] Moreover, until the twelfth century at the earliest, north-west Wales was westward-looking and belonged to a political world encompassing the Isle of Man, the Norse-controlled isles of western Scotland, and Ireland.[20] It was to Ireland that Welsh princes fled in the eleventh and early twelfth centuries and a century later it was there also that sulking or treacherous Marcher barons such as William Marshal and William de Braose sought refuge. The rumored plan of Edward of Caernarfon, prince of Wales and king of England to escape across the Irish sea in 1327 brings a certain symmetry to the theme.[21]

The description of Muirchertach MacLochlainn as "king of Munster" would be more forgiveable were it not indicative of Walker's lack of awareness of Wales's connections with Ireland in general.[22] The intervention of Strongbow and the Geraldines in Ireland in the years after 1169 is treated only cursorily yet it was central to the politics of Wales at the time, being the product both of pressure from the resurgent Welsh under Rhys ap Gruffydd and Henry II's distrust of Marcher independence.[23] The author's interest in Gerald of Wales might have led him to consider in greater depth the reasons why his kinsmen, the Geraldines, became involved in Ireland.[24]

Walker aptly compares the imposition of English law in Wales in 1284 with the more comprehensive transmission of writs to Ireland in 1227, but an even more appropriate point of comparison might be the attitude of Edward I to the native laws of Wales, Ireland, and Scotland, all of which felt the force of his intolerance in the last quarter of the thirteenth century.[25] Again, the society of the Welsh March and March law, about which Walker says very little, offer obvious scope for comparison with Ireland.[26] Finally, the efforts of Robert and Edward Bruce to forge a "Celtic alliance" of Scots, Irish, and Welsh against the "Saxons" between 1315–18 surely deserve at least passing mention, particularly when the Welsh and Scots had shown themselves capable of alliance on previous occasions.[27] Walker's book, of course, is not intended to replace Professor Davies' histories of Wales and the Welsh March, but the latter has shown how an understanding of Irish history can be of benefit to the historian of medieval Wales, just as the Welsh perspective he has brought to medieval Irish history has greatly enlivened that subject.[28]

To say as much is to acknowledge one advantage of a broader British approach and Professor Davies's contribution to it. British history, however, is about more than comparing the experiences of Wales,

Ireland, Scotland, and England in the Middle Ages. As Dr Frame has said, "...comparisons by their very nature assume, and even reinforce, the solidity and separateness of whatever is being compared. As well as looking over the partition-walls, we need to do some thinking about the design of the building itself."[29]

In *Domination and Conquest,* Davies shows how Anglo-Norman domination of Britain was underpinned by historical myth, economic advantage, and a sense of cultural superiority which was closely linked to the intolerant reforming policies of the church.[30] Davies is particularly good when discussing the attitudes which shaped mens' outlook and his superb use of chronicle material is of exceptional value in this regard. Anglo-Norman power came to be felt in Britain thanks to the energy and acquisitiveness of the nobility and particularly the *juvenes*: the youger sons and illegitimate offspring of great lords, who had much to gain and little to lose. However, as Henry II and John demonstrated, there was no question of the nobility fully escaping royal control in the more remote regions of the British Isles in the late twelfth and early thirteenth centuries—and not much evidence that many of them wanted to in the first place.[31]

The middle of the thirteenth century saw a hardening of English attitudes towards native custom and variation in other parts of Britain which went hand in hand with the growth of bureaucracy around the king.[32] Edward I's reign saw English power in Britain at its most convincing, with the parliament of 1305—hearing as it did petitions from Wales, Ireland, Scotland as well as Gascony—representing the high-water mark of English control. Davies argues convincingly that while English domination of the British Isles did not require conquest, by the end of the thirteenth century "concepts of domination had given way to an ideology of unity, uniformity and conquest."[33]

The 1305 parliament is also central to Robin Frame's analysis of the politics of the British Isles from 1100 to 1400.[34] He and Davies cover much the same ground although differences of approach and interpretation do exist between them. Whereas Davies concentrates on the experience of Scotland, Wales, and Ireland, Frame integrates developments in England more explicitly in *The Political Development of the British Isles.* Indeed, not the least of the merits of his book is the insight it gives into developments in England such as the growth of the common law and administrative structures, the emergence of the political community, and the significance of parliament.[35] In extending his previous work on the "aristocratic nexus" throughout the British Isles in the thirteenth century and in his comparison of the various frontier regions of Britain, Frame has shown the value of the experiment on which he has embarked.[36]

The weak link in both Davies's and Frame's interpretation of medieval British history is Scotland. The phrase "of course Scotland was different ..." occurs in both books.[37] Scotland obviously conforms to the picture of the growth of feudal kingship and French culture in the British Isles.[38] It can also be accommodated in the story of English attempts to exercise lordship throughout Britain, particularly in the reign of Edward I [39] However, as Frame himself acknowledges, Scotland falls beyond the scope of what he has to say about the growth of political communities in the British Isles and, for all Davies's subtlety, English attitudes to the Scots kingdom after 1296 do not really bear comparison with the character of Anglo-Norman conquest in Wales and Ireland.[40] One suspects that the most critical comments about the validity of "British history" and the assumptions upon which it rests will come from Scottish historians.

From an Irish perspective much is explained when examined in a British context which would otherwise be distorted. To give one example, the idea that John as lord of Ireland and later king of England had any particular interest in Ireland—as might be surmised from the growth of royal power which took place there during his reign—is shown to be anachronistic when viewed as part of his efforts to exploit his position throughout his lands as a means of financing his proposed recapture of Normandy. His reign saw similar attempts to strengthen his authority in Wales and Scoland.[41]

It is, of course, possible to disagree with much of what Davies and Frame have to say about Ireland in the context of British history, and indeed they differ among themselves on important issues. How English power should be measured in the country is one topic on which they diverge. For Davies the limits of the diffusion of common law are a broad guide to the limits of the Anglo-Norman advance, while for Frame the Lordship of Ireland extended beyond the area of common law to include English lords in Ireland, such as the earls of Desmond, "who stood outside the conventional scheme of English administration" and who, in turn, were often able to "manage Gaelic leaders."[42] Was the Lordship of Ireland all-inclusive, then, since even Neill Mor O Neill, the most powerful and independent Gaelic lord of his day, could tell Richard II in 1394–5 that "I did not deny your lordship, for I have ever recognised your lordship"?[43] Might it not be argued with equal plausibility that Gaelic Ireland extended to any region controlled by the English where native chiefs grazed their cattle or to any part where a settler lord commissioned Irish bards to sing his praises?[44]

This last point brings us to a subject notable by its virtual absence from both Davies's and Frame's books: the "Gaelic revival." This may be defined as the self-conscious reassertion by the native Irish population of their political and cultural separateness from the English settlers with whom they shared the island. Why this central theme in medieval Irish history should be omitted from consideration is difficult to understand since, as Davies has pointed out elsewhere, such a reaction is "one of the best-known responses to colonial rule" of any native society.[45] In other words, it is a phenomenon that can be accommodated within a British context and, indeed, adds credibility to such an approach. Frame's apparant suspicion of the concept of a Gaelic revival may spring from his skepticism about the notion of Gaelicisation: the process by which the settlers became culturally assimilated with the native Irish.[46] The two concepts, however, are not the same. Simms has recently shown how the revival of historical studies in Gaelic Ireland from the middle of the fourteenth century was exclusive in character. The historians simply ignored the arrival of the English and their impact on Ireland, unlike the bardic poets who sought patronage from the newcomers. The important point here is that the settlers in turn encouraged the historians to include them in the Irish historical scheme as laid down in the great pseudo-historical compilation, *Lebor Gabala* (The Book of Invasions). It is at this stage that the Gaelic revival and Gaelicization meet and merge.[47]

Frame's concentration on "trans-regional landholding" may also lead him to dismiss too quickly the existence of an "Irish politics" in the thirteenth century. Indeed, he has elsewhere argued that "for the student of thirteenth century politics and lordship" the distinction between English and Irish history is "profoundly unnatural."[48] His view may be modified in time when more work is done on those early English settlers who held in Ireland only or who deliberately made Ireland the center of their activities while also holding elsewhere.[49] King John certainly had no hesitation in recognizing the existence of an Irish baronage when he sought their support in his dispute with the pope in 1212.[50] The conquest of Connacht of 1235 and the colonization which followed it were carried out by those who already had land in eastern and southern Ireland; it was a case of internal expansion.[51] The barons of Ireland demonstrated their solidarity and self interest beyond question when they advised Edward I against extending English law to the Irish in 1280.[52]

From the outset Ireland was a frontier and one does not have to be a disciple of Turner to accept that frontiers breed their own politics very quickly. Might we not say that Irish politics began with Maurice FitzGerald's assertion in 1170, as reported by Gerald of Wales, that "just as we are English as far as the Irish are concerned, likewise to the English we are Irish"?[53] The speech itself is no doubt apocryphal, but might it not reflect a genuine attitude among some of the earliest invaders? Frame remarks on the popularity of Gerald's work among the English in Ireland from the middle of the fourteenth century and one imagines that the folio containing this speech was particularly well thumbed.[54]

To say all this is not to detract from the merits of British history, but rather to reinforce Frame's point that it is a complementary approach rather than an alternative one to national history. To recognise as much may help to take some of the heat out of the current debate about whether Ireland has the right to a separate history at all after 1169.[55] It hardly seems either controversial or revelationary to suggest that some parts of Ireland's medieval past can best be understood in the context of the island itself while others must be placed in a broader context which naturally fixes most often on England but which takes into account the experiences of Scotland and Wales as well. It is a remarkable fact that no historian has yet written a history of medieval Ireland from the coming of the English to the middle of the fourteenth century which fully integrates the experiences of both native and newcomer.[56]

Finally, Ireland's place in medieval British history will not fully be understood until the views of the Irish about the British Isles are examined. That they had a view about this matter from as early as the ninth century is, I think, demonstrated by the quotation which begins this essay. In the matter of attitudes of cultural superiority the Irish had nothing to learn from the Anglo-Normans. *Scoti sumus non Galli,* was the memorable put down delivered to St. Malachy, the Irish church reformer and friend of St. Bernard, when he attempted to build a church in the French fashion at Bangor in 1140. Two and a half centuries later a Spanish visitor to the court of O'Neill remarked of the Irish that "they consider their own customs the best and most perfect in the world."[57]

The Irish were not only self-conscious, they were also aware of their position in a region, the British Isles, which was increasingly dominated by the English. This was particularly obvious in the reign of Edward I. In 1287 it was reported that "on account of the Welsh war the Irish are elated beyond their wont."[58] A sympathetic attitude to the Welsh is also shown in the annal entry for 1295:

> The king of England subdued the Welsh and brought many of them with him to Gascony to the war which was being waged between him and the king of France. That indeed was a pity, for the English cared not whether they (the Welsh) fell there or survived.[59]

An equally interesting attitude to the Scots is revealed by the same annals in the following year, 1296, when it reports

> A great hosting by the king of England and the nobles of England, Ireland and Wales, to Scotland, and the king of Scotland and Scotland itself were taken by them without opposition or strife. And that was a disappointment to the Gaedil [Irish], for the Scots had previously a very great reputation for prowess.[60]

This is a line of investigation which seems likely to complement rather than undermine what Davies and Frame have to say about the history of the British Isles in the Middle Ages.[61] It is simply to approach the same reality from a different angle. It may even transpire that those who will have the most questions to answer in the light of a broader British context are the historians of medieval England.

Brendan Smith
(Newman Scholar), Department of Medieval History
University College Dublin.

Notes

1. Quoted in D. O Corráin, "Prehistoric and Early Christian Ireland" in R. F. Foster (ed.), *The Oxford Illustrated History of Ireland* (Oxford, 1989), p. 6.

2. Frame, *Political Development of the British Isles*, p. 3; R.R. Davies, "In Praise of British History," in R. R. Davies (ed.) *The British Isles 1100–1500; Comparisons, Contrasts and Connections* (Edinburgh, 1988), p. 17.

3. Frame, *Political Development of the British Isles*, p 3; idem, "Aristocracies and the Political Configuration of the British Isles," in Davies (ed.), *The British Isles 1100–1500*, p. 150.

4. Ewan, *Townlife in Fourteenth Century Scotland*, p. vii.

5. Ibid., p. 4; E. Ewan, "The Community of the Burgh in the Fourteenth Century" in M. Lynch, G. Stell and R. M. Spearman (eds.), *The Scottish Medieval Town* , (Edinburgh, 1988).

6. Ewan, *Townlife in Fourteenth Century Scotland*, pp. 8, 11, 64-65, 94–113, 130.

7. Ibid., pp. 34–35.

8. Ibid., pp. 76–91

9. Ibid., pp. 120–5, 134, 147–154.

10. Ibid., p. 161.

11. Ibid., p. 69; T. O Neill, *Merchants and Mariners in Medieval Ireland*, (Dublin, 1987), pp. 23–24, 61–62, 119–21; R. Nicholson, "A Sequelto Edward Bruce's Invasion of Ireland" in *Scottish Historical Review*, xlii (1963) 30–40; R. Frame, *English Lordship in Ireland, 1318–1361.* (Oxford, 1982) pp. 138–42.

12. K. Walsh, *A Fourteenth Century Scholar and Primate, Richard Fitz Ralph in Oxford, Avignon and Armagh*, (Oxford, 1981), pp. 341–43; A. Cosgove, *Late Medieval Ireland, 1370–1541* (Dublin, 1981), pp. 76–77, 95; G. Mac Niocaill, a "Socio-Economic Problems of the Late Medieval Irish Town", in D. Harkness and M. O Dowd (eds.), *The Town in Ireland*, (Historical Studies, 13, Belfast, 1981), p. 17.

13. "Nowhere was the spirit of conquest and of racial superiority so vigorously and selfishly kept alive as in the Edwardian boroughs. It was little wonder that they were the most consistent target of Welsh resentment throughout the fourteenth century." R. R. Davies, *Conquest, Coexistence and Change: Wales 1063–1415* (Oxford, 1987), p. 373. For a comparison of the problems of Scottish and Irish towns in the later middle ages see K. Nicholls, "Gaelic Society and Economy in the High Middle Ages" in A. Cosgrove (ed.) *A New History of Ireland. II, Medieval Ireland 1169–1534* (Oxford, 1987), p. 420.

14. Ewan, *Townlife in Fourteenth Century Scotland*, p. 1.

15. The best discussion of medieval Irish towns remains G. Mac Niocaill, *Na Buirgéisí, 12–15 aois* (1 vol. in 2, Dublin, 1964). Part 1 consists of relevant Latin charters while part 2, which analyses the social structure of the towns, is written in Irish without an English translation. *V* also the work of Mac Niocaill cited above, n. 12.

16. *V* below p. 167.

17. Walker, *Medieval Wales*, p ix.

18. Ibid., pp. 38–39, 180–85.

19. H. Pryce, "Church and Society in Wales, 1150–1250. An Irish Perspective," in Davies (ed.), *The British Isles, 1100–1500*, pp. 27–47.

20. Davies, *Conquest, Coexistence and Change*, pp. 9–11; A. Candon, "Muirchertach Ua

Briain, Politics, and Naval Activity in the Irish Sea, 1075 to 1119" in G. Mac Niocaill and P. Wallace (eds.), *Keimelia, Studies in Medieval Archaeology and History in Memory of Tom Delaney*, (Galway, 1988), pp. 397–415.

21. M. T. Flanagan, *Irish Society, Anglo-Norman Settlers, Angevin Kingship* (Oxford, 1989), pp. 61–69; F. X. Martin, "John, lord of Ireland, 1185–1216" in Cosgrove (ed.), *New History of Ireland*, pp. 138–52; Frame, *English Lordship in Ireland*, pp. 138–40.

22. Walker, *Medieval Wales*, p. 49. Mac Lochlainn was king of the North (also styled king of Ailech) from 1136 to 1143 and from 1145 to 1166. D. O Corráin, *Ireland Before the Normans* (Dublin, 1972), pp. 150–74.

23. Walker, *Medieval Wales*, pp. 49–50. Walker argues that relations between Henry II and Rhy sap Gruffydd, king of Deheubarth, improved in the late 1160s after Strongbow became involved in Ireland. This is in accord with the case put forward by Flanagan in *Irish Society*, pp. 161–64. Frame, on the other hand, has argued that it was the agreement between Henry and Rhys which encouraged Strongbow and other Marchers to go to Ireland in the first place. R. Frame, *Colonial Ireland 1169–1369*, (Dublin, 1981), pp. 6–7.

24. Walker, *Medieval Wales*, pp. 74–80.

25. Ibid., pp. 141–42; P. Brand "Ireland and the literature of the early common law" in *The Irish Jurist, new series*, 16 (1981), pp. 95–113; R. R. Davies," "Lordship or Colony?" in J. F. Lydon (ed.), *The English in Medieval Ireland*, (Dublin, 1984), pp. 156–57.

26. R. R. Davies, "Frontier Arrangements in Fragmented Societies: Ireland and Wales", in R. Bartlett and A. MacKay(eds.), *Medieval Frontier Societies*, (Oxford, 1989) pp. 77–100, idem, " The Law of the March," *Welsh History Review*, 5, (1970–71), pp. 1–30; G. Mac Niocaill, "The Interaction of Laws," in Lydon (ed.), *The English in Medieval Ireland*, pp. 105–17.

27. Walker, *Medieval Wales*, p. 113; S. Duffy, "The Bruce Brothers and the Irish Sea World" in *Cambridge Medieval Celtic Studies*, 21 (1991), pp. 55–86

28. Davies, *Conquest, Coexistence and Change*, idem, *Lordship and Society in the March of Wales 1282–1400* (Oxford, 1978). *V* also the works by Davies cited above.

29. Frame, "Aristocracies and the Political Configuration of the British Isles," p. 154.

30. Davies, *Domination and Conquest*, pp. 1–24.

31. Ibid., pp. 32–34, 75–82.

32. Ibid., pp. 94–96, 103–108; K. Nicholls, "Anglo-French Ireland and After," *Peritia; Journal of the Medieval Academy of Ireland*, I (1982), p. 371.

33. Davies, *Domination and Conquest*, pp. 127–28.

34. Frame, *Political Development of the British Isles*, p. 142.

35. Ibid., pp. 74 –85, 170–79.

36. Ibid., pp. 50–71, 198–224; idem, "Aristocracies and the Political Configuration of the British Isles," pp. 142–59; B. Smith, "The Concept of the March in Medieval Ireland: The Case of Uriel" in *Proceedings of the Royal Irish Academy* 88, C, (1988) pp. 257–69.

37. Davies, *Domination and Conquest*, pp. x, 8, 39, 47; Frame, *Political Development of the British Isles*, p. 58.

38. Ibid., pp. 39–44; Davies, *Domination and Conquest*, pp. 19–20.

39. Ibid., pp. 75–76, 81, 100–106; Frame, *Political Development of the British Isles*, pp. 160–68.

40. Ibid., pp. 187–97; Davies, *Domination and Conquest*, pp. 47–65.

41. Ibid., pp. 79–82; Frame, *Political Development of the British Isles*, pp. 60–3.

42. R. R. Davies "Introduction" in idem (ed.), *The British Isles, 1100–1500*, p. 6; Frame,

Political Development of the British Isles, p. 206.

43. Quoted in Davies, "Lordship or Colony?," p. 143.

44. K. Simms, "Nomadry in medieval Ireland: The Origins of the Creaght or *Caoraigheacht,"* in *Peritia v* (1986), 379–91; idem, "Bards and Barons: The Anglo-Irish Aristocracy and the Native Culture," in Bartlett and MacKay(eds.), *Medieval Frontier Societies,* pp. 177–97.

45. The standard exposition of the theme remains E. Mac Neill's chapter "The Irish Rally" in his book *Phases of Irish History* (Dublin, 1919, reprint 1968), pp. 323–56; Davies, "Lordship or Colony?" p. 158 Davies is mistaken in his belief that for the Irish an awareness of national identity emerged only when they became subject to the English. D. O Corráin, Nationality and kingship in pre-Norman Ireland" in *Historical Studies.* XI. T. W. Moody (ed) *Nationality and the Pursuit of National Independence* (1978), 1–35.

46. The most he will allow is "the tendency of the aristocracy to acquire provincial colourings" in the outlying parts of the British Isles, *Political Development of the British Isles,* pp. 51–52; idem, "Power and Society in the Lordship of Ireland, 1272–1377," *Past and Present,* 76 (1977), 3–33; K. Nicholls, *Gaelic and Gaelicised Ireland in the Middle Ages,* (Dublin, 1972), pp. 3–123; idem, "Gaelic Society and Economy in the High Middle Ages," pp. 421–24; B. Smith, "The Medieval Border: Anglo-Irish and Gaelic Irish in Late Thirteenth and Early Fourteenth Century Uriel" in R. Gillespie and H. O Sullivan (eds.). *The Borderlands: Essays on the History of the Ulster-Leinster Border.* (Belfast, 1989), pp. 41–54.

47. Simms, "Bards and Barons," pp. 177–97; B. Cunningham, 'Seventeenth Century Interpretations of the Past: The case of Geoffrey Keating' in Irish Keating'in *Irish Historical Studies,* 25 (1986–7) pp. 116–28; R. Mark Scowcroft, "Leabhar Gabhala, part. 2, the growth of the tradition" in *Eriu: Foùnded as the Journal of the School of Irish Learning,* 39 (1988) 1–66.

48. Frame, *Political Development of the British Isles,* pp. 53–60; idem, "Ireland and the Barons' War" in P. R. Coss and S. D. Lloyd (eds.), *Thirteenth Century England,* 1(Woodbridge, 1986), p. 167.

49. R. Bartlett, "Colonial Aristocracies of the High Middle Ages," in Bartlett and MacKay (eds.) *Medieval Frontier Societies,* pp. 23–48; J. R. S. Phillips, "The Anglo-Norman Nobility" in Lydon (ed.) *The English in Medieval Ireland,* pp. 105–18.

50. A. J. Otway-Ruthven, *A History of Medieval Ireland,* (London and New York, 1980), p. 85.

51. Frame, *Colonial Ireland,* pp. 40–41; J. F. Lydon, "The Expansion and Consolidation of the Conquest," in Cosgrove (ed.), *New History of Ireland,* pp. 164–66.

52. A Gwynn, "Edward I and the proposed purchase of English law for the Irish, c. 1276–80" in *Transactions of the Royal Historical Society,* 5th ser., 10 (1960), p 111–27; A. J. Otway-Ruthven," The Native Irish and English Law in Medieval Ireland" in *Irish Historical Studies,* 7 (1950–51), 1–16; J. F. Lydon, "Lordship and Crown: Llywelyn of Wales and O Connor of Connacht" in Davies (ed.), *The British Isles, 1100–1500,* pp. 51–52.

53. Quoted in J. F. Lydon, "The Middle Nation" in idem (ed.), *The English in Medieval Ireland,* p.2; A. Cosgrove, "Hiberniores ipsis Hibernis" in A. Cosgrove and D. Mc Cartney (eds.), *Studies in Irish History Presented to R. Dudley Edwards,* (Dublin, 1979), pp. 1–14.

54. Frame, *Political Development of the British Isles,* pp. 179–87.

55. S. Ellis, "Nationalist Historiography and the English and Gaelic Worlds in the Later Middle Ages" in *Irish Historical Studies*, 25 (1986–87), pp. 1–18; B. Bradshaw, "Nationalism and Historical Scholarship in Modern Ireland" in *Irish Historical Studies*, 26 (1988–89), 329–51; A. Cosgrove, "The Writing of Irish Medieval History" in *Irish Historical Studies*, 27 (1990–91). S. Ellis; "Historiographical Debate: Representations of the Past in Ireland: Whose Past and Whose Present?" in *Irish Historical Studies*, 27 (1990–91), 289–309.

56. Cosgrove's, *Late Medieval Ireland* succeeds in this respect for the later medieval period.

57. Martin, "John, Lord of Ireland," p. 155; Cosgrove, *Late Medieval Ireland*, p. 98.

58. Duffy, "The Bruce Brothers," p. 80

59. Ibid., p. 81.

60. Ibid., pp. 81–82.

61. Davies, "Introduction" in idem, *The British Isles, 1100–1500*, pp. 6–7; Frame, *Political Development of the British Isles*, pp. 140–41.

BOOK REVIEWS

Book Reviews

Graeme Clark, ed., with Brian Croke. Alanna Emmett Nobbs, Raoul Mortley, *Reading the Past in Late Antiquity*. Canberra, Australia: Australian National University Press, 1990. Pp. xv, 370.

The history of late antiquity used to be left largely to clergymen and lawyers. From the end of the nineteenth century, however, it began to attract the attention of historians of antiquity and the Middle Ages. The names of J. B. Bury, Otto Seeck, and Ernst Stein spring to mind, but even they were often haunted by a Gibbonian sense of decline. It is really only since the Second World War that the period from the fourth to the seventh century has been perceived no longer as a kind of degenerate and inglorious appendix to classical Greece and Rome, but rather as a crucial epoch in the formation of European and Near Eastern society, with its own peculiar characteristics and its own logic of development. The last thirty years have seen an unprecedented out-pouring of studies of various aspects of late antiquity, sometimes paint-ed with the broadest of brushes, sometimes concentrating in minutest detail on a single topic, a single region, or a single source. To name names is inevitably invidious among so many distinguished scholars of so many nationalities. But, if one may confine oneself to works in English, A. H. M. Jones's *The Later Roman Empire* (1964) and Peter Brown's *The World of Late Antiquity* (1971) were each in its own way path-breaking studies.

One aspect of the new—or renewed—interest in late antiquity which has recently come to the fore is how men and women in this epoch of change perceived, interpreted, and made use of their own past, real or imagined. This has been the subject of several conferences, the proceedings of which have been published as books. Australian scholars have been especially active in this domain. Nineteen eighty-three saw the appearance of *History and Historians in Late Antiquity*

(Pergamon Press, 1983), edited by Brian Croke and Alanna Emmett, and embodying contributions to a conference held at Macquarie University, Sydney, two years earlier. A similar conference held at the Humanities Research Centre in the Australian National University in 1988 provided the material for *Reading the Past in Late Antiquity* (Canberra, ANU Press, 1990), edited by Graeme Clarke, the Director of the Centre, with the assistance of an editorial team which included among its members Brian Croke and Alanna Emmett Nobbs.

The contributions not unexpectedly vary in range and depth. They vary also in how they choose to understand the concept of the past. Philip Rousseau's "Basil of Caesarea: Choosing a Past" (pp. 37–58) is concerned with the way in which a man edits his own past in order to impose a rationally satisfying structure on his life. In Basil's case the structure had also to be spiritually satisfactory. The most noteworthy example of this procedure which comes to mind is Augustine's *Confessions.* Basil was no Augustine, and he had perhaps a less complicated past. Yet this study of one of the Cappadocian Fathers tidying up his own life brings out many of the problems facing deeply religious men in an age of conflict and change. C. E. V. Nixon's "The Use of the Past by the Gallic Panegyrists" (pp. 1–36) looks at a different kind of problem—when did the past become exemplary and "safe"?—by studying the practice of the Latin panegyrists from Gaul. What emerges is that mention of the recent past—the events of the speaker's and his hearers' own lifetime—is on the whole avoided except in straightforward narrative, while anything more than two or three generations ago is free from dangerous implications and can be safely used to illuminate the present.

Averil Cameron's "Models of the Past in the Late Sixth Century: The Life of the Patriarch Eutychius" (pp. 205–24) is a partial preview of her forthcoming study of this neglected sixth-century text. It offers a perceptive and suggestive examination of the way in which persuasive citations from the Cappadocian Fathers were becoming, already in the late sixth century, an essential method of justifying the various positions adopted by a prominent churchman. As time went on, Cameron observes, the number of texts quoted becomes smaller and smaller. *Mutatis mutandis,* it reminds us of the way the more superficial Marxists of our own day used quotations torn from their context as a proof of orthodoxy. In the case of Eutychius these quotations carry with them a structure of typological comparisons, in particular with the story of Moses, which recurs through the centuries in panegyrics on Byzantine patriarchs.

Two of the contributions are concerned with the *Chronicle* of John Malalas, to the study of which Australian scholars have recently made notable contributions. Elizabeth Jeffreys (pp. 121–46) examines the series of dates from Adam in the reconstructed Malalas, from which she infers an interest in millennial calculations, based on the equation of millennia since the creation with the six days of creation. This kind of calculation, which goes back to Sextus Julius Africanus, had gone out of fashion by the sixth century. Jeffreys suggest that Malalas' purpose in reviving it is to demonstrate that the fateful year 6000 had passed uneventfully, and that his own age was well into the "safe" seventh millennium. Against whom was Malalas arguing? Jeffreys suggests that some obscure Syrian sects with whom Malalas was familiar may have believed that the end of the sixth millennium was at hand. There is no surviving evidence for such a sect. But Malalas' occasional and seemingly random use of dates from Adam clearly indicates some kind of millenialist interest either on the part of the chronicler or of his source. Roger Scott in "Malalas' View of the Classical Past" (pp. 147–64) observes that the chronicler perceived the mythological past exclusively in terms of his own late antique present, which is perhaps scarcely surprising, but furthermore that he virtually omits both classical Greece and the Roman Republic from his narrative. His perception of the past was of a series of empires, culminating in the Roman Empire. This kind of historical thinking has Hellenistic and perhaps also Judaic roots, and even found its way into Latin historiography via Pompeius Trogus-Justin. Scott will no doubt develop his arguments more fully in the forthcoming *Studies on Malalas*.

Brian Croke in "City Chronicles of Late Antiquity" (pp. 165–204) argues that the continuing existence of official city chronicles like the *Annales maximi* and the *Acta urbis*, not only in Rome but also in Constantinople and elsewhere, is a necessary hypothesis to explain the kind of events and anniversaries recorded by fourth-century historians. His argument is complex and rather slow in getting under way, but it is thoughtful and challenging. What he is trying to do is to put flesh on the dry bones of nineteenth-century *Quellenforschung*.

T. D. Barnes in "Literary Convention, Nostalgia and Reality in Ammianus Marcellinus" (pp. 59–92) convincingly rejects the concept of Ammianus as a neutral and dispassionate historian, a kind of rationalist recording angel in an age of passionate partiality. He sees throughout Ammianus' work a dominating nostalgia for a lost, and partly imaginary, past. It is this which makes him choose to overlook the increasingly political role of the church among other things. This analysis rejects the view that was canonical from Gibbon to E. A. Thompson, and puts Ammianus squarely in the camp of the militant pagans. This penetrating essay, one of the best in the collection, was evidently written before the appearance of John Matthews's massive and magisterial book on Ammianus. One wonders whether it would have led Barnes to modify his conclusions. I suspect not.

Space does not permit more than a mention of the remaining contributions to this interesting book. They are Kathleen Adshead's "Procopius' Poliorcetica: Continuities and Discontinuities" (pp. 93–120); R. Mortley's "The Hellenistic Foundations of Ecclesiastical Historiography" (pp. 225–50); Alanna Emmett Nobbs's "Philostorgius' View of the Past" (pp. 251–64); Pauline Allen's "The Use of Heretics and Heresies in the Greek Church Historians: Studies in Socrates and Theodoret" (pp. 265–90); G. W. Trompf's "Augustine's Historical Theodicy: The Logic of Retribution in the De Civitate Dei" (pp. 291–322); Peter Brennan's "Military Images in Hagiography" (pp. 323–46); and Cynthis Stallman's "The Past in Hagiographic Texts: S. Marcian of Syracuse" (pp. 347–66).

All those concerned with the world of late antiquity will find in this book something to interest them, occasionally something to provoke them, and always something which points to further research to be done.

Robert Browning
London

Alan Harvey, *Economic Expansion in the Byzantine Empire, 900–1200*. Cambridge and New York: Cambridge University Press, 1989. Pp. xx, 298.

In these days, when economic history is in something of a decline, and its practitioners almost apologetic, it is rather refreshing to see a book which approaches the subject with conviction and with firm ideas about what constitutes a medieval economy. The book is primarily concerned with the rural economy, studying its expansion in close connection with the development of social relations, that is, with the growth of what the author calls "feudalism." His concept of this term owes a good deal to Marxist historiography, which has seen it as describing not a political system but rather a mode of production, describing by this term what is also known as the seigneurial régime (p. 7). Much recent non-Marxist historiography has eschewed the use of the word "feudalism," not only for Byzantium but also for Western Europe, and some scholars may find the concept outdated. To this reviewer, terms in themselves seem less important than the content assigned to them, and Harvey's definition of "feudalism" as "the exploitative relationship between landowners and dependent peasants" does carry a meaning.

The main arguments of the book are as follows. The Byzantine economy was primarily rural, and its "social formation consisted over-whelmingly of peasant producers" (p. 1). The household unit, the basis of production, was not capable of fuelling economic expansion. Furthermore, there were no great technological developments in Byzantium. Therefore, increased production could only come about through an increase of the area under cultivation (p. 47). A demographic expansion, starting, it would seem, in the tenth century, and continuing for the next two centuries, provided the impetus. It went hand in hand with the expansion of large estates, and with the reduction of the rural population to the status of dependent peasant. An intensification of exploitation came in the early twelfth century, through the fiscal reforms of Alexius I. These developments increased the revenues of both the state and the great landlords, but at a different rate. The state, by granting fiscal privileges to the aristocracy, laid the foundations for the economic power of the aristocracy, thus, in the long run, undermining its own power. The growth of "feudal relations," according to this argument, would be a cooperative enterprise between the state and the great landlords, although the author himself does not express the argument in this way. In the same period, the towns experienced a resurgence, although, according to Harvey, they remained primarily centers of consumption rather than production.

There are, the author points out, two major points of interpretation where he differs from some earlier scholars. One is his insistence that the Byzantine economy was expanding throughout the twelfth century, whereas other historians have considered that time a period of stagnation. It should be noted, however, that this theory is not entirely novel, since Michael Hendy and Alexander Kazhdan, among others, have also regarded the twelfth century as one of expansion. As far as demography and the rural economy goes, the argument has also been made by Jacques Lefort. The second important point is the idea that increasing "feudalization" was a positive rather than a negative development in economic terms, since the great landlords could stimulate production both through land-clearance and through their own increased demand.

The argumentation rests on a considerable amount of research. The author has analyzed carefully the often elusive evidence, has made an effort to differentiate between regional developments (primarily between the European provinces and Asia Minor), and is sometimes sensitive to the fact that economic expansion is not a simultaneous and all-embracing process, as, for example, when he finds signs of both expansion and contraction in the same area (p. 61). His main conclusions regarding demographic growth and its effects on the economic and social development of the countryside seem to this reviewer persuasive.

There are, of course, some points with which one may take issue. Chapter 1 ("The Early Medieval Period"), where the argumentation seems heavily dependent on preconceptions, is somewhat weak. This period (seventh through ninth centuries) is said to be one of transition, in which the origins of Byzantine "feudalism" may be traced (p. 14). However, it is nowhere made clear in what this transition lies, unless it be simple chronology, surely not an interesting analytical category. The author himself subsequently says that the first indications of "feudal social relations" appear in the early ninth century (p. 33). It is also stated that the economic stratification of the peasantry, which may be perceived in these early centuries, later led to the expansion of the large estate (p. 16), an assertion which is neither proven nor sustained. Some statements are baffling: thus, it is hard to see how the Slavic origins or otherwise of the widow Danelis can have affected her economic activities (p. 32). Chapter 3 ("Taxation and Monetary Circulation") makes good use of archaeological finds to argue for increased monetary circulation in the eleventh and twelfth centuries. On the other hand, it is much more difficult to prove the statement that the peasantry suffered from a shortage of cash (pp. 116–18), and so the author draws upon examples ranging from the tenth to the fourteenth centuries. A similar, and dangerous, use of observations from different historical periods (the Roman period and the early nineteenth century) in order to describe developments of the eleventh–twelfth centuries appears in the discussion of farming (pp. 142 ff). Finally, the extent of the reduction of the peasantry to a status of dependency during the period in question is exaggerated.

The book deals primarily with the rural economy, and this is what it should be judged on. The discussion of trade and manufacturing is inadequate. The author does not consider commercial activity to have been important, at least until the time the Italian merchants acquired a powerful presence in Constantinople. However, the role of trade in the Byzantine economy before the twelfth century has not yet been adequately studied; that book remains to be written. Similarly, the argument that cities were primarily centers of consumption rather than production is somewhat undermined by the fact that most of the cities the author discusses had manufacturing activity that was sometimes very considerable; were they exceptions, as the author argues, or should the original statement be revised?

In his conclusion, the author states that the pattern of economic development in the Byzantine Empire was much closer to that of western Europe than is usually assumed (p. 242). The point is reinforced, somewhat startlingly, when he uses Georges Duby's discussion of the phases of expansion and tries to apply it to Byzantium. Other scholars, too, have recently seen Byzantium as having a development *grosso modo* similar to that of western Europe. While this trend of thought is appropriate, and productive, it holds an inherent danger. Western medievalists, fortunate in having a much greater volume of surviving evidence, have produced interpretations of high explanatory value; however, these are not entirely valid for all western societies, nor are they entirely valid for Byzantium. The specificities of this society—the role of the state, of the village community, the particularities of production, must be kept in mind. This book is most useful and interesting for its analysis of the Byzantine data; the degree of similarity between this economy and western European ones is a subject which invites further elaboration.

Angeliki E. Laiou
Dumbarton Oaks

Seth Lerer, *Literacy and Power in Anglo-Saxon Literature.* Lincoln: University of Nebraska Press, 1991. pp. xii + 268 pp.

Medievalists are beginning to move with the times: the "resistance to theory" is wearing thin; more and more modern scholars of the Middle Ages are turning to Derrida, Foucault, or de Man for guidance in their studies. And those who are mystified by much of the post-modern deconstructionist jargon in turn look hopefully to those who have mastered the arcanum, and having mastered it, make their researches available in the common language of medievalists. Lerer's book is timely and, at least by some, the present reviewer included, eagerly awaited.

Lerer's five chapters carefully examine the changing concept of literacy during the Old English period; specifically, Lerer focusses on Bede's story of Imma *(Historia Ecclesiastica* 4, 22), Asser's *Life of King Alfred,* the riddles of the Exeter book, *Daniel,* and *Beowulf.* In the first chapter Lerer opposes the forces of pagan runes to Christian literacy and argues that Bede wishes to show the superior power of Christian literacy as exhibited, for example, in the liturgy; in the second, he demonstrates how Asser portrays Alfred's gradual literary maturing until at the end of the biography Alfred appears as an authority no longer relying on the scholars around him; in the third, he offers an interesting comparison of the Exeter book with Cambridge University Library manuscript Gg.5.35, both of which are collections of very disparate work, one in Old English, the other in Latin. Here, in the third chapter, he concentrates primarily on riddles and their glosses and considers them a "dialogue between the student and the the teacher ... on the folio." In chapter four, he concentrates on the *baswe bocstafas* in which the "mene, mene, tekel" was written, and moves from there to the "textuality of God's word." The last chapter presents Hrothgar "reading" the hilt which Beowulf has brought back from Grendel's mere, a reading which is opposed to the orality of much of the rest of the poem. This chapter also draws conclusions from the differences between the poet's narration of Beowulf's fight with Grendel and Beowulf's recounting of the same event to Hygelac.

This brief summary must necessarily omit many of the learned asides to other texts which Lerer introduces, and it can provide only a very rough sketch of the often highly sophisticated and detailed arguments. There can be no doubt that this book heightens one's awareness and appreciation of scenes of reading in the Old English poems studied. Even if one does not agree with Lerer's conclusions, he nonetheless forces one to foreground scenes that had hitherto been marginal, or to regard them in a new critical light.

If the above summary says little about "power," which, according to the title, should be a major part of the discussion, it is primarily because Lerer himself pays less attention to this subject than to "literacy." "Power" features most prominently in the first chapter, where runic power is contrasted to the power of Christian literacy, and in the second, where Alfred's political power increases in proportion to his abilities of mastering literature and literacy. It re-surfaces in chapter four, where Daniel's ability to "read" God's signs gives him "power," though Lerer does not clarify whether Daniel's "power" is over more than just God's signs. The third and fifth chapters have little to say about "power," except in the very widest sense of the word. In chapter three, for instance, Lerer claims that "Riddle 42 [of the Exeter Book] exemplifies the power of the written text to name and codify the range of living and imagined things" (p. 125). Oral speech, too, has this power; but what"power" is it to be able merely to "name and codify" rather than manipulate and control? The book clearly does not intend to be a Marxist tract attempting to demonstrate the means by which the literate gained and maintained power over the illiterate masses, but in moving "power" away from the political and social scene and almost completely into the world of the book, Lerer weakens the word. A somewhat less misleading title might have been "The Power of Literacy" rather than "Literacy and Power."

Lerer tends to overestimate the power of literacy especially in relation to that of speech. On page 102, he asks rhetorically: "Where could, say, the one-eyed seller of garlic and the sun and moon meet, save on the page of their transcription?" They could just as easily meet in speech; there is nothing inherently "literary" about riddles or catalogues. Both exist in ordinary speech as well, and therefore speech, like writing, can "enclose" and "unify" elements that are separate and unlikely to meet in Nature. Since deconstruction has taught us to examine the metaphors used by speakers and writers to determine their hidden biases, Lerer would have done well to examine some of the speech metaphors that consistently appear in connection with books and literacy because they show that the separation between the two is very difficult to maintain (Derrida's *Of Grammatology* notwithstanding). "Glosses," for instance, are identified as essentially literate responses to a literary work (p. 108), but the term "gloss" derives from Greek and literally means "tongue." The Conclusion of Lerer's book is entitled "Ðes ðe writ seggeð," where the emphasis seems to be once again on the oral performance of the book. Christianity itself, which Lerer seems to identify as a basically literate system (in opposition to Derrida, who claims that it is "logocentric"), takes the "word" of God, who is himself the "Logos," writes it down in the archetypal book, that is, the "Bible," and then expounds on it in "sermons", which in turn are sometimes written down. The border between literacy and orality is a fluid, not a fixed one, and hence such rhetorical questions as "where could, say, a one-eyed seller of garlic and the sun and moon meet, save on the page of their transcription?" point to oversimplification of highly complex material.

In his search for scenes of self-conscious reading, Lerer sometimes ignores the text in front of him. He quotes, for instance, the closing lines of Aldhelm's *De Creatura:*

Auscultate mei credentes famina uerbi,
Pandere quae poterit gnarus uix ore magister
Et tamen infitians non retur friuola lector!
Sciscitor inflatos, fungar quo nomine, sophos

and proceeds: "That the *magister* will be scarcely able to explain these words orally (*ore*) implies, I think ... that the engagement with these words is to be done in writing instead of speech" (p. 107). He then demonstrates that the glossator of CUL Gg. 5. 35 has done exactly that by providing cryptographic solutions to the riddles within *De Creatura.* The problem is that CUL Gg.5.35 has a different reading at this point which completely overturns Lerer's premise. The line *pandere quae poterit gnarus* continues with *uxore magister,* and not, as in the critical edition, with *uix ore magister.* Gg.5.35 therefore does not contain a challenge to the reader to engage with Aldhelm's words "in writing instead of speech." Of course the reading in Gg.5.35 is corrupt and incorrect, but the very fact that *uxore* has not been emended to *uix ore* indicates that the "engagement ... in writing" has not taken place. Similarly, Lerer sometimes forces the text into saying what he wants it to say. On page 109 he quotes a marginal gloss from Gg. 5.35 as follows:

Hic co*n*uertit se poeta ad lectores sup[erbos] *et* allo*qui*tur eos. ut dicam [...] singularu*m* creaturar[um] *et* si n*on* potueri[nt] [di]cta[re] eu*m* falsa aut uana dicere arbitrabuntur.

He translates: "Here the poet turns to the proud readers and addresses them: 'So that I may speak ... of individual creatures' and if they (i.e., the readers) were not able to put them into writing, then they will think that he (i.e., the poet) talks nonsense." I think it highly questionable whether "dictare" can be translated as "put into writing," since the root of the word stresses the oral rather than the literary meaning. In addition, the word *dictare* is entirely a product of Lerer's emendation: he emends to find a word suitable for his meaning, and even then he has to twist the translation of the word, and yet this emended word whose translation has to be twisted becomes a main witness for Lerer's contention that the glossator understands Aldhelm's invitation to respond "in writing." (Lerer's *dicam* should be *dicant* according to my photocopy of the manuscript.)

Lerer's tendency to fit the text he examines into his theory unfortunately often undermines his otherwise intelligent insights. To give additional examples: Lerer discusses Bede's account of Imma, whose captors were baffled by the fact that they could not bind him with fetters; they suspected that magic runes freed him, but in reality the fetters were loosened every time mass was read for him. Lerer summarizes: "Bede's vagueness on the magic ... is not the product of a bad memory but an act of literary suppression" (pp. 38–39). Bede supposedly suppresses the text of the magic runes, despite the fact that there were no runes on Imma. What is being suppressed? How could Bede quote some magic runes only to add that such could *not* be found on Imma? On page 63 Lerer speaks about the scene in which the young Alfred is attracted by the beautiful initial of a book full of *carmina Saxonica* and memorizes them in order to obtain the book. Lerer analyzes: "Alfred's mother's book of English poems ... comes to stand as the engagement of the future king with a tradition of literature ... in his mother tongue. This inheritance of vernacular learning will contrast ... with the teachings of the Scriptures which the king ... will learn to translate under Asser's tutelage." Asser does not mention the content of the *carmina Saxonica;* if, as is quite possible, they were poems of the Caedmonian style such as *Genesis,* or if they were truly *Saxonica,* for example an early copy of the Old Saxon *Heliand,* then the contrast between "vernacular learning" and "the teachings of the Scriptures" collapses because the Scriptures can be taught in the vernacular. On page 155 Lerer claims that Aelfric in his homily *De Populo Israhel* implies that "the word of God itself is to be more than simply heard: ... God's word is to be *read.*" I agree that God's word "is to be more than simply heard"; it is to be obeyed as well. But I cannot agree that Aelfric would even implicitly condemn the large masses of illiterate Anglo-Saxons for their inability to read God's word. Aelfric, more than Lerer, would be aware of the large number of good Anglo-Saxon Christians who had never learned to read, and who yet fully deserved to enter into Heaven. On page 178 Lerer states that Grendel "cannot be an audience for literature," but lines 87b–88a in *Beowulf* read: *dream gehyrde hludne in healle.* If he is not an audience for literature, what is he? Lerer makes much of Grendel's "muteness" (e.g., p. 175); but if Grendel is mute, what form does the spell take which he puts on weapons (1. 804 in *Beowulf*) and is the "song" he sings in lines 786–87 really as wordless as is convenient for Lerer's theory? Maybe he speaks a language the Danes do not understand? Page 167 categorically states that "the verb *writan* appears only here [i.e., 1. 1688] in *Beowulf,*" ignoring that the compound *forwritan* appears in line 2705. For some curious reason Lerer completely neglects to mention the occurrences in lines 979, 2574, and 106 of the word *scrifan* or a compound thereof, even though this "writing" word would seem to be essential to his argument. On page 171 Lerer considers lines 1687 and forward of *Beowulf* "the biblically flavored accounts of a war in heaven." The flood that killed the giants did not inundate heaven but the earth. These, and unfortunately quite a few other misreadings or superficial readings, suggest that Lerer was more preoccupied with the theory he wished to apply than with the texts to which he was applying it.

Lerer calls his book a "preliminary study." It is, but in more ways than he suggests: he considers it preliminary because it intends to provoke future work on scenes of reading and writing in Anglo-Saxon literature, because it does not include all the Anglo-Saxon texts relevant to his topic, and because it does not make any claims "for a historical development of Anglo-Saxon literacy." Regrettably, it is also preliminary in that quite a number of passages need to be read more carefully than Lerer has done. Doubtless it will fulfill its ambition of provoking future work, and it will be a useful guide in the generally uncharted regions of applying theory to Anglo-Saxon literature: useful in what to examine and how to examine it, but also useful in what to avoid.

Gernot Wieland
University of British Columbia

Joseph Shatzmiller, *Shylock Reconsidered: Jews, Moneylending, and Medieval Society*. Berkeley and Oxford, UK.: University of California Press, 1990. Pp. viii, 255.

On April 11, 1315, Bondavid of Draguignan, Jew and citizen of Marseilles, lent the modest sum of sixty shillings to his fellow citizen Laurentius Girardi. The debt was duly recorded on a notarial register, and a promissory note handed over to Bondavid. When Bondavid sought repayment of the sum, however, Laurentius claimed that he had paid the debt already, and that Bondavid was acting fraudulently in attempting to collect it again. Laurentius' claim was supported by

Petrus Guizo, a local laborer with whom he lived and to whom he was related by marriage. All suggestions of compromise being refused, the case went to trial between February and July of 1317. More than two dozen Christian witnesses were called on Bondavid's behalf to testify to his praiseworthy character and to the untrustworthiness of Petrus Guizo, Laurentius' sole witness. The trial verdict has not survived; but it seems nearly certain that Bondavid did indeed win his case.

Working from these trial depositions, ably transcribed and edited in an appendix, Joseph Shatzmiller offer us an unusually detailed look at the friendly relationships of confidence and trust which might exist between a Jewish lender and his Christian clients in early fourteenth century Provence. In the highly monetized economy of thirteenth and fourteenth century Europe, credit arrangements of one sort or another were a ubiquitous feature of life in both rural and urban areas. Attitudes toward moneylenders were as ambivalent then as they are today. Hostility toward exacting creditors and exorbitant interest rates was balanced by a sincere appreciation for lenders who supplied needed funds.

Especially appreciated were lenders who would prolong without penalty the repayment periods on loans, lend money without collateral, and remit some part of a debt in cases of poverty or need. Bondavid was apparently such a man. One of his witnesses remarked, indeed, that Bondavid was "more righteous than anybody he ever met in his life. He does not believe that there is one more righteous than he in the whole world." (p. 118).

Justice, however, was never simple in cases which pitted Christians against Jews, even in Marseilles where Jews enjoyed citizenship and Jewish lawyers practiced in the city courts. Shared values of generosity and good will lay in uneasy tension with conflicting religious loyalties and the uncomfortable reversals of deference and power that accompanied Christian indebtedness to Jews. Bondavid's witnesses wished to see justice done in the case. "Nevertheless", several of them remarked, they "loved [their] Christian brother [i.e., Laurentius] more." (pp. 135, 138, my translation)

As Shatzmiller shows, medieval Jewish lenders were not the Shylocks of legend, or even of Jacques Le Goff's recent, and unfortunate, *La Bourse et la Vie*. They could not afford to be. Provencal Jews generally lent at lower interest rates and to a lower class, more predominantly rural clientale than did the Christian merchants, Italian bankers, and ecclesiastical institutions with whom they competed in the lucrative business of lending money. Similar Jewish lending patterns obtained widely across Mediterranean Europe, and are beginning to be traced in northern Europe as well. Shatzmiller's synthesis of the secondary literature on this subject is very well done, and will render this material much more accessible to non-specialists than it has ever been before.

Canon lawyers too were divided in their views of usury, in my view even more divided than Shatzmiller allows (pp. 45–46, 51–53). Although many canonists from the late twelfth century on declared all interest to be usury, and all usury unacceptable, the popes themselves did not adopt such views until the 1311–12 Council of Vienne; and even then there is some doubt whether the provisions of this council, which equated usury with heresy, were intended to apply to Jews. Strictly speaking, only Christian usurers fell under the jurisdiction of church courts and hence of the canon law. Jews were judged by the civil courts; and it was not therefore until kings, princes, and municipal councils began to outlaw rather than simply regulate usury that moneylending by Jews was proscribed. Saint Louis IX of France began this process in 1228, to be followed in 1275 by Edward I of England. But in most of the rest of Europe, including Provence, Jewish loans at controlled rates of interest remained enforceable in civil courts until at least the fourteenth century.

Although lending itself thus remained licit, the legal status of both Jewish and Christian lenders became increasingly problematic, even in places like Bondavid's Marseilles where Jewish loans were recorded on notarial registers as a matter of course, and where mid-thirteenth century civic legislation still spoke straightforwardly of the enforceability through the city courts of interest at the approved rate of three pence per pound per month (15% p.a. simple interest). After 1309, however, in keeping with a new statute pronounced by Count Charles II of Anjou and Provence, anyone convicted of accepting interest on a loan would be forced to pay back all the interest he had ever received on every loan he had ever made, plus a punitive fine of five times the total sum of interest collected. For lending to continue at all, borrowers in Marseilles now had to hide the usurious nature of their transactions with a lender, or the lender himself would be ruined. The widespread willingness of borrowers to cooperate in this deception speaks eloquently of their need to borrow money. But it was also, of course, an extremely dangerous position for a lender. If a single client succeeded in convicting him either as a usurer or a false creditor, his career could be ruined. As Shatzmiller shows, Bondavid went to court in 1317 not because repayment of the sixty shilling debt meant that much to him—he was a wealthy man, to whom such a small sum was inconsequential—but rather to avoid the legal consequences which might have stemmed from Laurentius' public accusations against him.

A year later, however, the case might not have gone so well. In February 1318, the statute book of Marseilles was expunged of any references to the legal enforceability of usury, in explicit conformity with the prohibitions pronounced at the 1311–12 Council of Vienne. Why it took these decrees six years to affect Marseilles is something of a mystery. Shatzmiller suggests that the decrees may not have been known until 1317, when they were published along with the rest of the Clementine Decrees by Pope John XXII. This may indeed be correct. On the other hand, the Council of Zamora in Spain knew of the Vienne decrees by the end of 1312, and incorporated them into its proceedings. Shatzmiller's other suggestion, that this change in municipal policy was motivated by the upcoming translation of the relics of St. Louis of Anjou, which was expected to bring many eminent visitors to the city including the pope, may thus be the more likely one. Whatever the explanation at Marseilles, however, it appears that a more wide-ranging examination of the impact of the Vienne decrees on fourteenth century moneylending is now called for, especially in view of the very different assessment of their significance in Ken Stow's new edition of Grayzel's *The Church and the Jews in the XIIIth Century II.* (pp. 229, 309).

This is an attractive and useful book which both specialists and generalists will read with profit. Its main arguments will not surprise specialists, but they are important, and deserve to be placed before a wide audience. Indeed, if the University of California Press were to bring out a paperback edition of the book, omitting perhaps the Latin appendices, it could be adopted for course use. This might also provide an opportunity to correct the rather large number of typographical and other errors which mar the book. The 1287 synod of Leodiensis (p. 24), is not London, but rather Liège; Robert de Curzon (p. 45), and Robert de Courçon (p. 47), although separately indexed, are the same person, as are Simon David (p. 46) and Simon Davit (p. 80), also separately indexed. Simon de Criclada is Simon of Cricklade; in the index he appears as Simon de Crilada. The index has also confused St. Louis of Anjou with St. Louis IX, King of France. Notes 93 and 94 on p. 200 are reversed; and the editor of *Letters of Robert Grosseteste* in note 99 is H. R. Luard; M.A. is his degree, not his initials. In Table 7 on page 92, the pound signs have been replaced by # marks, and on page

69, an interest rate of 4 pence per pound per month is in fact a 20 percent rate of interest, not 25 percent. Further typographical errors occur on pages 6, 87, 89, 102, 115, 171 n.28, and 211 n.47. Some errors are inevitable, but a scholar as good as Shatzmiller seems to me to deserve better than this from his press.

On substantive matters, I would demur from Shatzmiller's judgments on only two points, both minor. The account on page 63 of Robert Grosseteste's 1231 letter to the Countess of Winchester misses the vituperative tone of this letter. Grosseteste wrote not to urge the Countess to accept the Jews whom he had just had expelled from Leicester, but rather to urge her to expel them from Winchester also, unless they were willing to give up moneylending and live by handiwork alone. And the account on pages 63–64 of Louis IX's Jewish policy can now be revised somewhat in light of William Chester Jordan's new book on *The French Monarchy and the Jews* (1989), which appeared while Shatzmiller's book was in press. Otherwise, the book seems to me very much in accord with the picture which Jordan has now painted in such admirable detail, and can be confidently recommended as an engaging overview of the realities of Jewish moneylending in the thirteenth and fourteenth centuries.

Robert C. Stacey
University of Washington

Kozo Yamamura, ed., *The Cambridge History of Japan*, III: *Medieval Japan*. Cambridge and New York: Cambridge University Press, 1990. Pp. xviii, 712.

This volume is the third in a series of six, of which four have now been published. The primary objective of the project is to "put before the English-reading audience as complete a record of Japanese history as possible." The third volume covers Japan's middle ages, encompassing the late twelfth through the sixteenth centuries. Essays by six American and six Japanese specialists provide readers with significant new perspectives and detailed information on political and economic institutions, foreign relations, and cultural developments. Bibliographic suggestions and a lengthy glossary are included. The tome is hardly an easy read; but it is a book that will be required reading for anyone wishing to take the measure of medieval Japanese historiography in English.

The specialized study of Japanese premodern history prior to 1600 is quite new in Western historiography. Since publication in 1966 of John Whitney Hall's pioneering *Government and Local Power in Japan*

500 to 1700, an increasing but still small number of Western historians have been trained. The vast majority of those studying medieval Japan are Japanese producing scholarship in Japanese. This is actually a broadening and dynamic factor for the field, which of necessity is an international one that synthesizes various historical perspectives and historiographical traditions. Understandably, the selection and translation of important scholarship written in Japanese is a critical task; and the editor of this volume, Professor Kozo Yamamura, is to be commended for his strenuous efforts in this regard.

Medieval Japan has often been called "the age of warriors." Recent scholarship has succeeded in broadening discussion to include the courtier world, for at least through the Kamakura age (1180–1333), the imperial court at Kyōto maintained to a significant extent its authority, status, and wealth; and even thereafter courtiers remained influential arbiters of culture. If there is one thing that emerges from poring through the thirteen essays in this volume, it is the sense that the discussion of medieval Japan must be expanded even more aggressively to include the stories of monks and nuns, peasants, merchants, artisans, fishermen, entertainers, and bandits—and their families and social units as well. The scholars whose work comprises the third volume of the *Cambridge History of Japan* have succeeded in sketching the canvas for a panoramic landscape that teems with suggestions as to how much additional work must be done before the rich *comédie humaine* of Japan's medieval age actually reveals itself to English readers. It is an auspicious beginning.

The volume contains a variety of historical writing, some of it retrospective and some brimming with new research. In limited space I can provide only a sampling of its riches.

Jeffrey P. Mass's article on the Kamakura Bakufu distills twenty years of research and publications on this early warrior government. In his crispest style yet, Mass hones his central theses: the political immaturity of warriors prior to the Gempei War of 1180; the dyarchic nature of the Kamakura-age polity; the criticality of the stewardship *(jitō)* post in the institutional structure of the Bakufu; and the primary importance of judicial rather than administrative functions in the Kamakura polity. Kozo Yamamura's essay on commercial and urban development and Martin Collcutt's essay on Zen Buddhism and its institutions are also retrospectives of previously published research.

Startling new historical vistas are revealed by H. Paul Varley's study of "high culture" and Barbara Ruch's inquiry into "the other side"—popular culture, particularly as represented by female religious practitioners and by entertainers. Varley's contribution represents the first scholarly analysis in English of medieval culture from the combined perspectives of literature; the fine arts; and the "practiced arts" of noh drama, linked-verse composition, and the tea ceremony. He succeeds in highlighting some of the key elements in a cultural and intellectual continuum that joined the medieval age both with the classical past and with early modernity. In a particularly interesting discussion of fourteenth and fifteenth-century intellectuals, Varley describes how courtiers tutored warrior clients in courtly arts while undertaking a "scholarship of nostalgia," to plumb Japan's classical past. Eventually their work flowered in the "national studies" movement of early modern times. Varley and Ruch agree that medieval culture leaders, elite and popular, together shaped arts that contributed to a new sense of national community in the fifteenth century. Their shared conclusion is nothing less than a "finger pointing to the moon," a clear sign of the need for future research to further elucidate this assertion.

Several essays translated from the Japanese concern socioeconomic and political developments in the countryside, bringing a new level of understanding to these topics.

Professor Kyōhei Ōyama's essay provides the clearest discussion in English concerning land tenure, social organization, and authority patterns in specific provinces and estates. Of special interest is his observation that two tenure systems actually overlapped in Japan's medieval countryside, one based on absentee lordship and one on local lordship. Warrior governance via the *bakufu,* he asserts, worked long and well because it enforced coexistence between the two systems. The *bakufu* also succeeded in preserving the authority of the imperial center throughout the long span of medieval history.

Professor Keiji Nagahara analyzes the flow of peasant history, rural lifestyles and technologies, and the decline of the estate system. He describes how small villages comprised of scattered households at the beginning of the medieval age increased in productivity and wealth, and by contracting with absentee landlords for self-managed collection and payment of estate dues, gradually fashioned autonomous structures for self-government. Unified village units *(sō)* joined province-wide and regional leagues *(ikki)* to resist enemies in the fifteenth century. Nagahara pronounces this a key moment in peasant history, when "Japan's original democratic institution"—the self governing village—reached the peak of its development. Thereafter, local warriors, responding to the threat posed by autonomous villages and leagues, proceeded to ignore the orders of the *bakufu,* demolished the estate system, and incorporated the villages into their own local domains.

Professor Shoji Kawazoe's chapter on Japan's foreign relations is a veritable cornucopia of new insights into a heretofore little explored field. Kawazoe notes that in the thirteenth century, forty or fifty Chinese ships were docking yearly in Kyushu. Influential Chinese merchants lived in the port of Hakata where they patronized Zen and other cultural imports, which then spread up the Inland Sea to the courtier and warrior capitals at Kyōtō and Kamakura. Underlying the Mongol invasions of the 1270s was Khublai Khan's belief that Japan had to be subordinated to assure success for the final Mongol assault on the Southern Sung. Kawazoe also offers a persuasive explanation as to why, given Japan's traditional rejection of tributary status vis-a-vis China, Shogun Ashikaga Yoshimitsu (ruled 1368–1408) accepted the title of "King of Japan" from the Ming Chinese monarch. During the civil war then blazing between contenders to the imperial throne, the representative of the Southern Court in Kyūshū accepted designation as a Ming tributary in 1370. When Yoshimitsu, whose ancestor had placed the northern emperor on the throne, eventually gained ascendance in the war, he was forced to consider appropriating tributary status, with its accompanying use of the "King of Japan" title, for the northern court.

Looking at the volume as a whole, a major contribution is its compilation of a formidable body of translated terms and concepts indispensable for the study of medieval Japan. The glossary will prove useful to specialists and new readers alike. I do wish, however, that more Japanese terms had been struck from the text, thereby improving readability. I also think readers would have benefitted from more complete bibliographic citations in chapter footnotes and a more detailed map.

There are some specific complaints to be registered. A host of typos, misspellings, and punctuation peccadillos were overlooked. Still more serious are errors in the text, such as muddled references to the temple Tōji where Tōdaiji is meant, and vice versa (pp. 346, 348, 367, 370); Ōta no Shō has been mistaken for Ōyama no Shō (p. 311); the Togashi *shugo* has been called a *jitō* (p. 339); Daigoji in suburban Kyōto has been located in Nara (p. 349); the Gion Shrine has been called a temple (p. 354); and Hosokawa Yoriyuki's name has been misread as Yoriyuri (p. 425). The Chinese character for *shiki* is wrong in the glossary (p. 698); and there are misses in romanization. For instance, the gazetteer termed "Mineaiki," cited a number of times in the text (pp.

171–77), proved unidentifiable by that name but appeared as *Hōsōki*. Tracking down this correct reading cost significant time because Chinese characters for personal names, place names, and primary sources have been left out of the volume. There was also the puzzling reference to a port in Kyūshū called "Bōnotsu" (p. 399), which many English readers would mistakenly pronounce "Bon'otsu". A better notation would have been "Bō'no'tsu". Both cases demonstrate why Chinese characters should always be included in a work such as this, preferably in text but certainly in glossaries and indices. These are only a sampling of the misinformation in the volume, all easy enough for a specialist to spot but misleading to less informed readers. This reviewer would urge Cambridge University Press to publish an exhaustive list of *errata* to add to copies for future sale.

We might, in conclusion, consider what the volume lacks—if only to suggest directions for future research and publication. First, I would like to have seen a concluding discussion of "medieval" in the Japanese context, based on insights from the volume. Such a discussion was in fact initiated at the 1990 annual meeting of the Medieval Academy of America in Vancouver, where two panels of specialists with members from Japan and the United States presented thoughts on the subject to an audience of Western medievalists. There is much to be gained in continuing that discussion. Second, there are some notable chronological gaps—the mid-thirteenth century and the sixteenth century are the most thinly covered. It is to be hoped that the fourth volume of the *Cambridge History* will begin with the early sixteenth century, thereby filling one of those breaches. Finally, one misses treatment of specific topics of importance, such as the changing structure and functions of religious institutions; the transformation in women's status throughout the medieval age; family history; developments in Shintō; and, of course, the evolution of the imperial institution. This is simply to say that much remains to be done to bring the broader landscape of Japan's medieval history before the eyes of English-speaking readers. This book has surely propelled the process forward.

Joan R. Piggott
Cornell University

Lee Palmer Wandel, *Always Among Us: Images of the Poor in Zwingli's Zurich.* Cambridge and New York: Cambridge University Press, 1990. Pp. vii, 199.

The poor are always with us, but what people think should be done about them does not always stay the same. Certainly attitudes towards poverty underwent significant changes in sixteenth-century Europe. There were many reasons for this. The demographic upsurge which began in the late fifteenth century seems to have increased the total number of paupers. A new set of ideas which historians group together under the rubric of "social discipline" generated a strong impetus to regulate and control the poor. And the dramatic religious changes of the sixteenth century stimulated new attitudes about poverty. The older view which linked supposedly Protestant concepts about idleness and labor to the new systems of poor relief is rarely advanced today: there is too much evidence of parallels between Catholic and Protestant initiatives in dealing with the poor. But nobody doubts that the religious impulses of the Protestant and Catholic Reformations did contribute to the reorientation of attitudes towards poverty and poor relief in many parts of Europe.

The impulse was general but the manifestations were usually local. Much has already been written about the restructuring of poor relief in specific communities in the sixteenth century. Less, it seems, has been said about perceptions of the poor in specific towns and cities. It is this topic, rather than the institutional framework for dealing with poverty, that Lee Palmer Wandel explores in her study of "images of the poor" in Zurich between 1519 and 1525. During these years, under the guidance of Ulrich Zwingli, Zurich became a leading center of the Reformation. Zwingli and his supporters faced a challenging task: they had to root out allegiance to the old church while also deflecting the appeal of the vigorous new Anabaptist movement. To do so effectively, they had to offer a clear and persuasive vision of their city as a Christian community in which all (or almost all) of the inhabitants had a legitimate role. This in turn meant that the political and religious leaders of Zwingli's Zurich needed to have a clear image of who the poor were and how they fitted into the whole social order.

Wandel explores the image of the poor in Zurich by examining three kinds of contemporary sources. First she considers three of Zwingli's own treatises in which poverty and the poor were significantly addressed. Then she explores the visual images which were printed as title-page illustrations for these three treatises. Finally she considers two major acts of Zurich legislation: the Alms Statute of 1520 and the Poor Law of 1525. Altogether this is not, as such, a very large body of evidence. But Wandel subjects her sources to a close analysis and offers useful comparisons to other relevant writings and images. In the end the author makes a persuasive case that a new sensibility towards the poor emerged in Zwingli's Zurich.

Medieval piety had honored those who, like St. Francis, voluntarily adopted a life of poverty. But Zwingli and his followers saw no virtue in this. To become poor by a religious vow seemed no more holy to them than to become poor due to a dissolute or spendthrift way of life. Involuntary poverty, however, was a different matter. From the legislative point of view, people who fell into poverty through no fault of their own were the "deserving poor" and were thus entitled to civic charity. From the religious point of view, however, the involuntary poor were also the very "images of God," certainly more so than the statues and pictures whose veneration the Zwinglians were so eager to stamp out. As legitimate objects of help, the deserving poor provided wealthier Zurichers with an opportunity to carry out those principles of fraternal love which were central to Zwingli's vision of the Christian community. Individual acts of charity—alms handed personally to a beggar—would be replaced by a general transfer of wealth from richer to poorer citizens, administered through the kind of central agency which was being established in Zurich as in many other cities during the early sixteenth century.

But if the poor were to be the visible images of God in this new fraternal community, there had to be some clear mark of their being so. As long as they continued to receive charity they were to wear conspicuous metal badges so that all could see how effectively the Zwinglian notion of fraternal love was being carried out. What kind of community Zurich had become should be made visible to all. An image, after all, must be seen.

This much of the author's argument is highly convincing, based as it is on a detailed study of the relevant texts. The author's use of visual imagery to support her argument is a bit more problematic. Two of the three visual images she discusses include striking representations of Jesus reaching out dramatically to a group of common people; the third shows a cross-bearing Jesus surrounded by ordinary folk. These were certainly unique images at the time—and they were not inconsistent with the Zwinglian vision of a community in which the poor were "images of God." But the interpretation of these pictures

ultimately rests on one's understanding of the textual sources. Though
the author argues that visual images themselves can represent a kind of
language, these images do not speak to us quite as clearly as she thinks.
For the language on which Wandel primarily bases her argument is still
the familiar language of words and texts.

Christopher R. Friedrichs
University of British Columbia

Robert S. DuPlessis, *Lille and the Dutch Revolt: Urban Stability in an Era of Revolution,
1500–1582*. Cambridge Studies in Early Modern History. Cambridge and New York:
Cambridge University Press, 1991. Pp. xv, 372.

Writing the history of something that did not happen is notoriously difficult. Robert DuPlessis succeeds because he discusses the lack of a
revolt in the town of Lille in the 1570s as an examination of the sources
of stability. From the first outbreak of image breaking in 1566 down to
the early 1580s each town in the Low Countries was repeatedly faced
with a choice of maintaining the status quo or carrying out dramatic
political changes. Despite pressures from various forms of central government, from groups in other nearby towns and from Protestants in
the local hinterland, Lille kept the same government staffed by the
same people and stayed faithful to Roman Catholicism. There were
occasions where the issue was in doubt and where only violent action by
the town government, the Magistrat, and the urban militia succeeded
in keeping order and retaining the integrity and independence of civic
authority. But until 1582 when, with the full agreement of the town government, Spanish troops entered the town, Lille fiercely guarded its
privileges, its autonomy, and its stability.

 The question then is why, while so many other towns went
through upheaval, Lille did not. With a population of at least 30,000
she was perhaps the sixth largest town in the Low Countries. She had a
social structure similar to that of other textile towns with a small group
of very rich merchants who did business with each other and a mass of
producers. She had a growing population and a rapidly expanding
economy. She faced rising food prices with no increase in wages and,
so, a long-term deterioration in the standard of living for both skilled
and unskilled workers in the years before the Revolt. There are two
ways given to approach the answer in this study of urban behavior. In
the first two-thirds of the book DuPlessis lays out in precise detail the

structure of government, of the economy and society of the town from 1500 to 1566. Aware of similar scholarship, he addresses all the now well-known issues of urban elites, social stratification as well as political relations. The remainder of the book is a description of the day-to-day events from 1566 to the final reconciliation of Lille with Spanish royal authority, all well-placed in a description of the easily confusing general political events of the period in the Low Countries. The argument is that it is impossible to understand the latter without knowing the former. What is not clear is if all of the detail about the society and the economy, about structure, is needed to comprehend what was a set of sometimes haphazard events where, for example, careful planning, crowd manipulation, or good slogans weighed heavily in the final outcome.

DuPlessis argues consistently that the ruling elite, faced with a threat, both consolidated itself and never lost its resolve. Lille was also the capital of Walloon Flanders and, though relations were far from perfect between the Magistrat and the governor, the two levels of authority usually worked in concert. He also argues that the choice of the Magistrat consistently through the sixteenth century to legislate against larger scale textile manufactories meant that not only was there a thriving industry in new draperies but also that a sharp division between wage laborers and entrepreneurs did not develop in the town. The merchant elite which dominated the government did not invest in weaving, but did promote through legislation a small commodity system with artisans rather than a proletariat. It was among weavers in the nearby countryside tied to a putting-out system and textile workers dependant on wages in other towns that Calvinism flourished. In Lille, it never gained more than a tenuous foothold. The Magistrat was consistent in suppressing Calvinist worship, always within the confines of the law of the land. The Magistrat was also conscious of the need for charity and DuPlessis tracks the expenditures of the generous public welfare scheme—overhauled extensively between 1500 and 1566—which always rose in times of distress, both economic and political.

The city archives of Lille, as well as the regional and national archives of Belgium, have been scoured for a wide variety of information about every aspect of town life in the sixteenth century. For the story of what happened during the critical years 1566–1582, much of the information must come from letters and from chroniclers and DuPlessis is very conscious of the problems of relying too much on the reminiscences of what were typically Catholic city government officials who recorded, after the fact, their own success. With the statistics of population, wages, prices, incomes DuPlessis is also painfully aware of the shortcomings of the data and uses seven appendixes to explain what he has done with the numbers and why. There is a discussion of the sources but there is no bibliography, an unfortunate oversight given the broad range of secondary material marshalled by the author and buried in footnotes. At times the report of the theory being used or of the precise nature of information or misinformation serve as a barrier to presentation of the argument. At times too little is given, for example in his comparison of the history of the Revolt in a number of towns in the Low Countries.

DuPlessis uses Henri Pirenne's analysis of the Revolt in towns as the place to start. In the end DuPlessis finds that Pirenne is not right in claiming that the revolution was progressive. Equally DuPlessis does not find that those favouring the Revolt were enemies of change and defenders of established privilege, a position typically held by scholars of collective action. He sees rather an "... interaction of both forward-looking and defensive forces that gave rise to the Dutch Revolt, at least in the cities" (p. 319). He finds in the history of Lille during a time of continuing political upheaval a case which demonstrates all of the currents, including religious ones, which dominated the history of Europe in the sixteenth century. In using a town where the decision was to remain the same rather than to change, he finds an excellent way to lay out the choices which faced those who were politically active in the period. Though it will never be possible to know with certainty why, under the varying circumstances, individuals made the choices they did, at the very least DuPlessis has laid out with care and clarity what those choices were and the context in which they were made.

Richard W. Unger
University of British Columbia

Richard Kieckhefer, *Magic in the Middle Ages.* Cambridge Medieval Textbooks. Cambridge and New York: Cambridge University Press, 1990. Pp. 219.

The Cambridge Medieval Textbook series is intended to serve the needs of both teachers and students, and in this particular case, the needs of undergraduates. Kieckhefer, therefore, after a handsome tribute to Lynn Thorndyke, has kept references to a minimum and has tried to clarify difficult matters without embarking upon the histories of arcane points. The inquiring undergraduate (or graduate indeed) will

find plenty of direction for further study in the twelve pages of bibliographical references conveniently arranged by the topics of seven of
the eight chapters.

The introductory first chapter attempts to isolate the terms of
the inquiry to indicate what constitutes magic and what does not. In
the end, "magic" appears always to need a qualifying adjective. What
Kieckhefer discusses is either "natural magic" which invokes the power
thought to inhere in some objects—not as a natural property of the
object but as emanation from elsewhere—or "demonic magic", the
invoking of the power of a set of malicious and non-human creatures. A
person is sick; afterwards, that person is well. A person is well, then is
sick. If there is more than a temporal connection between the two
states, then it must be a causal, and the problem is to identify the cause
so as to determine a remedy for the sickness. Is a sick liver helped by a
tea made from liver-shaped leaves (natural magic), by deflection of
malicious creatures (demonic magic), by prayer (religion), or by the
avoidance of fatty foods (science)? Kieckhefer makes a bold attempt to
distinguish among these, although a jaundiced person might find, not
surprisingly, some blurring along the edges. That is not surprising
because confidence in the remedy plays a large part in the cure both
then and now, just as confidence that an ordeal will work to display
guilt is a good part of the working of a lie-detector test.

Kieckhefer wants to examine not just magic itself (with or
without adjectives) but the role of magic in medieval culture, and he
promises that we can compare "popular with learned notions" and discover their crossing point. Herein lies a problem. How are we to discover what "popular" notions are, if, as the author well realizes, we are
dependent upon the "learned" for access? "In what ways did the literate
elite share or absorb the mentality of the common people? Do some
writings reflect the views of ordinary people better than others? Can we
accurately reconstruct popular notions from learned attacks on them?
Do the definitions of magic used by the intellectuals reflect or distort
popular ways of viewing things?" There is plenty of matter here to provoke much methodological discussion among students of history. If, in
fact, we cannot reach "popular" mentalities except through "learned,"
the assumption that there are these two "mentalities" co-existing
throughout the period is not demonstrable and, indeed, it is not clear
why there should not be any number of mentalities existing at the same
time in different places or even in the same places.

Popular attitudes are taken up particularly in chapter four

which occupies about a quarter of the text. Unfortunately, it is not clear whether charms, amulets, *lacnunga* remedies and the like were used, and if so, what the users thought about them. Court records provide anecdotal evidence of what people were charged with doing or confessed to doing, but, again, not usually what they or anyone else thought about what they were doing. Chapter eight on prohibition, condemnation and persecution, rests heavily on the evidence of trials where those who frame the charges, make the judgments, and construct the record are all part of the literate minority or "mentality."

Chapters two and three investigate historical origins—classical, Christian, Norse, and Irish—of some of the practices. Kieckhefer seems to be on firmer ground when he reaches the later period. Chapter five has an interesting discussion of the trivialization of "magic" as words like "bewitching" and "enchanting" are no longer always charges or accusations but compliments, and transformations may be reduced to sleight of hand. Arabic learning and the occult are the subjects of chapter six while seven deals with necromancy, a particular interest of the author who had forthcoming at the time of publication, *A Necromancer's Manual from the Fifteenth Century*.

There are a number of illustrations produced probably to hold the price of the book within the reach of the undergraduate with better eyes and less money than I. There are also a few misprints only one of which is likely to confuse the reader. On p. 97, the date of the charge against Eleanor Cobham should be 1441 not 1414.

A. Jean Elder
University of British Columbia

Ian W. Archer. *The Pursuit of Stability: Social Relations in Elizabeth London.* Cambridge Studies in Early Modern British History. Cambridge and New York: Cambridge University Press, 1991. Pp. xvi, 307.

Ian Archer's *Pursuit* attempts a comprehensive examination of the loyalties, tensions, and anxieties that shaped the social mosaic of early modern London. A critical survey of current scholarship introduces the study, and is followed by a brief outline of some of the "dynamics of interaction between rulers and ruled," including civic riot. Discussion of earlier periods of political instability in London then establishes the context for further analysis of what is perceived as "the lack of controversy in the Elizabethan period." Archer's subsequent assessment of the composition of the city elite stresses both its homogeneity and its solidarity in relations with the crown. A chapter on local government, neighborhoods, and communities delineates the civic hierarchy and various substructures of government, and attempts to contrast parish loyalties with social divisions. Another explores how the livery companies generated institutional loyalties, and so ensured that the pursuit of redress remained institutionally focused. Here, a strongly revisionist tone, which characterizes the prefatory remarks of several chapters, comes to the fore. The allegation that "an exaggerated impression of either conflict or consensus" has been created by the "preoccupations of historians" seems to infer the existence of whole schools of thought which adhere to either one or the other of these impressions. Yet, by way of illustration, only the admittedly dated work of George Unwin and a recent study by Steve Rappaport are offered. Then, in support of his own (pre)conceptions of the reasons why tensions were largely contained, Archer proceeds to outline various aspects of both conflict and consensus within and between the companies. The next chapter deals with the demography of the impoverished, and charts the sources and distribution of relief for London's poor. The book then concludes with a sojourn into the city's seedy underworld and a look at both the perceived and real threat of petty criminals to social cohesion, and how their punishment reinforced entrenched values.

Archer's conclusions are mainly that the overall cohesion of London's governing elite was essential to the maintenance of social stability in the face of popular disorder, and that the populace over which the elite ruled was weak and divided. At the same time he emphasizes the vulnerabity of the elite to a concerted challenge from below, and the consequent responsiveness of London's rulers to popular grievances.

The book is thorough and serious, and as a whole it benefits from a clear organizational format. It is based largely on a broad range of manuscript sources from several British archives, and is supported with numerous statistical tables relating to taxes, poor relief, patterns of philanthropy, and treatment of crime. Clear announcements of principal themes lead the reader into each chapter. It must also be said, however, that Archer has written without much concession to non-specialists in the urban social history of the later Tudor period. Numerous esoteric terms are left undefined, and, although the early chapters contain invaluable sketches of governmental institutions, considerable knowledge of the central and civic administrative structures is assumed. In a sense, the work is still a doctoral thesis written for an audience of examiners. The documentation of sources is meticulous and extensive to the point of being cumbersome at times. When, for instance, three consecutive sentences in the narrative offer examples of how parish vestries exercised control over communal resources, three separate footnotes (p. 85 nn. 112, 113, 114) hardly seem warranted, given that the archival source cited is the same for each point. This sort of awkwardness (another example is the notes on p. 155) does little to enhance the narrative, which itself is rather densely written. Sentences tend to be long and occasionally are convoluted, and for the most part, the book demands much of the reader. In Archer's defence, we should not forget that this is a complex subject to write about in any manner and a difficult one to write about with any flair. This product of exhaustive research is an instructive and scholarly monograph on an esoteric subject, written for a specialized readership. It constitutes a useful contribution to our understanding of customs and societal relationships in Elizabethan London.

J. D. Fudge
University of British Columbia

John Matthews, *The Roman Empire of Ammianus*. London, Duckworth, 1989. Pp. xiv, 608.
J. den Boeft, D. den Hengst and H. C. Teitler, *Philological and Historical Commentary on Ammianus Marcellinus XXI*. Grõningen, Egbert Forsten, 1991. Pp. xiv, 344.
F. M. Clover and R. S. Humphreys, eds., *Tradition and Innovation in Late Antiquity*. Madison, The University of Wisconsin Press, 1989. Pp. xx, 343.

The rediscovery of Ammianus Marcellinus has been one of the achievements of the last forty years of classical scholarship. He was always known and appreciated by a few: he was Gibbon's "accurate and faithful guide" and for Ernst Stein he was the greatest literary genius between Tacitus and Dante whom "nul historien par la suite n'a probablement surpassé, ni même égalé, dans l'art d'émouvoir l'âme du lecteur."[1] But when E.A. Thompson published his *The Historical Work of Ammianus Marcellinus* in 1947, there was little in English with which to compare it. The situation is now completely changed. Late antiquity has been rediscovered and we have a spate of books on Ammianus, three concordances and several volumes of commentary, one of which is reviewed here.

Matthews's book is the fullest, and by and large, the best study that has been produced on Ammianus thus far. The title is chosen with intent: this is a study of the *Res Gestae* of Ammianus in its cultural and historical setting. Yet our evidence for this historian is still remarkably tenuous. From Ammianus' text, which has an autobiographical thread to it, we can infer a good deal, such as that his sympathies lay with paganism,[2] but in addition, we have only Libanius' *Epistle* 1063, dated to 392, and addressed to a Marcellinus who has confidently been identified as our historian. This identification has become the rock upon which a theoretical edifice has been built, that makes Ammianus a native of Antioch known to Libanius who was perhaps his teacher.[3] Matthews accepts the identification (on pp. 478–79, he notes only to dismiss a suggestion by Charles Fornara that Libanius' correspondent was someone else) and Barnes[4] recently has asserted that "no one has seriously cast (the identification) in doubt", but it is perhaps less soundly based than either scholar would admit. M. L. West[5] has recently detected the names of Magnus and Marcellinus in several acrostics from the Cyranides, which comes from the milieu of fourth-century Alexandria, and Libanius knew a Magnus of Nisibis who was a physician in Alexandria. Could the Marcellinus who was the recipient of Magnus' poems be the Marcellinus of *Epistle* 1063? And could our historian belong to Alexandria rather than Antioch? The evidence is shaky and I for one would not rush to accept it. But West has managed to demonstrate how fragile the basis of our hypothesis about the background of Ammianus is.

The second book under review here is a commentary on Ammianus' twenty-first book, prepared (in English) by three Dutch scholars. Book twenty-one begins with Julian at Vienne, beginning to prepare for the conflict with Constantius II which never happened, and still making a pretense of Christianity. It ends with Constantius' death. Den Boeft, den Hengst, and Teitler are continuing this commentary started by Dr. P. de Jonge, who read this book in manuscript, and it is done with care and learning.

The papers in *Tradition and Innovation in Late Antiquity* are the product of two seminars, the first held at the University of Wisconsin (Madison) in spring, 1984, and the other later the same year at the University of Chicago. They stretch from late antiquity to the 'Abbasid period. Here I can cite only a few of particular interest: Katherine Shelton's "Roman Aristocrats, Christian Commissions: The Carrand Diptych," which treats the problem of pagan imagery on objects d'art commissioned by Christians; Walter Kaegi's "Variable Rates of Seventh Century Change"; and Terry Allen's "The Arabesque, the Beveled Style and the Mirage of Early Islamic Art," which charts the artistic continuity from the Byzantine world to the early Moslem one. This is a wide-ranging but important collection of papers.

J. A. S. Evans
The University of British Columbia

1. *Histoire du Bas-Empire* I: *De l'état romain à l'état byzantin (284–476)*. (J.-R. Palanque, trans.) Paris, 1959, p. 215.

2. R. L. Rike, *Apex Omnium. Religion in the* Res Gestae *of Ammianus* (Berkeley, 1987); T. D. Barnes, "Literary Convention, Nostalgia and Reality in Ammianus Marcellinus," in Graeme Clarke et al, (eds), *Reading the Past in Late Antiquity* (Rushcutters Bay, NSW, 1990), pp. 59-92.

3. Cf. E. A. Thompson, "Ammianus Marcellinus" in T. A. Dorey, ed., *Latin Historians* (New York, 1966), pp. 143–57; Andrew-Wallace-Hadrill, Ammianus, *Marcellinus: The Later Roman Empire (A.D. 354–378)*. Harmondsworth, 1986, pp. 14–16.

4. *V* n. 2, p. 61.

5. *Classical Quarterly* 32 (1982), 480–81; cf. G. W. Bowersock, *Journal of Roman Studies*, 80 (1990), pp. 247–48.

BOOKS RECEIVED

Listing of a book here does not preclude a review of it in a later issue of *Studies in Medieval and Renaissance History.*

Arnold, Benjamin, *Princes and Territories in Medieval Germany,* Cambridge and New York: Cambridge University Press, 1991. Pp. xiv, 314.

Blair, Peter Hunter, *The World of Bede.* Cambridge and New York: Cambridge University Press, 1991. Pp. xii, 342.

Blumenfeld-Kosinski, Renate and Szell, Timea, eds., *Images of Sainthood in Medieval Europe.* Ithaca and London: Cornell University Press, 1991. Pp. vii, 315.

Bonnassie, Pierre, trans. Jean Birrell, *From Slavery to Feudalism in South-Western Europe.* (Past and Present Publications). Cambridge and New York: Cambridge University Press, and Paris: Editions de la Maison des Sciences de l'Homme, 1991. Pp. xii, 352.

Calabria, Antonio, *The Cost of Empire. The Finances of the Kingdom of Naples in the Time of Spanish Rule.* (Cambridge Studies in Early Modern History). Cambridge and New York: Cambridge University Press, 1991. Pp. xii, 285.

Cameron, Averil, *Christianity and the Rhetoric of Empire. The Development of Christian Discourse.* Berkeley and Oxford, UK.: The University of California Press, 1991. Pp. xv, 261.

Copeland, Rita, Rhetoric, *Hermeneutics and Translation in the Middle Ages. Academic Traditions and Vernacular Texts.* (Cambridge Studies in Medieval Literature). Cambridge and New York: Cambridge University Press, 1991. Pp. xiv, 295.

Edbury, Peter W., *The Kingdom of Cyprus and the Crusades, 1191–1374.* Cambridge and New York, Cambridge University Press, 1991. Pp. xviii, 241.

Farmer, Sharon, *Communities of Saint Martin: Legend and Ritual in Medieval Tours.* Ithaca and London: Cornell University Press, 1991. Pp. xii, 358.

Haldon, J. F., *Byzantium in the Seventh Century: The Transformation of a Culture.* Cambridge and New York: Cambridge University Press, 1990. Pp. xiv, 229.

Israel, Jonathan I., ed., *The Anglo-Dutch Moment: Essays on the Glorious Revolution and Its World Impact.* Cambridge and New York: Cambridge University Press, 1991. Pp. xv, 502.

Jeffreys, Elizabeth, with Brian Croke and Roger Scott, *Studies in John Malalas.* The Australian Association for Byzantine Studies. Department of Modern Greek, University of Sydney, Sydney, NSW, 1990. Pp. xxxvii, 370.

Lerer, Seth, *Literacy and Power in Anglo-Saxon Literature.* (Regents' Studies in Medieval Culture). Lincoln: University of Nebraska Press, 1991. Pp. xii, 268.

Maddox, Donald, *The Arthurian Romances of Chretien de Troyes: Once and Future Fictions.* Cambridge and New York: Cambridge University Press, 1991. Pp. xii, 180.

McKitterick, Rosamond, ed., *The Uses of Literacy in Early Medieval Europe.* Cambridge and New York: Cambridge University Press, 1990. Pp. xvi, 345.

Miller, Edward, ed., *The Agrarian History of England and Wales, Volume III: 1348–1500.* (General Editor: Joan Thirsk). Cambridge and New York: Cambridge University Press, 1991. Pp. xxv, 982.

Morse, Ruth, *Truth and Convention in the Middle Ages. Rhetoric, Representation and Reality.* Cambridge and New York: Cambridge University Press, 1991. Pp. xv, 372.

Paxton, Frederick S., *Christianizing Death: The Creation of a Ritual Process in Early Medieval Europe.* Ithaca and London: Cornell University Press, 1990. Pp. xiv, 229.

Pounds, N. J. G., *The Medieval Castle in England and Wales: A Social and Political History.* Cambridge and New York: Cambridge University Press, 1990. Pp. xvii, 357.

Richmond, Colin, *The Paston Family in the Fifteenth Century: The First Phase.* Cambridge and New York: Cambridge University Press, 1991. Pp. xxii, 269.

Roberts, Michael, *From Oxenstierna to Charles XII: Four Studies.* Cambridge and New York: Cambridge University Press, 1991. Pp. 203.

Uozumi, Masoyoshi, ed., *Essays in Honour of the Seventieth Birthday of Professor Kiyoko Takeda Cho. I. Feudal Systems of Asia: An Attempt at a Comparative Historical Inquiry. Pp. 112, II. Tradition and Modernization.* Tokyo: International Christian University Asian Cultural Institute, 1990. Pp. 298.

Watt, Teresa, *Cheap Print and Popular Piety, 1550–1640.* (Cambridge Studies in Early Modern British History). Cambridge and New York: Cambridge University Press, 1991. Pp. xix, 370.

Waugh, Scott L., *England in the Reign of Edward III.* (Cambridge Medieval Textbooks). Cambridge and New York: Cambridge University Press, 1991. pp. xi, 303.

Werner, Ernst, *Jan Hus. Welt und Umwelt eines Präger Frühreformators.* Forschungen zur Mittelalterlichen Geschichte, XXXIV. Weimar: Verlag Hermann Bohlaus Nachfolger, 1991. Pp. 256.

CONTENTS OF
PREVIOUS VOLUMES

VOLUME VI (1983)
RICHARD C. HOFFMANN
Outsiders by Birth and Blood: Racist Ideologies and Realities around the Periphery of Medieval European Culture.

KATHRYN L. REYERSON
Land, Houses and Real Estate Investment in Montpellier: A Study of the Notarial Property Transactions, 1293–1345.

D. L. FARMER
Crop Yields, Prices and Wages in Medieval England.

VOLUME VII (1986)
BERNARD S. BACHRACH
Geoffrey Greymantle, Count of the Angevins 960–987: A Study in French Politics.

ROSLYN PESMAN COOPER
The Florentine Ruling Group under the "governo populare," 1494–1512.

JENNIFER L. O'REILLY
The Double Martyrdom of Thomas Becket: Hagiography or History?

VOLUME VIII (1987)
MAVIS MATE
The Estates of Canterbury Prior before The Black Death, 1315–1348.

SHARON L. JANSEN JAECH
"The Marvels of Merlin" and the Authority of Tradition.

M. PATRICIA HOGAN
The Labor of their Days: Work in the Medieval Village.

MARY ERLER and NANCY GUTIERREZ
Print into Manuscript: A Flodden Field News Pamphlet.

JAMES D. ALSOP and WESLEY M. STEVENS
William Lambarde and Elizabethan Policy.

INDEX

Aachen, Council of, 121, 123,125,132
Abbasid period, 206
Acrostics, 206
Acta urbis, chronicle, 179
Adam, 179
Abshead, Kathleen, 180
Aelfric, 187;
  De Populo Israhel, 187
Aerial photography, 3
Aldhelm, 186–87;
  De Creatura, 186
Alexandria, city of, 206
Alexius I, Byzantine Emperor, 181
Alfred, king of England, 54, 187
Allen, Pauline, 180
Allen, Terry, 206
Alms Statute of Zurich, 198
Alphabetic script, 141
Ammianus, 39–40, 44, 62–63, 179–80, 205–6
Anabaptist movement, 197
Anchor, 55, 57
Andreas, poem, 54
Anglo-Saxon Chronicle, 54, 58, 61,67
Anglo-Saxon, literacy of, 54;
  literature of, 39, 54–56, 62
  migration of, 33, 35, 37–38, 54–55, 58–59, 67;
  ships of, 35, 42–44, 48, 50, 52–54, 56, 58, 65–66
Annales maximi, chronicle, 179

Apollinaris, Sidonius. See Sidonius
Apostles, 119
Archaeology, 3–4, 162, 182
  nautical, 33–38, 43, 56–61, 66
Archer, Ian W., 203–5
  The Pursuit of Stability: Social Relations in Elizabethan London, 203–5
Archers, 17–18
Armor, 19
Ashby Dell, ship of, 36
Askekarr, ship of, 35
Asser, 184, 187;
  Life of King Alfred, 184
Auerbach, Eric, 142
Augustine, Bishop of Hippo, 151–52, 180;
  De civitate Dei, 180;
  De doctrina christiana, 151;
  Confessions, 178
Augustinians, 121
Ausonius, 150
Australian National University, 178
Avienus, Roman geographer, 46–47, 63
AVISTA, 1, 3–4

Bachrach, Bernard, 7, 11–12, 14–16, 20, 24–29
Bannockburn, Battle of, 17

217